FREE SPEECH IN AN
INTERNET ERA

Free Speech in an Internet Era

Papers from the Free Speech Discussion Forum

Edited by

Clive Walker

PROFESSOR OF CRIMINAL JUSTICE STUDIES
UNIVERSITY OF LEEDS SCHOOL OF LAW

Russell L. Weaver

PROFESSOR OF LAW & DISTINGUISHED UNIVERSITY SCHOLAR
UNIVERSITY OF LOUISVILLE LOUIS D. BRANDEIS SCHOOL OF LAW

CAROLINA ACADEMIC PRESS

Durham, North Carolina

Library of Congress Cataloging-in-Publication Data

Free speech in an internet era : papers from the free speech discussion forum /
[edited by] Clive Walker and Russell L. Weaver.
     pages cm
  Includes bibliographical references and index.
  ISBN 978-1-61163-407-5 (alk. paper)
  1. Freedom of speech--Congresses. 2. Freedom of expression--Congresses.
3. Internet--Law and legislation--Congresses. 4. Information technology--
Law and legislation--Congresses. I. Walker, Clive, Professor, editor of compilation. II. Weaver, Russell L., 1952- editor of compilation.

  K3254.A6F74 2013
  323.44'3--dc23

                         2013001696

CAROLINA ACADEMIC PRESS
700 Kent Street
Durham, North Carolina 27701
Telephone (919) 489-7486
Fax (919) 493-5668
www.cap-press.com

CONTENTS

Introduction:
Free Speech Discussion Forum

Clive Walker* & Russell L. Weaver**

The fifth Free Speech Discussion Forum was held at the University of Notre Dame's London Law Centre on June 12–13, 2012, and was co-sponsored by the University of Notre Dame's London Law Centre, LexisNexis, the Emory University School of Law, the Windsor University Faculty of Law (Canada), the University of Alabama School of Law, the University of Western Ontario Faculty of Law (Canada), the University of Poitiers Faculty of Law (France), and the University of Louisville's Louis D. Brandeis School of Law. The gathering brought together a combination of scholars and practicing lawyers from the United States, Europe, and Canada. The topics for the 2012 forum included two issues: "Free Speech in the Internet Era" and "The Meaning of, and Complications for, Media in an Internet Age." The papers printed in this volume reflect the "discussion papers" on which the deliberations were framed.

Some of the chapters dealt directly with issues related to the media in an Internet age. The chapter by professors Russell Weaver, Clive Walker and Geoffrey Bennett poses a poignant contemporary question: *Can Newspapers Survive in an Internet Era?* The chapter notes that, with the advent of the Internet, the fortunes of traditional print newspapers have seriously declined so they may be unable to survive in their current form. In some instances, print newspapers are being replaced by online investigative outlets. The chapter goes on to suggest that a legitimate question remains regarding whether online investigative reporting services can adequately replace traditional newspapers as the "watchdog of democracy." Online publications arguably have significant ad-

---

* Professor of Criminal Justice Studies, University of Leeds School of Law.

** Professor of Law and Distinguished University Scholar, University of Louisville, Louis D. Brandeis School of Law.

vantages over print publications in terms of speed and sometimes in terms of coverage. Indeed, traditional newspapers have not historically provided sufficient coverage of local issues, but blogs and online news services are capable of providing that coverage since there is effectively limitless space on the internet and much lower process costs. In other words, even though society might be losing the traditional "guardian" or "watchdog of democracy," it may be acquiring a new and somewhat different type of watchdog. However, questions have been raised regarding whether the new forms of media will be as "reliable" or even as informative as traditional media. Because of the democratic nature of the Internet, allegations can come from a variety of sources, and it can be difficult to discern whether an online publisher is a "journalist" as opposed to a "political activist" or both. Video images can be altered, "old" images can be passed off as "new" ones.

The possibility of technology misuse is raised by Professor Jon L. Mills' *The New Media in the New World: Are They Behaving Badly or Doing Their Job?* He begins by recognizing that new technologies have facilitated the collection and publication of information. For example, a "smart phone can record an image of an event and send it to a global audience" with "immense and positive" impact. He notes that "images of government abuses turned global opinion in the Arab Spring of 2011 and fostered opinion within those countries." Nevertheless, he suggests that "the harm fostered and made possible by new technologies cannot be ignored," and he contends that both the new and the old media should be held accountable when they behave badly. "The challenge is to maintain free speech and to protect the individual right to privacy and to be let alone from intrusion."

Likewise, because of media convergence, it has become increasingly difficult to categorize and define with precision "media" organizations. Convergence extends to all types of media, including the traditional press, broadcasters, satellite communications, cable communications, and the Internet. So the saying goes, "a screen is a screen," and the dividing lines between the different types of media is rapidly disappearing. This situation raises profound questions regarding the meaning of the term "the press." That issue is addressed by Professor William Araiza's *The Institutional Press, the Internet, and the Paradox of the Press Clause*, which examines the press clause in light of recent technological developments. He notes that court have struggled to define "the press" in an Internet age, and accordingly have encountered difficulties in reaching a coherent, stable understanding of who is entitled to constitutional protection. He goes on to express doubt about whether the term "the press" should be defined by the courts, and instead suggests that the task of defining the press "is best undertaken as a combined effort of legislatures, with their greater responsiveness and line-drawing flexibility, and courts, reviewing such definitions for compliance with the basic principles underlying the Clause."

Other chapters in the symposium deal with the question of whether the existence of the Internet should cause us to reconsider our approach to freedom of expression, or to particular types of free speech issues that may arise. Professor Arnold Loewy's explicitly raises this issue: *Does the Internet Require Rethinking First Amendment Theory?* He notes that each speech technology has historically been accompanied by its own legal approach in the United States, but expresses doubt about whether the Internet requires special rules.

Professor Christina E. Wells' *The Promise and Peril of Protesting in the Internet Era* discusses some of the issues that may arise with protesting through electronic means. She notes that the "Internet presents opportunities and pitfalls to protestors." Although the Internet offers protesters significantly enhanced communications possibilities, it also creates opportunities for repressive officials to control protest movements. In any event, these "new forms of protest can potentially destabilize the Court's existing narrow paradigm involving protestors," and "the very newness of these forms of protest can frighten regulators causing them to overreact and overregulate."

Professor Joseph A. Tomain's chapter, *Advancing Technology & Aging Democracy*, examines Internet speech through the lenses of intellectual property, privacy, election law, and net neutrality, and concludes "that free speech in the internet era is a topic of broad scope and there is much to resolve." This essay also raises the question about whether citizens in our aging democracy are able to rise to the challenge to curtail or avoid the speech-threatening developments that technology supplies to those with the power and incentive to expand. Tomain wonders whether "American citizens [will] sleepwalk through these changes before it is too late (or at least significantly more difficult) to reverse."

A number of the chapters from the symposium deal with specific areas of speech. For example, Professor Indra Spiecker genannt Döhmann's *The Difference between Online and Offline Communication as a Factor in the Balancing of Interests with Freedom of Speech* notes that free speech principles can sometimes collide with other values affecting opinion and information, such as protection of privacy or data protection, and she suggests that a balancing of interests is often necessary. She notes that the balancing of these interests requires a determination of the intensity in which interests are hindered and rights infringed and in the way protection is necessary. She also notes that both sides of the balancing of interests can be influenced by the means in which freedom of speech is expressed and by the dangers and misuses possible, and that both influences have to be taken into account. She concludes that the Internet produces contradictory effects. It allows for more freedom of information, for easy, quick, and inexpensive access to information with little restrictions for time, space and other resources. However, it also changes the impact of communication considerably. Therefore, some of the effects which are almost unnoticed and of little importance in the offline world become major factors in an online environment. As a result, the "internet poses new challenges and new questions. But often, it asks us some of the old questions again. We should not be afraid to find new answers—and to allow for a differentiation between the offline and the online world."

Professor Eric Barendt's *Defamation and Net: Anonymity, Meaning and ISPs* deals with the problem of defamation in the context of anonymous postings and the use of pseudonyms on the Internet. He argues that proposals to discourage the use of pseudonyms should be supported in order to avoid making it difficult for defamation claimants "to enforce their reputation rights." Nevertheless, he believes that "courts are right to curtail actions for what is really only vulgar abuse or offensive childish speech on the Net," because such speech often involves "hyperbole and exaggerated claims that nobody is likely to take seriously." He considers such speech as no different from speech published in other formats. However, he argues that it "would be wrong to go further" and "apply a more lenient libel law for the publication of defamatory allegations on the Net." He argues that anonymous "rumours initiated by blogs can cause enormous financial loss or ruin someone's social standing." He concludes that we "should take equally seriously arguments that its exercise may, and sometimes does, cause significant damage to reputation (and other) rights."

Mr. Paul Tweed's *Free Speech in the Internet Era: Developments "Online" in Defamation and Privacy Law—Brief Observations*, discusses a variety of topics encountered by practitioners, from superinjunctions, to the WikiLeaks scandal, pending British defamation legislation, and a recent British defamation decision. The chapters focuses on the inevitable conflict between freedom of expression and protection of reputation evident in these areas. He concludes that "legislative changes and the shifting and often inconsistent common law decisions, still leave a totally unsatisfactory situation on any view, whereby the worldwide web remains very much a law onto itself." He adds his hope for the future: "The next few years will therefore be very interesting indeed, and may no doubt be expected to serve as a yardstick, not only for the future development of regulation for online publication, but also for the harmonisation of privacy and freedom of speech laws and regulation of use of the internet that may establish universal standards for future generations to come."

Professor Christopher J. Roederer's chapter, *Now Trending: Loving the Internet Terrorist?*, raises issues related to Internet terrorism. He argues that American society has created this "bogeyman" of the "Internet terrorist" because it "feeds our unhealthy needs and sustains on our unhealthy fears." He expresses concern that we have allowed these fears to "undermine the rule of law, weaken our democracy, and diminish our human rights (including our First Amendment rights and freedoms—among others)." In his view, these attitudes have "hurt us morally" and "cost us severely." He expresses concern about how we can "exercise our First Amendment rights, much less our civic duties, if we cannot talk to or listen to those whose actions appear to be directing many of our domestic and international policy decisions, namely those we suspect of terrorist activities."

Last in order is Professor Kevin Saunders' chapter, *Obscenity, Community and the Internet*. His chapter suggests that the United States and Europe have taken into account differences among communities in making determinations regarding what materials may be held to be obscene. However, he notes that these assessments were undertaken prior to the development of the Internet, and he notes that the Internet, "a medium with no firm attachment to any particular geographic location, calls into question the earlier reliance on geographic community and requires an analysis of community in the Internet era."

In conclusion, the impact of the Internet is having potentially profound impacts on the delivery of mass free speech. Analysis by the contributors to this book does not necessarily result in the demand for fundamental legal change in every corner of the law. However, those who continue to ignore the Internet's transformative capacity in offering their prescriptions for change, a criticism levied against the recent Leveson Report in the United Kingdom,[1] invite the fate of early redundancy or easy evasion. Thus, the chapters in this book offer an insight into a debate that is ignored by lawyers at their peril.

---

1. See *An inquiry into the culture, practices and ethics of the press* (2012–13 HC 780). Compare Finkelstein, R., *Report of the independent inquiry into the media and media regulation* (Canberra, 2012).

FREE SPEECH IN AN INTERNET ERA

1

CAN NEWSPAPERS SURVIVE IN AN INTERNET ERA?

Russell L. Weaver, * *Clive Walker** * &*
*Geoffrey Bennett****

Although the history of free expression is inextricably intertwined with advances in speech technology, the most dramatic technological advances have come in recent decades. The Internet, personal computers, and assorted handheld devices have all revolutionized communication,[1] enabling ordinary people to speak to large audiences. As a result, users of contemporary communications devices can circumvent the traditional "gatekeepers" of communication, such as the owners of broadcast or print, and their reporters, editors and producers.[2] Because of the Internet, political communication is no longer the sole purview of the rich or the powerful or even the professional, but now also resides with the masses.

The results of this technological revolution are evident throughout the world. When the Chinese government claimed that air quality was improving, disbelieving activists purchased air quality monitors, and began posting environmental readings on the Internet, and ultimately forced governmental officials to acknowledge problems with air quality.[3] In Russia, when a local mayor offered cash to veterans in exchange for votes, a Russian recorded the offer on his smartphone and posted it on YouTube, thereby prompting the mayor's conviction for violating Russian election rules.[4] Perhaps the most striking illustration of the power of the Internet is the recent political upheavals in the Middle East, commonly referred to as "The Arab Spring." The Internet and social media have played a critical role in toppling the Tunisian government,[5] as well as in bringing down Egyptian President Hosni Mubarak.[6] As these examples reveal,

 * Professor of Law and Distinguished University Scholar, University of Louisville, Louis D. Brandeis School of Law.
 ** Professor of Criminal Justice Studies, School of Law, University of Leeds.
 *** Professor of Law & Director, University of Notre Dame London Law Centre.

Internet activism has shown the capability of developing from self-referent, local or sectional applications to national or transnational impacts.[7]

As the Internet has assumed an increasingly prominent role in political discourse, some have begun to wonder whether the traditional media—sometimes referred to as the "Watchdog of Democracy"—can survive. If newspapers do not survive, who will investigate governmental corruption, and provide a check on governmental abuse? Will new entities emerge that will serve this function? In this paper, we sketch out some views regarding the future of the traditional media in the United States and United Kingdom. The first section will examine the decline of traditional media and its attempt to reassert power through such tactics as charging for online content. We then turn to the question of whether the online communications media offers a more attractive model for political communication, or whether the traditional print and broadcast media will absorb any attractive attributes and compete successfully with the *parvenus*.

I. The Decline of Traditional Media

As new communication devices have gained in significance, traditional media (newspapers and broadcasting) have suffered a corresponding decline. Although the traditional media's role as a gatekeeper of information has not disappeared, traditional media is facing a host of challenges, some of them monumental and unprecedented.

The present situation stands in stark contrast to the situation that existed in the United States forty to fifty years ago. At that time, many people obtained their news through one of the (then) three major broadcast networks (CBS, ABC and NBC).[8] In the absence of cable and satellite television or the Internet, network news programs were able to capture a sizeable market share, and to play a prominent role in politics and society. In addition, because such a large percentage of the population watched the three networks, their news programs had a homogenizing effect on society and societal attitudes.[9] At one point, a CBS anchorman was referred to as "the most trusted name in news."[10] At that time, newspapers also held a dominant place in American society. Most citizens subscribed to one or more local newspapers, and local dailies were capable of influencing and shaping public opinion. Because of their prominence, newspapers were able to attract significant advertising resources, thereby enabling them to employ more staff and reporters.

In the United Kingdom, the BBC has always played a dominant and to some extent unique role in broadcast journalism. Public good purposes are written into its Royal Charter and Agreement,[11] and its universal license fee[12] secures funding that offers a level of riches and a degree of security far surpassing any other broadcaster. The United Kingdom newspaper sector includes both national and local variants, with the national editions being viewed as especially important in the formation of public opinion and the investigation of wrongdoing.[13]

In modern times, the grip of the major broadcast networks is eroding. In the United States, the three networks have morphed into four (Fox News has now been added to the mix), have been supplemented by multiple cable and satellite offerings,[14] and no longer dominate news coverage. The same applies within the United Kingdom where the growth of British Sky Broadcasting Group (commonly known as BSkyB or Sky), which is controlled by News Corporation, has secured a prominent position as the largest pay-TV broadcaster in the United Kingdom and Ireland with over 10 million subscribers. One important element of the service is Sky News, a 24-hour outlet which was said in November 2005 to be the first choice for "key opinion formers" by the then head of BBC News, Peter Horrocks.[15] Thus, people who do not like the major networks can ignore them altogether, and still obtain news through lots of cable and Internet options. The array of cable and satellite radio and television channels, as well as blogs and other new Internet forms of communication, would have been mind-boggling to the inventor of the printing press, Johannes Gutenberg. The outcome is that the major networks no longer have the power to shape public opinion in the same way that they did decades ago.

Newspapers are also in decline. Indeed, the problems confronting daily newspapers may be more daunting than those confronted by radio and television networks, and it is not clear how many of them can or will survive functionally or financially in their current form.[16] Because of the Internet, people are no longer limited to reading only their local newspapers, and can access newspapers (and other news outlets) in quite distant places. Indeed, when Americans travel in Europe, or Europeans travel in the United States, it is possible for them to continue reading their hometown newspapers via the Internet. As a result, most newspapers have seen a steady decline in their circulation numbers.[17] The net effect is that many cities have watched their papers slide into bankruptcy, while some others are being served by dailies with newsrooms that have shriveled by half.[18]

Newspaper circulation and newspaper advertising have been declining steadily in recent decades. Throughout the 1990s and the early 2000s, the decline was approximately 1 percent per year.[19] During the economic downturn of the late 2000s, the decline began to accelerate.[20] In early 2009, newspaper advertising declined by as much as 30 percent,[21] with print circulation declining by 7 percent,[22] and total circulation of all newspaper dailies dropping to 44 million copies a day—the lowest level since the 1940s.[23] Illustrative of the decline is *The Los Angeles Times* which saw total circulation fall from 1.1 million to 657,000 between the years two thousand and two thousand nine.[24] *USA Today* has suffered declines in both circulation and advertising.[25] Overall, United Kingdom newspaper circulation fell by 25 percent between 2007–09, when the decline in the United States decline was 30 percent.[26]

During the 2008 economic downturn, the signs of economic distress for traditional newspapers were widespread and deep. Many newspapers suffered severe budget shortfalls, and were forced to furlough[27] or reduce staff,[28] lower salaries,[29] suspend retirement contributions,[30] consider reductions in home delivery,[31] or file for bankruptcy protection.[32] For example, the McClatchy Company, which controls approximately thirty daily newspapers and another fifty nondaily papers, laid off 15 percent of its staff.[33] Conde Nast, faced with a steep decline in advertising revenue, engaged in aggressive cost-cutting measures.[34] *The Washington Times* was losing money and its future was uncertain.[35] The industry, as a whole, shed twelve thousand jobs in a recent year.[36] *The Rocky Mountain News* closed down because of financial difficulties,[37] and major Chicago[38] and Philadelphia[39] newspapers were either forced into bankruptcy,[40] or faced the possibility of bankruptcy.[41] Two Philadelphia newspapers, *The Inquirer* and *The Daily News*, were both sold at public auction.[42] A number of United States newspapers folded.[43] Most newspapers that remained had substantial debt.[44] Some of these negative trends began to turn around somewhat in the United States by 2011.[45]

The decline of United Kingdom newspapers has continued unabated as reflected in the fact that they print fewer editions. However, the only major newspaper closure involved the best-selling Sunday newspaper, the *News of the World*, which was for policy rather than financial reasons.[46] It is interesting to note that the only rises in circulation have been for free newspapers (especially *Metro* which is handed out at transport interchanges) and low cost newspapers (20p) such as the *I* version of *The Independent*.[47]

The changes in the United States have been dramatic, reflecting a more fragmented (and therefore more vulnerable) industry. Many newspapers that survived suffered serious financial reverses, including the *Washington Post*,[48] *Detroit Free Press*,[49] *The Detroit News*,[50] *Seattle Post-Intelligencer*[51] and *San Francisco Chronicle*.[52] The *Seattle Post-Intelligencer*, which desperately sought a purchaser,[53] ultimately decided to discontinue print publication and become an entirely online publication.[54] With the shift, *The Seattle Times*, the *Post-Intelligencer's* chief competitor, returned to profitability.[55] The *San Francisco Chronicle* has also been in dire financial straits,[56] and the McClatchy Company lost four million dollars in 2009.[57] Of course, the stock valuations of many newspapers declined significantly, sometimes by as much as 90 percent,[58] and many newspapers were saddled with high debt levels.[59] To some extent these bankruptcies were beneficial because they allowed organizations like the Tribune Co. to reorganize.[60] Even the venerable *New York Times* announced temporary salary cuts.[61]

Because of these stresses, a number of United States cities have gone from being multi newspaper cities to single newspaper cities,[62] and some daily newspapers no longer publish every day.[63] There are suggestions that some cities will be left with no newspapers at all.[64]

At the very least, those newspapers that survive will be forced to take drastic steps. *The Christian Science Monitor* and *The Kentucky Post* jettisoned their print versions and now publish completely online.[65] Other newspapers, in an effort to save money, no longer publish on a daily basis,[66] have significantly downsized,[67] or are sharing coverage with competitors.[68] *The Washington Post* saw significant declines, and was forced to eliminate its Saturday print edition, Sunday Source section, and its Book World section (as a separate section).[69] *The New York Times* took out a large loan,[70] eliminated a quarterly dividend to conserve cash, folded its Metro section into the paper,[71] and reduced newsroom staff.[72] One newspaper accepted a governmental credit guarantee despite obvious implications for the paper's independence and impartiality.[73] The *San Francisco Chronicle* reduced its newsroom staff by 300 people or about 50 percent.[74] Other major newspapers have reduced their staffs by 20 percent or more, including *The Washington Post* and *Los Angeles Times*.[75] In addition, the New York Times Co. threatened to shut down *The Boston Globe*, which it had purchased for a record price some years earlier.[76] It ultimately decided to keep the paper open, but only after forcing *Boston Globe* workers to accept substantial pay reductions.[77] In 2009, it ordered temporary pay cuts for employees of *The New York Times*.[78]

Some believe that newspaper staff cutbacks have affected both the quantity and the quality of newspaper coverage. As one reporter noted, "Nearly every large paper in the country prints fewer pages and fewer articles, and many have eliminated entire sections. Bureaus in foreign capitals and even Washington have closed, and papers have jettisoned film criticism, book reviews and coverage of local news outside their home markets."[79] As the *Chronicle's* Editor-at-Large suggested, cutbacks of this magnitude inevitably affect the ability of newspapers to report the news: "It's objectively true that there's less in the paper ... You can't deny that a loss is a loss."[80] There is evidence suggesting that these conclusions are correct, and that newspaper staff reductions are affecting the ability of newspapers to cover governmental issues and politics.[81] "Only one TV station in Virginia still has a reporter at the capital. Many newspapers have decided to cover the capital by phone, if at all."[82] A similar situation prevails at the Maryland capital.[83] Symptomatic of the times is the fact that the American Society of Newspaper Editors cancelled a recent convention because too many editors decided to stay home.[84] Some newspapers have laid off copy-editors despite the obvious implications for the quality of the finished news product.[85]

The decline of the traditional media has been used as an argument in 2007 by the BBC for the maintenance of its statutory license fee.[86] However, the age of austerity that befell public services after the 2010 United Kingdom General Election has now been extended to the BBC itself, which has experienced a budget cut of 16 percent and a freeze on the license fee for six years.[87]

The bottom line is that the newspaper elite, as a gatekeeper to communication, is in full-scale retreat.[88] As newspaper subscriptions have declined, and fewer and fewer young people read hard-copy newspapers, hope for a revival fades. The net effect is that many newspapers are desperately seeking new economic models.[89] While tens of millions of people still read daily newspapers, many now read the news entirely online.[90] The problem for the traditional print media is that they have higher operating costs related to ink, paper and news print distribution than online publishers.[91]

II. Attempts to Charge for Online Content

Some newspapers are attempting to deal with the decline by charging for online content. A major problem for newspapers is that advertising, usually the largest revenue source for newspapers, is declining,[92] and is declining so quickly that newspapers cannot cut their budgets quickly enough to remain profitable.[93] A significant percentage of advertising has migrated to the Web,[94] or to other electronic competitors (*e.g.*, cable television).[95] For example, even Twitter makes its income off advertising.[96] Over just the last couple of years, newspaper advertising has dropped by 25 percent.[97]

Today, instead of scouring the local daily newspaper for job openings, many applicants conduct their job searches online using services like Monster.com[98] or Hotjobs.com in the United States,[99] or jobsite[100] or fish4[101] in the United Kingdom, obviating the need to search through newspaper classified advertisements.[102] In addition, many people are using eBay[103] and Craigslist[104] to buy and sell goods,[105] thereby eliminating the need to purchase comparatively expensive newspaper ads.[106] As one industry observer noted, "Web sites like Craigslist have been to classified ads what the internal combustion engine was to horse-drawn buggies."[107] Even blogs are beginning to attract advertising revenue.[108] Although most bloggers do not attract sufficient revenue to allow them to quit their day jobs, some do.[109]

Of course, newspapers also seek to attract online advertising, but online newspaper advertising revenue is still less than print advertising (and sometimes does not yet cover the costs of the online operation) although it is rapidly gaining ground on print advertising.[110] The fundamental difficulty thus persists that the new online revenue and print advertising that remains is not sufficient to support traditional newspapers in their historical form and at historical staffing levels.[111]

In a desperate search for ways to make money and remain viable,[112] some have suggested radical solutions (*e.g.*, government subsidies and tax exemptions for newspapers).[113] Another possibility is for newspapers to accept donations, and a website has been established that allows individuals to donate to their newspapers,[114] but it is hard to believe that voluntary donations will save existing newspapers.

National newspapers in the United Kingdom at least are under the ownership of profit-making corporations (such as News Corporation in the cases of *The Times* or *The Sun*) or powerful individuals (such as the reclusive tycoons, the Barclay brothers, in the case of *The Daily Telegraph* or Alexander Lebedev, a Russian oligarch, in the case of *The Independent*). These ownership arrangements hardly represent deserving causes for charitable donations. In any event, the reliance on a state subsidy is not an attractive fate for a sector that is meant to be fiercely independent from the state.[115]

A much more feasible solution is that some news outlets are considering whether to charge for their online content.[116] A few U.S. newspapers do charge for content,[117] as do some European newspapers,[118] and the technology that would support charges is readily available.[119] Among the newspapers that charge for content are *The Wall Street Journal* and the *Financial Times*,[120] as well as some of their subsidiaries,[121] but few other media outlets have followed their lead.[122] Although *The Wall Street Journal* has nearly one million subscribers, the *Financial Times* has only slightly more than 100,000.[123] The *Financial Times* remains profitable because it charges $300 for a subscription and $100 more for the print edition, and has even moved to increase revenue from subscriptions.[124] Some suggest that the *Financial Times'* strategy of charging for content was a wise one,[125] but others question whether the *Financial Times'* success is primarily due to the nature of the publication as a provider of specialized financial information to a relatively wealthy audience.[126] The other attempts to charge for online news involved *The Times* and *The Sunday Times* in 2010. The immediate result was a loss of 90 percent of online readership,[127] and there were only just under 120,000 subscribers by 2012.[128] No other mainstream daily has followed its example so far.

The Wall Street Journal has adopted more of an intermediate approach to charging for its content. *The Journal* decided to charge for its content right from the beginning,[129] but it placed approximately 70 percent of its content outside the paywall, including sports coverage, arts and entertainment articles, and selected stories.[130] "It's a pretty standard strategy for business, rights? I mean, you allow people to come in, sample your wares, but then say, if you want it all folks, you have to pay."[131] Although some of *The Journal's* business and financial news are freely available online, most of it is behind the paywall.[132] *The Journal* rarely attempts to charge for popular mainstream stories that can readily be found on free websites.[133] Since it is possible to find *The Journal's* content on the Web through targeted Internet searches, this approach has its limits.[134] *The Financial Times* recently modified its policy to permit "micropayments" that allow users to purchase individual articles rather than general subscriptions.[135]

Whether other news outlets will be able to charge for their content, is far from clear. The three publications that have been most successful in imposing paywalls have been financially-oriented publications that publish specialized financial information (*The Financial Times, The Wall Street Journal* and *The Economist*).[136] Nevertheless, at least one commentator has argued that each news outlet must determine what is unique and valuable to its particular readership (*e.g.*, a Houston newspaper might choose to charge for content related to the oil industry),[137] and doubts whether newspapers can survive based on online advertising alone.[138]

Not everyone agrees. For most newspapers and media outlets, there is a delicate balance between charging for online content, which can generate subscriptions and income, and risking the possibility of discouraging online advertisers by limiting online traffic through paywalls.[139] Many publishers have decided that they cannot risk the possibility of alienating online advertisers who constitute a significant and growing source of their income.[140] Alan Rusbridger, Editor of *The Guardian* newspaper, argues that "the future is going to be a world in which everyone—and by everyone I mean everything in science, academics, politics—is going to be open and linked and collaborative."[141] He doubts that newspapers can simply "withdraw from that world."[142] At the time of his statement, *The Guardian* was making approximately 40 million British Pounds per year.[143] However, even Rusbridger questioned whether *The Guardian* could survive long-term based solely on online advertising revenue, and he suggested that newspapers may ultimately be forced to enter into more collaborative relationships.[144] His musings must, however, be set in the context of the fact that *The Guardian* made an overall loss in its last published accounts, which were for years 2010–11.[145]

Most United States newspapers have moved to impose paywalls for at least some of their content. For example, *The Louisville Courier-Journal* originally allowed online readers to access its current content for a period of one week. After that, only abstracts were available for free, and readers were charged for viewing the full text of archived articles.[146] *The New York Times* twice attempted to impose paywalls without success.[147] Undeterred, *The New York Times* is moving again in that direction,[148] as have a number of French publishers.[149] *The New York Times* gives online readers free access to twenty articles per month (a number that it recently reduced further), but attempts to charge for reading additional articles.[150] The *Courier-Journal* is trying to follow this approach by providing readers with access to only five free articles per month.[151]

News Corporation's other newspapers have also flirted with the idea of charging for online content.[152] As Rupert Murdoch recently stated, "Quality journalism is not cheap, and an industry that gives away its content is simply cannibalizing its ability to produce good reporting … We intend to charge for all our news Web sites."[153] Amazon markets the Kindle and charges subscription fees to download news.[154] Nevertheless, the largest and most popular United Kingdom newspaper online website, Mail Online, retains free access. It was reputed to be the second most popular newspaper website in the world in 2011—second only to the *New York Times* and that was before paywalls were reintroduced for its site.[155] By January 2012, Mail Online was reported as having overtaken the *New York Times* in web traffic, with the largest increase in the United States itself.[156]

Unquestionably, online readership continues to grow.[157] Between 2007 and 2009, total online readership grew from 60 million visitors a month to 72 million visitors a month.[158] As people spend more and more time connected to the Web, online advertising will necessarily increase.[159] For some publications, for example *The New York Times*, digital advertising revenue is rapidly approaching equivalence to print advertising revenue.[160] Even at that paper, overall, print advertising has declined, while digital advertising has increased, so that overall advertising revenue has remained flat.[161] The bright spot for newspapers is that the rates for digital advertising are generally higher than the rates for print advertising.[162]

Whether *The New York Times* or *The Times* (or any other newspaper) will ultimately succeed in profitably charging for their online content is far from clear.[163] Because so many other publishers offer free online content, a single publisher (or groups of publishers) may not be able to successfully impose charges without seeing large numbers of readers migrate to other news purveyors on the web.[164] After all, an inherent and fundamental attraction of the web is its networked connections, which provide the facility for almost infinite choice and the publication of information at almost no cost, especially when copyrighted value is taken for the benefit of others. The latter point is involved in a complaint lodged against Google News, whose method of aggregation did not breach any copyright. Widespread complaints from the media did however result in Google agreeing to restrict free access.[165]

The web market for news in the United Kingdom (and perhaps beyond) is also affected by the economically anomalous position of the BBC. Because it has no need to turn a profit,[166] has a secure income stream, and has public good objectives, the BBC Online has been able to develop what is probably the largest and most popular news and current affairs web site in the world (and certainly within the United Kingdom). There are said to be 20 million regular users just in the United Kingdom alone.[167] The BBC's situation has been the subject of complaint from other players in the market, notably James Murdoch, who in a 2009 lecture complained that "We seem to have decided as a society to let independence and plurality wither. To let the BBC throttle the news market and then get bigger to compensate."[168] Of course, his views may be not entirely divorced from his private commercial interests, but they did receive wide acclaim from that sector and perhaps some resonance in government financial restraints after the 2010 General Election (including a 25 percent cut in the budget for BBC Online).

III. A Media Revolution?

Some believe that the trends affecting traditional media suggest that the media is in the midst of a revolution. In an editorial, *The New York Times* quotes Internet observer, Clay Shirky, who notes that many traditional media outlets have fallen by the wayside,[169] and notes that "this is what a revolution looks like."[170] He goes on argue that,

> The old stuff gets broken faster than the new stuff is put in its place. The importance of any given experiment isn't apparent at the moment it appears; big changes stall, small changes spread. Even the revolutionaries can't predict what will happen. Agreements on all sides that core institutions must be protected are rendered meaningless by the very people doing the agreeing…. Ancient social bargains, once disrupted, can neither be mended nor quickly replaced, since any such bargain takes decades to solidify.[171]

From inside the media industry, the James Murdoch suggested in 2009 that the revolution had already happened:

> … talking about a coming digital future, or a digital transformation, is to ignore the evidence that it has already happened. Why do I think we are getting this wrong? Why do I believe we need to change direction as a matter of urgency? It's quite simple. Because we have analogue attitudes in a digital age. We have business models and a policy framework based on spectrum scarcity. We have limited choice, and we have central planning. The result is lost opportunities for enterprise, free choice and commercial investment. If we recognise that truth and change in the right way, the opportunities and benefits for all of us and—more importantly—for consumers and society are powerful and attractive. We know we have to change: the digital present is forcing us to make urgent choices.[172]

Some argue that the decline of traditional media and the rise of the Internet will have troubling implications for the democratic system. As noted, the traditional media have historically played a "watchdog" role in society by investigating and challenging the government.[173] Perhaps the most famous United States example of this watchdog function is provided by Woodward and Bernstein's Watergate investigation for *The Washington Post*; an investigation that ultimately led to President Richard Nixon's resignation from the presidency.[174] But numerous other examples abound, and investigative reporting is a proud tradition among newspapers.[175] It is also recognized as a constitutional imperative by western democracies. In the words of the European Court of Human Rights in *Goodwin v United Kingdom*, "freedom of expression constitutes one of the essential foundations of a democratic society and … the safeguards to be afforded to the press are of particular importance" because of "the vital public-watchdog role of the press."[176]

The difficulty is that newspapers are able to conduct investigations because they maintain paid staff who can devote time and effort to investigations and to effective communication. As advertising revenue has declined, some newspapers no longer have sufficient resources to support strong international or investigative reporting.[177] The continued decline of the traditional media, and the movement of more news organizations online, creates the risk that investigative journalism will decline still further. In some instances, online content is not necessarily the same in nature or content as print content even for the same newspaper. A good illustration is Mail Online where the content heavily accentuates more pictorial based lifestyle content (especially celebrities) in ways that are not reflected in the printed *Daily Mail*.[178]

This situation has caused some commentators to express concern that there will be a net loss to democracy if newspapers are no longer available to perform an investigative function, and can no longer serve as a check against governmental misconduct and abuse.[179] As a former Executive Editor of the *Miami Herald* put it: "nobody else will step in and do the occasionally extraordinary reporting that newspapers do. The difference that a good newspaper makes to the quality of life in any community is vital. It's like a healthy heart."[180] Nicholas Lemann, Dean of Columbia University's School of Journalism, agrees, arguing that: "In a world where content is free, original news gathering doesn't happen. We really need to face up to the fact that this is going to be lost."[181] Steve Coll, former Managing Editor of *The Washington Post*, has argued that traditional newspapers provide certain essential advantages to reporting: "audiences of a global scale," the "independence that comes with scale," legal departments and deep pockets and an imperviousness to threat, particularly in these libel-shopping, globalized days.[182] In addition, traditional organizations help train journalists and give them the time to do quality work.[183] Increasingly, unable to fund their own reporters, some newspapers are relying on wire services for information.[184] Of course, newspapers can also make use of the profusion of free Internet sources, but, as Bob Woodward recently commented, the proposition that "somehow the Internet was a magic lantern that lit up all events" amounts to a false and lazy belief since ultimately "the truth resides with people. Human sources."[185] Those sources must be found and questioned and analyzed, all of which takes considerable skill and resources.

Certainly, individuals can undertake investigations on their own, but it is not clear that individuals will choose to devote their free time to such investigations or that they will have the skills or resources to do so effectively. Moreover, it is less likely that online allegations, not backed up by the imprimatur of newspapers (or by the status of radio or television stations), will be considered "reliable" or will be taken seriously by the public. As the Dean of Columbia University's School of Journalism stated, "If you don't have people out working as full-time reporters, there's this category of information that's not going to appear magically out of nowhere."[186] Even those involved in online news organizations have expressed doubts about their capabilities to supplant the traditional media. Mr. Joel Kramer, who formerly worked for *The Star Tribune* and now edits an online journal, *MinnPost.com*, questions whether online journals can completely replace traditional newspapers: " 'It would be a terrible thing for any city for the dominant paper to go under, because that's who does the bulk of the serious reporting.' "[187] He went on to note that: " 'Places like us would spring up, ... but they wouldn't be nearly as big. We can tweak the papers and compete with them, but we can't replace them.' "[188]

Others disagree and believe that virtually all serious reporting will eventually migrate to the Internet. Jeff Jarvis of the City University of New York's graduate school of journalism argues that the "death of a newspaper should result in an explosion of much smaller news sources online, producing at least as much coverage as the paper did ... Those sources might be less polished, but they would be competitive, ending the monopolies many newspapers have long enjoyed."[189] The head of *Talking Points Memo* (TPM), an online investigative website, admitted that online investigative reporting cannot now replace the investigative journalism being done by print reporters: "If all the big papers disappeared right now and we replaced them with 50 TPMs, it wouldn't come close to doing the job."[190] However, he believes that online journalism will evolve to fill that void, noting that the industry is "in a broader transformation where models like ours and others are going to evolve that can fill the void."[191]

Some of the concerns about the future of traditional newspapers miss the point. The critical question is not whether traditional ink and paper publications will survive, but whether the traditional investigative and watchdog functions will continue. As one commentator noted, "I think that the policy should not necessarily be to try to preserve ink printed on newsprint and thrown on people's doorsteps every morning, because what's important here is not that method of delivering the information. It's all of the reporting and organizing of information that goes on in newsrooms."[192] Matthew Yglesias, a blogger and a fellow with the Center for American Progress Action Fund, holds a similar view: "The question is, do you want to try to channel [your efforts] into this dying model that isn't exactly working any more, or is it more important to find ways to fund new kinds of institutions?"[193]

In recent years, new methods of investigative journalism are being developed online, and there are many non-traditional media outlets that conduct investigations (such as the Drudge Report in the United States[194] and Guido Fawkes in the United Kingdom[195]). Of course, online newspapers are not an entirely new phenomena,[196] and some online publications began entirely online rather than shifting from print to online. This trend was no doubt influenced by the availability of skilled journalists after layoffs by traditional newspapers. Illustrative of this new approach is GlobalPost whose staff includes former journalists from *Newsday*, the *Boston Globe* and the *Los Angeles Times*.[197]

These new types of organizations may actually have "watchdog" advantages over traditional newspapers. Most existing newspapers have biases, personal or political, that can affect their reporting on matters of public interest.[198] So, democracy may actually benefit if journalism shifts from a single newspaper with monopolistic control (as is the case in many cities), or a small range of national titles, to multiple online news entities with different perspectives.[199] Multiple online entities are more likely to present more diverse perspectives on the issues of the day.[200]

The "new media" now includes a variety of models, including "smaller groups, those devoted to journalism, those operating out of universities, those operating from advocacy groups and think tanks, [and] all these things are already happening."[201] Illustrative are blogs which include both one-person operations, and organizations like the *Huffington Post* and the *Daily Beast* that publish blog posts by a host of unpaid bloggers.[202] There are also "hyperlocal" blogs (defined as coverage focused on "50 to 60,000 people who have common interests, things like school system, parks, tax base") or that focus on issues that may be overlooked by larger and more traditional news organizations.[203] Some of these blogs collaborate with traditional newspapers.[204] Included in this category in the United States are websites such as EveryBlock, Outside.in, PlaceBlogger and Patch.[205] These sites might attempt to alert readers to government data reports, local arrests, restaurant reviews, and house sales.[206] EveryBlock was started with a grant in excess of $1 million, and has spread to several cities.[207] Because of small audiences,[208] some hyper-local blogs can have difficulty generating significant advertising revenue,[209] but there is hope that local businesses will eventually provide support for such sites.[210] Of course, the development of blog-based newspapers may further undermine traditional newspapers and news organizations.[211] *Huffington Post* and *Daily Beast* bloggers work for free, and some of them are professional journalists.[212] The irony is that "By joining the fray on these sites, journalists and their cousins in the punditocracy undermine the very newspapers and magazines that value their work enough to actually pay for it."[213]

Illustrative of the new types of organizations that are developing online is WikiLeaks.[214] WikiLeaks is difficult to precisely categorize, but it investigates and publishes articles about government and institutions, and it leaks confidential and classified documents to the public and sometimes to the press.[215] WikiLeaks has attracted worldwide attention, including both praise and condemnation, for its leaks of classified United States government documents. WikiLeaks fervently embraces its role and image as a leaker of information. On its website, WikiLeaks asks this simple but poignant question "Have documents the world needs to see?"[216] It then goes on to proclaim that "We help you safely get the truth out,"[217] and exhorts the public to help WikiLeaks in this effort: "Disclosed documents are classified, censored or otherwise opaque to the public record. We rely on readers to alert their communities and press to the revelations here. Go to it!"[218]

WikiLeaks attracted considerable controversy, created a significant amount of diplomatic uproar[219] and has forced governmental officials to scramble to deal with diplomatic and political pressures.[220] For example, WikiLeaks released video footage of U.S. helicopters in Iraq killing some eighteen people.[221] In November 2010, WikiLeaks created a worldwide uproar when it claimed to have gained possession of a quarter-of-a-million classified diplomatic documents.[222] These documents dealt with diplomatic issues, including secret bargaining, candid views of foreign leaders, and discussions of foreign nuclear and terrorist threats.[223] Although WikiLeaks initially released only a few hundred of those documents (a very small percentage of the total number of documents),[224] it followed that disclosure with additional releases.[225] The documents that were released contained an incredible array of information dating back to 1966, some of which might harm U.S. relations with foreign officials.[226]

Some of the information released by WikiLeaks was not only classified, but sensitive and potentially damaging to U.S. relations with foreign nations and foreign leaders.[227] For example, the documents contained criticisms by U.S. officials of foreign leaders,[228] including Afghan President Hamid Karzai,[229] and suggested that Afghan leaders were corrupt.[230] The leaked documents also contained critical views of then Prime Minister Sylvio Berlusconi of Italy,[231] unflattering references to a number of world leaders,[232] indications that Palestinian leaders were saying one thing in private and another (inconsistent) thing in public,[233] and secret information regarding Swiss bank accounts.[234] The cables also offered considerable insight into China's efforts to control Internet usage, including its attempts to pressure Google to help censor Internet content.[235] U.S.-Mexico relations were severely strained by some of the disclosures.[236]

Some of the information in the WikiLeaks disclosures may have played a role in bringing about the 'Arab Spring' revolts, including the demise of Tunisia's President Zine e-Abidine Ben Ali. The Tunisian revolt was rooted in a number of concerns, including allegations of corrupt practices by the President's family.[237] Among the disclosed WikiLeaks documents was a cable from the U.S. Embassy in Tunisia discussing corruption in the Tunisian government, and suggesting that the President's wife's family had benefitted handsomely from his position.[238] Some of the WikiLeaks documents were published by a Tunisian website, TuniLeaks, and they were posted on the same day as the WikiLeaks disclosure (suggesting collaboration between WikiLeaks and TuniLeak).[239] These documents included allegations that the former President's family was receiving benefits, and that bribery was commonplace.[240]

As the collaboration with TuniLeak reveals, WikiLeaks has become increasingly sophisticated about how it releases leaked documents. For example, in addition to publishing documents on its own website, WikiLeaks took on press partners in 2010 such as *The New York Times*, Germany's *Der Spiegel* magazine, Britain's *The Guardian* newspaper,[241] France's *Le Monde* newspaper[242] and Spain's *El Pais* newspaper.[243] These partnerships were ended after the entire archive was posted in 2011, though around 25 smaller scale media associates have emerged as backers and the *Daily Telegraph* has also continued to promote the files.[244] In all, WikiLeaks worked with more than fifty local partners, including the *Daily Taraf* in Turkey, *Expresso* in Portugal, and *The Hindu* in India.[245] In the 2011 disclosures, there were so many documents and so much information that editors have been unable to sift through it all, and it is likely that the leaked documents will have implications for business and private interests as well as government.[246] *The Guardian*, a British newspaper, was offered 500,000 military dispatches from Afghanistan and Iraq.[247]

WikiLeaks is not the only player in the 'leaks' field. For example, Cryptome has existed since 1996,[248] while LiveLeak has acted for an outlet for both news and non-news online media materials.[249] In the aftermath of Wikileaks, "Open-Leaks" was created.[250] OpenLeaks was founded by former WikiLeaks associates,[251] and operates on a different model. Rather than posting documents on its own website, OpenLeaks works directly with existing media and human rights organizations and connects the leakers with organizations who (in turn) publish the documents.[252]

Besides WikiLeaks, and other similar "leaks" organization, which essentially publish undigested data, there are a number of other online organizations that venture further. The spectrum ranges from mere opinion and commentary to full-blown investigations and traditional reporting online.[253] These online publications have grown in "number, size, financing and credibility," and now exist in many cities.[254] The Pulitzer Prize is now open to online publications,[255] with *ProPublica* being the first online publisher to win the award.[256] *Talking Points Memo* won the Polk Award for legal reporting,[257] and the *Voice of San Diego* won an investigative award from the organization, Investigative Reporters and Editors.[258] Many of these small organizations are financially viable. One commentator suggests that some bloggers are earning $10,000 to $200,000 a year in income, and therefore the economic basis exists to fund online journalism.[259]

In the United Kingdom, the Guido Fawkes blog is the most popular political site and advertising is prominent but its income is not disclosed. The Guido Fawkes blog is based on 'leaks' and commentary and functions with just two editors.[260] Of course, this mixture may not be entirely distinct from traditional journalism—both formats rely on 'insider' sources and then put their own gloss on the information.

There are some clearer examples of online journalism at least in the United States.[261] For instance, *Politico*, an online news organization that has teamed up with Reuters news service,[262] is conducting aggressive investigative reporting. *Politico* now has 200 employees, hosted one of the Republican presidential primary debates, and started the website 2012 Live to cover the elections.[263] 2012 Live publishes extensive information about candidates and local political leaders.[264] During the 2010 United States elections, traffic at its website reached two million to six million hits a month (which is still relatively small compared to the 20 million hits per month that CNN.com receives, and 15 million hits per month for NYTimes.com).[265] *Politico* expressly proclaims that its mission "is to carve out an even bigger place in the news media landscape" and "to take a leap forward in front of everyone else."[266] During the presidential campaign leading up to the 2012 presidential election, *Politico*[267] published an article claiming that Republican presidential candidate Herman Cain had sexually abused two female colleagues while he was the head of the National Restaurant Association.[268] It also broke stories, involving News Corps political contributions,[269] presidential candidate Jon Hunstman's past,[270] and President Obama's handlers' treatment of Muslim women.[271]

Other similar organizations are also engaged in political reporting. Although *Talking Points Memo* had only a single reporter in 2008,[272] it employed six a year later,[273] is expanding to 15 reporters,[274] and receives about 1.4 million hits per month on its website.[275] *Talking Points Memo* played a lead role in investigating allegations against former U.S. Attorney General, Alberto Gonzalez.[276] *Real Clear Politics* is also actively involved in covering the 2012 election.[277] Like its online competitors, *Real Clear Politics* is in the process of doubling its reporting staff to six (and, possibly, eight) reporters.[278] It receives about 2.6 million hits per month on its website.[279] Other comparable organizations include Politics Daily, started by AOL, and NationalJournal.com.[280]

The *Huffington Post* has expanded from 60 employees in 2008 to more than 200 employees by 2011.[281] Although originally focused on the aggregation of information, and commentary, it is now trying to emphasize original reporting.[282] A significant percentage of that reporting is political in nature.[283] Like Facebook and Twitter, *Huffington Post* relies on writers who work for free.[284] Indeed, some "content farms" like Demand Media, pay very little ($10 to $20 a story).[285] Presumably, many who provide this content are motivated by a desire to showcase their work, or to influence the political process.[286] *The Huffington Post* expanded its operation in 2011 to Canada, France, and the United Kingdom.[287]

New online newspapers take many different forms. The *Texas Tribune* focuses on Texas state government, and ignores unrelated news stories (even major ones).[288] The publication, which started with 12 employees in its Web-based organization,[289] emphasizes investigative reporting,[290] and operates as a not-for-profit organization on a business model that emphasizes premium content, as well as memberships and corporate sponsorships.[291] The organization began with $3.7 million that was donated by a venture capitalist, and others, as well as with grants from the Houston Endowment ($500,000) and the James L. Knight Foundation ($250,000).[292] In addition to its daily reporting, the *Texas Tribune* hosts blogs and databases on various issues (*e.g.*, spending by lawmakers, donations by PACs and lobbying expenditures).[293] The organization was able to attract the former editor and publisher of *Texas Monthly Magazine* as its CEO and editor-in-chief, and was able to attract other well-respected reporters and an accomplished editor.[294] The publication claims that its goal is to hold "politicians accountable," and it does that through news stories, video interviews, original audio stories, and the posting of raw data.[295]

Other online investigative services are also adding staff,[296] and are breaking significant stories.[297] A former Managing Editor of the *Chicago Tribune* (ousted after a dispute) founded a rival paper the *Chicago News Cooperative* that is completely online and directly competes with the *Tribune*.[298] New online publications have also opened in Washington, D.C., and Texas as well.[299] Organizations like the *Chicago News Cooperative* are competing for journalistic talent, and indeed are hiring staff away from traditional newspapers.[300] Similarly, *In Denver Times*,[301] established as a for profit operation by former journalists for the *Rocky Mountain Times* which closed down, seeks to pursue a financial model based on monthly pledge amounts from readers.[302] Although the organization will give anyone access to breaking news stories, only subscribers can obtain news updates on their iPhones and BlackBerrys and be able to chat online with other readers and columnists.[303]

Other online models are similarly revolutionary. For example, *Global Voices* works with volunteer bloggers and other individuals all over the world to report information.[304] The organization, which is operated as an independent nonprofit, is funded by grants from foundations and donations by private individuals.[305] The organization publishes blog posts and articles, as well as cellphone photos and videos, on sites such as Facebook, Twitter and YouTube.[306] Because of its reliance on volunteers in the affected countries, *Global Voices* was able to provide timely reports on the unrest in Tunisia and Libya, as well as the tsunami that hit Japan.[307] In addition, the organization provides links to other articles that the posters or bloggers may be relying on.[308]

Another news organization that has developed is "Democracy Now!," a nonprofit organization that produces a daily newscast,[309] which is streamed over the Web,[310] and aired through nearly 1,000 other media outlets such as public, community and college radio stations, public access television stations, some PBS affiliates, and the noncommercial satellite networks Free Speech TV and Link TV.[311] Although "Democracy Now!" Reports on the latest news developments, it devotes significant coverage to "struggles for justice and the effects of American foreign policy."[312] "Democracy Now!" has made a name for itself covering antiwar protests,[313] as well as its discussions of alleged torture by U.S. governmental officials,[314] the execution of a Georgia inmate,[315] and the Occupy Wall Street movement.[316]

Some online publications deal with special interest issues. For example, *PolitiFact*, an online publication run by *The St. Petersburg Times*, runs truth and accuracy checks on arguments and claims made by politicians.[317] Gawker.com addresses media issues, and Jezebel focuses on women's interest issues.[318] Jezebel's readers are 97 percent female, and it receives more than 37 million hits a month,[319] and its articles have been described as both "incendiary" and "cutting."[320]

There are also a number of microblogs. In New Orleans, some of these microblogs work with *The Times-Picayune* and other mainstream media to provide coverage that exceeds the capacity of the traditional media.[321] The system was started by a citizen journalist.[322] MinnPost.com provides coverage of Minnesota, *Voice of San Diego* provides coverage of San Diego issues, Kaiser Health News provides coverage of health care issues, and *ProPublica* provides national and local investigative reporting.[323] Some of these organizations are nonprofits who receive contributions from readers, and the *Voice of San Diego* was funded by a venture capitalist.[324] *The Voice of San Diego* does not attempt to cover all stories, but is rather focused on important stories not being covered by others or stories that it feels that it can report better than other news organizations.[325] In winning a coveted investigative award, the *Voice* acted on a tip that was sent to all media organizations, but one that only it decided to pursue.[326]

Online media have considerable advantages over traditional print newspapers. The obvious and notable advantage is that online newspapers eliminate many fixed costs because they do not require ink and paper, and do not require physical delivery of the finished print product by ground transport. Another advantage is that online papers can be more current with the news because they can be updated on an hourly basis.[327] Finally, online newspapers offer the possibility of interactivity in the sense that readers can participate in online fora where they can express criticism, support or opposition to a published article piece.[328]

Despite the decided economic advantages of the Web, hard-copy newspapers will not disappear. They have important and valuable attributes: a track-record of expert and resourced journalism, broad coverage, a familiarity of layout, the attribute of a permanent record that can be relied upon and revisited, and (for local media) geographical connection and the fostering of mutual community support and belonging. Even the Occupy Wall Street Movement, for example, has recognized that hard copy newspapers have distinct benefits. Although the Movement generally functions in a very high-tech manner, some protestors have created a hard-copy newspaper to accompany the movement[329] (there is no "official" newspaper because "nothing is official in the world of Occupy Wall Street").[330] Some in the Occupy movement believe that a hard copy paper has special value in this context: "newspapers convey a sense of place, of actually being there, that digital media can't. When is the last time that somebody handed you a Web site?"[331] As one of the producers of the newspaper noted, "A newspaper is tactile, engages all of the senses, and leads to more immersive reading than what people might do online."[332] In addition, unlike a protest sign, a newspaper can provide a more detailed analysis of a protest's grievances and history.[333] Interestingly, as part of the Arab Spring protests, a hard-copy newspaper was published by protestors in Cairo.[334]

As traditional newspapers attempt to stay afloat, they have increasingly begun to offer their content online. Many traditional newspapers are also beginning to offer interactivity as part of their service,[335] thereby allowing readers to participate in discussions, publish their ideas, and engage in discussion with other readers.[336] The difficulty with these interactive solutions is that the newspaper still sets the agenda by publishing (online) an article and by giving readers the opportunity to respond to that article. In other words, readers are not necessarily initiating their own discussion fora on topics that interest them, though some newspapers have attempted to address even this limitation. A notable example is *The Guardian*'s commentisfree,[337] which hosts hundreds of discussions every week and encourages debate on the original post. At the same time, even this facility is subject to the overall ethos of the newspaper (described as "progressive, liberal, left-leaning").

One might argue that the future of many existing newspapers may be entirely or mainly online. Just as much retail business is shifting from bricks and mortar stores to online shopping, more and more newspapers may become predominantly online publications, with print versions being truncated freesheets for commuters. Thus, *Metro* is published by the *Daily Mail* group and is made available to commuters in 50 United Kingdom cities, totaling the third largest readership of any newspaper. In this way, the media may be simply morphing into a different format, as it has done in the past.[338] As Professor Jarvis of City University of New York noted, many money-losing papers should "have the guts to shut down print and go online," and it "will have to be a much smaller product, but that's where we're headed anyway."[339]

The precise nature or form that these new online publications will take is not settled, and a number of different forms may ultimately develop. News

Corp. has taken steps to develop an iPad-only newspaper, *The Daily*.[340] The content is refreshed each morning, and subscribers are charged $40 per year (or $.99 per week).[341] In addition to providing content, *The Daily* has the ability to provide photographs, video and other interactive features,[342] and to tailor content to an individual reader's interests.[343] Freed from print, and print distribution methods, News Crop. is able to produce *The Daily* for the relatively cheap amount of $500,000.[344] Of course, the question remains whether the public is willing to pay for its online news content.[345]

Other traditional newspapers are making the move from ink and print versions to completely online versions.[346] The *Seattle Post-Intelligencer*, which was not viable as a traditional newspaper, decided to publish entirely online.[347] In doing so, the paper dramatically reduced its staff from 165 people to 20 people,[348] and questions were raised regarding whether this staff reduction affected the quality and scope of the organization's reporting.[349] The *Seattle Post-Intelligencer* is covering issues related to sports, transportation, courts and local government, and is also publishing Web links to stories in other publications, photo galleries, and comments from civic leaders.[350] However, the *Post-Intelligencer* is not trying to produce a traditional newspaper, in the sense that it is trying to cover all issues, noting that "few people come to our Web site and try to re-create the experience of reading a newspaper" and reading the publication "cover-to-cover."[351] Instead, the *Post-Intelligencer* is trying to cover a more limited range of topics.[352] As Joel Kramer, CEO of the *MinnPost*, another online publication, noted, it is simply not feasible for a Web-based publication to replicate a traditional print-based newspaper.[353] Kramer described the *MinnPost* as more akin to a news magazine since "most stories we don't cover every day."[354] In addition, the tone is different. As Kramer notes regarding the *MinnPost*, "Our writers have much more freedom to be analytical—they combine news with commentary."[355] In addition, the *MinnPost* is a nonprofit corporation that survives based on foundation grants, reader donations and revenue from online advertising.[356]

Similarly, when the *Cincinnati Post* died, the Scripps Co. (the owner of the *Post*) started an online publication, *KYPost.com*.[357] The publication has a limited focus because it centers on the Northern Kentucky suburbs near Cincinnati.[358] The publication features regional stories prepared by employees of the nearby Scripps-owned television station, and it also covers very local news and community events.[359] *KYPost.com* does not have a classified advertisements section.[360]

Of course, since both the *MinnPost* and *Post-Intelligencer* have traditional print-based newspapers in their cities (Minneapolis has both the *St. Paul Pioneer Press* and the *Minneapolis Star Tribune*), it is arguably unnecessary for them to cover as many topics as traditional newspapers. Nevertheless, it is not clear that online advertisements would be sufficient to maintain a comprehensive online publication. Although the *Post-Intelligencer* saves the cost of printing and hard copy distribution, it is not clear that the model is financially feasible because advertisers may not be willing to pay as much money for online advertising as they are willing to pay for hard copy advertising.[361] Perhaps, if a traditional print-based publication did not exist, advertisers might be willing to pay more, and it would be interesting to see if the online publishers would then feel compelled to expand the scope of their coverage.[362] One interesting side-effect of the *Seattle Post-Intelligencer's* shift is that the prospects for its former rival, *The Seattle Times*, have improved given the decline in competition.[363]

These examples of newspaper deaths are all taken from the United States experience. The United Kingdom experience is that newspaper offices are being closed and regionalized while journalists are made redundant,[364] but the closure of titles is perhaps less common: it is reckoned there were 32 closures in 2011, though 29 related to relatively recently established free papers.[365] One contra-indication of newspaper decline, especially of the local variety, is the growing investment by Warren Buffett's Berkshire Hathaway company in newspaper chains such as Media General.[366]

The move was perhaps partly inspired by sentiment in so far as Buffett was a former newspaper delivery boy. But there is also a business plan that is said to be based around newspapers serving locations with strong local identities and limited media competition, also giving rise to the future possibility that paywalls can be introduced effectively.

Although a decline in printed newspapers is already in process, their total demise appears unlikely, and other factors will mitigate the impact of the new media. For example, changes in media cross-ownership and competition laws could allow for media groups to secure economies and even to cross-subsidize.[367] The result may be less diversity and fewer voices, but at least the core activity of professional journalism will be allowed to survive somewhere within the media conglomerates. As the House of Commons Culture Media and Sports Committee observed, "We endorse the sentiment that it is local journalism, rather than local newspapers, that needs saving. The two are far from mutually exclusive, but newspapers need to be innovative in the way they train their journalists to work in a multi-platform world."[368]

A more general factor to be taken into account, encompassing media cross-ownership but going much further, is that media convergence may create a fight to the death between newspapers and the Internet. This paper has already examined the ways in which newspapers (and broadcasters) have become digitized and have developed substantial online activities. Another aspect of convergence is operating in the opposite direction. There is growing regulation of

Internet activities, and the result might be higher operating costs for online news outlets. The need to extend regulation in online news is currently being considered in the United Kingdom by the Leveson Inquiry,[369] which was set up following the revelation of widespread newspaper misconduct which included the hacking of private correspondence and (allegedly) the corruption of police and politicians. Evidence to the Inquiry has included, for example, a witness statement by Paul Staines (the owner of the Guido Fawkes site) in which he sought to warn off any inclination to extend regulation: "The Guido Fawkes website is based offshore and beyond the jurisdiction of the United Kingdom courts because of the oppressive libel law regime in the United Kingdom. Fortunately the frictionless and borderless nature of the worldwide web means that unless the United Kingdom authorities go down the authoritarian route taken by the Chinese, Saudi and Iranian regimes, there is no prospect of regulating foreign websites domestically."[370] Nevertheless, less libertarian Web activists might be more accepting of regulation, and the susceptibility of ISP businesses to regulation is being pioneered with restrictions on file-swapping,[371] which will no doubt be proliferated in the direction of pornography and other forms of speech.

Conclusion

The fundamental question raised by this chapter—whether online investigative reporting services can adequately replace traditional newspapers—remains to be played out. As a "watchdog of democracy," online publications arguably have significant advantages over print publications in terms of speed and sometimes in terms of coverage. In the 1980s, it might have taken long periods of time for information to make it to the end user, but now information can be distributed almost instantaneously.[372] In addition, as some commentators note, Internet-based coverage can include more micro coverage than can be provided by a large daily newspaper. Indeed, traditional newspapers have not historically provided sufficient coverage of local issues,[373] but blogs and online news services are capable of providing that coverage since there is effectively limitless space on the Internet.[374] In other words, even though society might be losing the traditional "guardian" or "watchdog of democracy," it may be picking up a new and somewhat different type of watchdog.

In the world of "new media," there are now many more potential watchdogs. Whether the new forms of media will be as "reliable" or even as informative as traditional media is much less clear. Some online publications claim to adhere to the same journalistic standards of "discretion" as traditional news outlets, including fact and source checking and an emphasis on objective reporting.[375] Of course, there are numerous question marks about whether the traditional media reports fairly or objectively, and the Leveson Inquiry in the United Kingdom was established because of their egregious failings. Nevertheless, given the range of Internet-devices available, entry into the news market is now wide open and an array of non-professional authors can attempt to communicate or to publish information so long as they have the time and inclination. Undoubtedly, some online publications attempt to adhere, and do in fact adhere, to traditional journalistic standards, and are undoubtedly as reliable as traditional newspapers. Nevertheless, it is clear that there have been significant problems regarding the credibility and reliability of some Internet communications, and the technology exists to alter pictures and other documents.[376] In other words, because of the inherently open nature of the Internet, allegations can come from a variety of sources, and it can sometimes be difficult to discern whether an online publisher is a "journalist" as opposed to a "political activist" or both.[377] Video images can be altered, "old" images can be passed off as "new" ones.[378]

With the development of a 24-hour news cycle (in the sense that stories and information are constantly being updated rather than being published once a day), which arose as much through the development of cable and satellite as because of the Internet, there will be inevitable accuracy problems attendant to quicker publication.[379] For example, in their haste to report on the event, some news organizations falsely reported that Congresswoman Gabrielle Giffords had been assassinated (instead of wounded) during the Tuscon assault on her,[380] and the Andrew Breitbart video that led a United States Department of Agriculture official, Ms. Shirley Sherrod, to resign because of statements that she allegedly made some twenty-four years earlier.[381] Eventually, the public may learn to distinguish between different types of Internet publications based on their accuracy and reliability,[382] just as they distinguish between the yellow press and reputable newspapers, or in the United Kingdom between the "broadsheets" and the "tabloids" (terms which are now materially almost redundant). There is no reason why similar distinctions cannot, or will not, be made by the public regarding online publications or that readers will not be able to discern which online publications are associated with quality reporting. In theory, although such distinctions can be made, the task is made more difficult by the proliferation and constant entry of new players in the new media market. In any event, it must be remembered that the "old media" is not entirely above reproach so it may be difficult to develop an acceptable standard.

In recent years, because of the fact of media convergence,[383] it has become increasingly difficult to neatly categorize and define media organizations. Convergence extends to all types of media, including the traditional press, broadcasters, satellite communications, cable communications, and the Internet. So the saying goes, "a screen is a screen," and "the old dividing lines between television, radio, Web and print disappear within the four corners of a tablet."[384] As a result, "CNBC and *The Wall Street Journal* are not in different businesses anymore."[385] Media convergence has tremendous practical implications for free speech and democratic communication, but its impact together with the globalisation of news agendas points to the future of the media as moving towards the format of the Internet whether for good or ill.

2

THE NEW MEDIA IN THE NEW WORLD: ARE THEY BEHAVING BADLY OR DOING THEIR JOB?

*Jon L. Mills**

The modern media have been a bulwark of democracy as well as a force in helping to promote new democracies and freedom worldwide. But there are limits, and the law recognizes that freedom of the press does not mean the freedom to do anything. The media intrude into the lives of individuals in many ways. Sometimes their intrusions are part of their job of keeping the public informed. Sometimes, however, those intrusions are not in the public interest and cause individuals harm. The law still needs to hold media accountable for misdeeds. The question is when? When are they doing their job and when are they behaving badly?

While we often think of media intrusions as stemming from the effects of stories that the media print or broadcast, the media may also violate privacy interests through the process of obtaining the information for those stories.[1] For example, in compiling a story a reporter might illegally trespass, wiretap, or harass. Advances in technology provide even more options to intrude legally and illegally. Generally, when a tort or a crime is committed by the media while newsgathering, the action will be punished.[2] Even though theorists and writers have argued for lower standards for the media, when they commit a crime in newsgathering,[3] most courts[4] will hold them accountable and treat them as they would any ordinary citizen.

* Dean Emeritus, Professor of Law, and Director of Center for Governmental Responsibility, University of Florida Fredric G. Levin College of Law. The author would like to thank Samantha Crawford, Heather Reynolds, Allison Fischman, and Tyler Hudson for research assistance in the preparation of this paper.

Lawfully gathered news might end up being intrusive because of its distribution.[5] For example, what if a reporter legally obtains otherwise confidential information or widely publishes previously obscure public information about an individual's sins or legal transgressions in the distant past? Even if a person is harmed, whether the media is legally liable for distribution of information is a complex question in the United States and in other jurisdictions. Making the question of liability even more difficult is consideration whether one medium of distributing information is more intrusive than another. In fact, courts have determined that some means are more intrusive than others. A video is more intrusive than a picture, and a picture has been found to be intrusive even when the written explanation concerning the same facts is not.[6] Should distribution on the Internet be treated differently than through a newspaper or television broadcast? In sum, a member of the media potentially may be accountable for illegal gathering of information or the illegal distribution of information.

Part A of this chapter introduces the legal framework for considering privacy issues related to media. Part B highlights this legal framework through an example of media intrusion in the newsgathering process. Part C lays out the broad spectrum of media intrusions arising from the different vehicles for publication: print, broadcast, and the Internet. The question throughout is this: were the media just doing their job or were they breaking privacy laws?

I. Evaluation of Media Behavior — The Privacy Matrix

Being morally reprehensible is not a sufficient legal standard. Media actions which may disgust general public notions of decency may also be legal. By comparison, media actions that seem morally admirable may be illegal. Privacy interests clash with free press principles because each of these values represents different sides of important rights in constitutional democracies. Free expression is a central tenet of democracies but so are individual rights and individual dignity. Therefore, the law seeks to protect both interests. The result is an unpredictable maze of widely varying and ever changing legal standards.

Unraveling this media-privacy knot requires complete understanding of all circumstances surrounding a specific alleged intrusion. Every case requires navigating a complex matrix of issues that will determine whether a particular media action will be seen as a violation of a legal privacy right. Adding to the complexity is the fact that the matrix of issues continues to shift due to new technologies and cultural changes in attitude.

To begin, it is important to note that most conflicts between the media and the right of privacy have one common factor—the disclosure of information that some individual finds intrusive. There are some intrusions the media may commit that are physical rather than relating to the disclosure of information. Those issues relate to trespass or such privacy torts as "intrusion upon seclusion." Whether any perceived media intrusion is an intrusion requiring a legal remedy is a question answered by walking through the legal maze that is contemporary privacy and media law. The matrix—the following six threshold questions—structures this legal analysis.

1. How and Where Was the Information Obtained?

The first question is "does the media have a legal right to obtain the information"? This issue is separate from issues dealing with the actual disclosure of information.[7] As previously mentioned, a media member has no additional license to obtain information that would be illegal for any ordinary citizen to obtain. As the Supreme Court has stated, "the First Amendment does not guarantee the press a constitutional right of special access to information not available to the public generally."[8]

Consequently, if truthful, newsworthy information was obtained illegally, then liability may exist for the disclosure of that information.[9] But the disclosure by media of information obtained by ambiguous means is more complicated. An important factor is if the media knew that the information was illegally obtained. Another important point is that there is heightened protection of the media's right to publish to avoid prior restraint.

Moreover, there are different degrees of intrusion depending upon the source of the information, ranging from reproducing online public records to electronic eavesdropping. Obtaining information from a public record[10] is far different than obtaining that same information from invading a person's home.[11] The value of a person's home might be found though an online search or by stealing that information. Even if it is the same information, one method allows publishing as it was legally obtained, while the other does not.

Disclosing illegally obtained information may result in legal liability.[12] If the publisher had present knowledge upon obtaining the information that the information was initially obtained illegally, then he may be liable for its disclosure.[13] However, the issue becomes even murkier depending on the nature of the information. If the information is of great public concern, the subsequent publication of illegally obtained information may be protected, particularly in the United States[14] Yet, if the publisher had more than mere present knowledge and was more involved in the illegal activity by actually advising the third party on how to obtain the information illegally, then the publisher may be liable as if he took part in the acquisition of the information.[15] Tangentially, if the publisher made a contractual agreement or promise not to disclose, the First Amendment is not implicated and will not protect the publisher from liability as it is not a shield to protect from breach of contract.[16]

Further, liability may exist even if no disclosure occurs at all. A member of the press, just like any other member of the public, may not trespass onto the physical property of another.[17] If, in the process of seeking information, a person intentionally enters land that is in the possession of another (or causes a third party or an item to do so) without authorized permission of the owner, then the seeker is liable for trespass.[18] Moreover, if a news gatherer pries into something private, something a reasonable person would object to as an intrusion, then the seeker may be liable under the tort of intrusion upon seclusion.[19]

If the information has already been disclosed, then no such protection exists to prevent the further dissemination of the information.[20] However, the doctrines of intentional infliction of emotional distress,[21] the right to publicity[22] and appropriation of likeness[23] attempt to provide remedies against the initial propagator. If the information has not been disclosed, then even if newsworthy, disclosure may be prevented or modified through an applicable statute preventing disclosure, or through an alternative disclosure that is less intrusive (e.g. written word) than the preferred medium of disclosure (such as a photo or video).[24]

Going forward, the advent of new technologies continues to change dramatically the way information is accessed and obtained. The question of where and how information is obtained is becoming metaphysical. The combination of new media and new technology creates new legal quandaries. For instance, once information is published on the Internet, especially anonymously, who is responsible for it? If information is re-published from the Internet then what is the source—the Internet or the original source of the story? Who is held accountable for the intrusion caused by an Internet posting? Is there an adequate recourse when information can never truly be removed from the web?

2. Is the Information True, False, or an Opinion?

In the United States, protecting the expression of speech is a well-defined and primary goal. Consequently, if a statement is pure opinion, then the free speech and the free press doctrines found within the First Amendment will almost always protect it.[25] An opinion is defined as a statement that cannot reasonably be interpreted as stating actual facts about an individual.[26] For instance, if on a dating website, someone posts that a person is a "creep and a jerk," that is an opinion. If the statement may imply a false assertion of fact, then it is not protected as an opinion.[27] In determining whether a statement is an "opinion," the entire work in which the statement is found, along with the context of the publication containing the statement as a whole, should be considered.[28]

Comparatively, if a statement is presented as a fact, then that information may fall outside of the traditional protections of the First Amendment, especially when the information is false or intrusive. False statements are more likely to lead to findings of intrusions, but true statements may also have this result. Although generally, if information is truthful, there will be no liability for the dissemination of that information, even a true statement may sometimes result in an illegal intrusion. One example of this is when true information is used to portray an individual in a manner that amounts to a distortion of his or her true attributes.[29] This distortion is protected under the doctrine of false light.[30] Similarly, under the theory of public disclosure of private facts, when a true statement contains sensitive facts, then its very disclosure may result in a privacy intrusion.[31]

If information is false, then publication will allow for an actionable intrusion under a defamation theory of liability. Minor inaccuracies usually do not amount to defamation and are typically forgiven by the courts.[32] However, when a false statement results in harm to an individual's reputation in the community, then liability for defamation may exist.[33]

3. Is the Particular Information Private in Nature?

There are laws and legal principles in place that attempt to protect private facts from intrusions by anyone, including the media. Of course, the threshold problem is defining the facts that are "private." In general, if information is publically known (such as where it is available in public records, obtained in public space or disclosed on the Internet), then the press is not punished for publishing it.[34] The logic of this is that there is no reasonable expectation of privacy if the information is freely available or can be publicly observed. However, there are particular exceptions to this rule, such as video voyeurism in a public space where it is a violation to take an image of private parts. The law can also protect information that is especially sensitive—information that is seen as so intimate that disclosure would outrage a community's sense of decency even if that information might be obtained in a public record.[35]

In the United States, that finding is unusual. American courts conclude that if something is obtainable in a public record, then there is no expectation of privacy. Other jurisdictions outside the United States have reached different conclusions. Those conclusions are based on that country's or community's belief that personal dignity is held in high regard.[36] Therefore, it is communities that define the meaning of "private" information. Since communities define private information, understanding the nature of "community" in the new media world is a necessary part of understanding the standards of privacy.

4. Who Is Seeking Privacy Protection?

When weighing an individual's privacy rights against the public interest, identity matters. A public figure has less protection against privacy intrusions due to his or her standing in the community and the public value of the information surrounding him or her. Entering the public eye acts as a voluntary relinquishment of some expectation of privacy. As a result, liability will attach only if the publisher of information is malicious in its disclosure of information against a public figure.[37] When this same disclosure consists of private facts concerning a private individual, the courts have held that the lower standard of negligence applies.[38]

In defining who is a public figure, jurisdictional differences will lead to different results. As seen below, jurisdictional differences are an important piece of the privacy puzzle. In this context, while the United States employs a broad interpretation of who is a public figure, some foreign jurisdictions do not. For instance, in Germany, a court has even determined that a royal princess, a public figure, is not considered a public figure when performing private activity.[39]

In the United States, presumably, if a person is a private non-public figure, then he or she is entitled more protection because he or she is less newsworthy. However, a non-public figure can become a public figure involuntarily if an event—such as a highly publicized car wreck or crime—in which the person has been involved is of public interest. Moreover, even the family of a murder or accident victim may come under increased scrutiny. If the information is particularly private, the court may go so far as to grant protection of the privacy interest of third party family members after the subject's death. This protection has been granted even though, normally, privacy rights usually do not survive the death of the subject.

5. Is the Information Newsworthy?

The concept of whether information is newsworthy is of overriding importance in the United States. Defining newsworthiness is defining the nature and characteristics of the information. The First Amendment acts as a strong shield for the media and its overall freedom to disclose. If information is deemed to be newsworthy, then U.S. courts offer the media broad protection for publishing it. In fact, the courts have gone so far as to say that if the media has lawfully obtained information about a matter of public importance (i.e. it is newsworthy), then the government may not constitutionally punish publication of the truthful information, absent some need to further a state interest of the highest order.[40] Further, even if a third party has illegally obtained the information, the media is protected for the disclosure of such information if it is of public concern if the media was not culpably involved in the wrongdoing.[41] As stated above, this protection of the media extends to disclosure of both information concerning public figures and information about private persons involved in newsworthy events.[42]

6. In What Jurisdiction or Jurisdictions Did the Intrusion Occur?

Due to the prevalence of the Internet as a news medium, and the rise of new technology, what was once a seemingly straightforward question of jurisdiction, is now a set of complex issues. Each of the other issues in the matrix explicitly depends upon jurisdiction. For instance, jurisdictional problems arise due to the differing definitions of "newsworthy" found worldwide. The result of this difference becomes clear when comparing a French court decision against an American court decision dealing with similar facts. In France, a court held that a man who had marched in a gay-pride parade had the right to oppose publication of a photograph of him marching in the parade.[43] Although this man had voluntarily exposed himself and his homosexuality to the public, and the parade was an event worth reporting, the court held that mere exposure does not relinquish all rights the man had as against the greater public.[44] By contrast, in the U.S., the *San Francisco Chronicle* published an article concerning the homosexuality of Oliver Sipple—a man who was involuntarily exposed to fame.[45] The court held that even though Sipple suffered pain, ridicule, mental anguish and embarrassment due to this forced outing, the nature of his sexuality was deemed to be newsworthy and thus protected.[46]

These differing definitions of "newsworthy," combined with each jurisdiction's unique set of remedies and protections, explain why jurisdictions vary greatly in determining privacy intrusions. Moreover, this new world of uncertainty has created a new global forum shopping including what is known as "libel tourism." Celebrities and businesspeople alike are using foreign courts to avail themselves of the privacy laws that are less protective of media.[47] In sum, worldwide communication and cross-border publication give rise to complex questions concerning the newsworthy standard.

II. Applying the Matrix

Applying the foregoing matrix to an example demonstrates the contextual and fact-specific nature of privacy intrusions. In this example, suppose Mayor Jones of Orlando, Florida is visiting London. While on her trip, Mayor Jones spends an evening with her brother, who lives in London with his wife. A local blogger, John Smith, follows Mayor Jones on the behalf of one of the mayor's political rivals from Orlando. Smith takes pictures of Mayor Jones leaving her brother's apartment and posts to his blog. The blog includes a written statement claiming that Mayor Jones slept at a man's apartment (not including that it was Mayor Jones's brother's apartment) while she visited London. Applying the matrix, the following considerations arise:

1. How was the information obtained? The photograph was gathered from a public place—the street outside of the Mayor's brother's apartment. It is unlikely that Smith can be held liable for his method collecting the information. Smith did not obtain the information by wiretapping or any other illegal means and was observing from a public space. Further, the fact that the apartment was owned by a man was a public record.

2. Is the information factual and truthful? Mayor Jones was seen leaving a man's apartment where she had stayed the previous night. That information is true. However, the information is also incomplete and misleading. By omitting the fact that the apartment belonged to Mayor Jones's brother, the blog implies that Mayor Jones was engaged in lascivious behavior. The false impression this creates may be actionable under the doctrine of false light or defamation by implication. However, everything that Smith reported was true—a court may also be unconvinced that any liability would attach for the disclosure of truthful information.

3. Is the particular information private in nature? The action of entering and leaving an apartment on a public street is not a private fact. Regardless of how private the nature of the community, this information would most likely not be a private fact. It is coupling the public fact of leaving an apartment with the implication that Mayor Jones might have slept with a man who was not her husband that makes the statement potentially damaging and potentially illegally intrusive.

4. What is the identity of the person seeking privacy protection? The fact that Mayor Jones is a public figure gives her a lower expectation of privacy due to the nature of the position that she holds. However, Mayor Jones may still have an argument that the information disclosed was related to her private life and was a private event. To receive re-

dress there may be a need to prove that Smith was malicious and intended to both deceive the public and to harm Mayor Jones. Resolution of these issues may depend on resolution of question 6—jurisdiction—below. In the United States, where private activities of public officials are relevant to their public office, Mayor Jones's argument might fail and the disclosure would then be protected under the First Amendment.

5. Is the information newsworthy? Smith would likely be free from liability by the broad protection offered to those who report newsworthy information unless malicious intent was provable. In these circumstances, the identity of Mayor Jones is directly tied to the newsworthiness issue. If Smith's blog did not involve Mayor Jones, then the "event" itself is of little or no newsworthiness.

6. Where did the intrusion occur? The event Smith reported happened in London but was posted to a blog focused in Orlando, Florida. The disclosure in Orlando might be protected speech. The legal test is quite different if the blog in question is read in London. There is clearly a "nexus" to England, so the question is whether an English court might take jurisdiction. If they did, it is likely they would find that Smith may be liable for a "breached confidence" of Mayor Jones. The British courts protected international celebrity Michael Douglas from having a picture taken of his wedding because it was a private matter and he could expect that such a photo would not be taken.

The example of Mayor Jones and local blogger Smith is very similar. In all, this example shows how relatively simple facts require complex analysis and the importance of keeping this matrix of issues in mind when evaluating various media actions.

III. Examples of Media, Good and Bad

The following examples describe a range of real actions by the media in pursuit of stories. These examples are divided based on the action of the media in acquiring information or the medium used to distribute the information—specifically through print, broadcast and internet. Some of these intrusions advance the cause of free press while others do not. As these actual cases demonstrate, liability depends on a multitude of factors including the location of the action, the type of information and the medium of delivery. An important aspect of some of these cases is the publisher's use, or potential use, of multiple mediums in publishing information—a newspaper may distribute a video on its website or a broadcast television news program may run a story based on its blog. Each medium of delivery is not equal, with some (e.g. video) having a far greater impact than others (e.g. written word). The question is "in obtaining and disclosing information was media behaving badly or merely doing their job"?

1. The Newsgathering Process

Heroes are sometimes formed from the newsgathering process. Witness the effect of the "Pentagon Papers" and the important revelations produced after the *New York Times* published information describing the government's mishandling of the Vietnam War.[48] The government sought to prevent the *New York Times* from publishing leaked documents that revealed unfavorable details concerning the war. The government based its argument on the fact that a source had illegally leaked the confidential information to the newspaper.[49] However, the Supreme Court held that despite the nature of the source of the information, the *New York Times* did not unlawfully acquire the documents and was thus free to disclose. The Court justified its position by recognizing that the story was newsworthy and the public interest would be served by the information's disclosure. As a result, the public, which was already highly suspicious of government, praised the reporting of the *New York Times* for exposing these secret details.

At the other end of the spectrum are the situations when the newsgathering process is so intrusive that the public questions the methods and motives of the media. The examples below demonstrate this dynamic.

In April 2011, *News of the World* chief reporter Neville Thurlbeck, former editor Ian Edmondson, and journalist James Weatherup were all arrested on suspicion of phone-hacking charges.[50] Further investigation into News Corp., parent company of the *News of the World* paper, revealed that thousands of phone messages had been hacked into by News Corp. employees. Targets of such hackings ranged from celebrities, including Hugh Jackman and Sienna Miller, to 9/11 victims, royal aides, families of killed veterans of Iraq and Afghanistan, sports figures and even murder victims. Perhaps the most astonishing account was the phone hacking of Milly Dowler. Having gone missing in March of 2002, Dowler's family held onto hope that she was alive based on the continual deletion of her voicemail messages. It was later revealed that a private investigator, working for *News of the World*, had been intercepting the cellphone messages, using them and deleting them to make room for more messages. It wasn't until September 2002 that Dowler's remains were found, and it was not until July 2011 that the hacking was reported.[51]

Another example, in 2010, involved WikiLeaks which began publishing confidential Pentagon documents concerning the United States war in Afghanistan.[52] WikiLeaks, an independent whistle-blowing website, was created to expose governmental secrets through worldwide dissemination of classified documents. Although the public tends to laud the exposure of governmental secrets, WikiLeaks has recently come under scrutiny for the unredacted release of some of the diplomatic cables that it had in its possession.[53] Although WikiLeaks claims that it had no part in the release, the unredacted cables reveal the identity of government informants and raise issues of both individual and national security.[54] We as a society like whistleblowers—we like the idea of exposing shady and corrupt practices. Yet, society itself is threatened when media exposure of government practices pose a threat to national security. The WikiLeaks exposure presents the following question: at what point does the scale tip from allowing media to feed the public interest to prohibiting media to protect public security?

Next, in 1973, former First Lady Jacqueline Onassis won a lawsuit against an overzealous photographer.[55] The photographer, Donald Galella, sued Onassis after members of her Secret Service physically restrained him while he was harassing a young John F. Kennedy, Jr. in public.[56] The court sided with Onassis, holding that even when seeking information about a public figure, the First Amendment does not allow Galella to engage in harassment.

In 1998, photographers swarmed the car and impeded the departure of Arnold Schwarzenegger as he and his wife picked up their child from daycare.[57] Recovering from recent open-heart surgery, Schwarzenegger believed the photographers were attempting a kidnapping attempt. The photographers were convicted of misdemeanor false imprisonment.

In 2001, a teacher's union and the local school board in Pennsylvania were engaged in heated collective-bargaining negotiation. A phone conversation between the chief union negotiator, Bartniki, and the union president, Kane, was intercepted and recorded by an unidentified person.[58] This person gave the recording to a local radio journalist who then broadcasted the conversation on his radio show. The union members sued the journalist alleging violations of state and federal wiretapping statutes. However, the Supreme Court held that, as applied to the journalist, the wiretapping statutes were an unconstitutional violation of his free speech. Since the journalist did nothing illegal in acquiring the conversation, his First Amendment right outweighed the union's privacy interest.

2. Print

The print category of media encompasses the traditional mediums of delivery—newspapers, magazines and books. However, this traditional category has expanded with the inclusion of corresponding websites by most newspapers and magazines. Books can also now be found or published through online sources. This difference sometimes matters. Although it appears well settled in the United States that the publication of lawfully obtained, truthful, and newsworthy information receives the highest level of First Amendment protection, there is a dichotomy between the protection of the words and the protection of photographs reproduced by the same source.[59] Consequently, photographers may be more readily liable for intrusion because of the medium in which they work.[60] Some of the cases presented below demonstrate this reality.

In 1990, Danny Rolling murdered six college students at the University of Florida.[61] Rolling was eventually arrested and pled guilty to the charges. At his sentencing, crime scene photos of the victims were introduced into evidence to show the cruelty and savagery of the murders and ultimately resulted in the death penalty for Rolling. The media sought to access and ultimately publish the crime scene and autopsy photos.[62] However, because this case dealt with public records, the right to access these photos applied equally to all citizens—thus, the issue of release concerned general access, not merely a media privilege. Yet, the media still had an important role in implicating First Amendment concerns. The presiding judge, Judge Stanley Morris, invoked a creative and unique solution in balancing the public's right to know against the privacy interests of the victims' families. The Court ordered the photos to be available for public viewing; however, they could not be copied, removed or reproduced (and so could not be published).

In 2001, Dale Earnhardt, on the last lap of the Daytona 500, ran into the outside wall and died. Earnhardt was pronounced dead at the track and his autopsy was performed shortly thereafter. Due to his enormous fame, members of the press sought access to the autopsy photos even though they already had access to the autopsy report. However, unlike the Rolling case, there was no criminal proceeding—the issue was not that public record photos were being withheld but rather that Earnhardt was a person of public interest. The press sued the medical examiner for release of the photos, arguing that NASCAR safety was it issue.[63] The parties—Earnhardt's family seeking to keep the photos private, and newspapers seeking to publish them—reached an agreement to have an independent medical examiner review the photos and the report and decide if the photographs provided any additional value to the report. After finding that they did not, the photographs were not made public. The court in denying publication opined that release of the photographs would most likely result in "immediate, widespread dissemination of [the] images, including posting on the World Wide Web."[64] Thus, similar to *Rolling*, although the autopsy report was public, the Court withheld the release and controlled publication of the photographs due to the heightened intrusion that comes with the medium of photography.

Extending one step beyond the intrusiveness of photographs is the medium of videography. In 2010, Sea World trainer Dawn Brancheau drowned when a killer whale dragged her under water and held her there while she was working at Sea World, Orlando. Sea World, which routinely takes video, happened to capture the drowning. The media sought access to the video record. The video record was obtained by the Orange County Sherriff's Department and Medical Examiner as they probed the possibility of any criminal activity and the cause of death. Although kept confidential throughout the course of the investigation, at its completion the video would be classified as a public record.[65] The family of Brancheau immediately sought a preliminary injunction to prohibit the release of the video. The release of the video touches on concerns of not merely the publication of a public record, but its disclosure—had the video already been made public, there would be no remedy to its release and almost certain wide dissemination across the Internet. The Court conducted a balancing test, relying heavily on *Rolling*, and ruled to prevent the video's disclosure. This case again highlights that the medium by which a privacy intrusion takes place has tremendous effect upon the degree of that intrusion.

In another example of print media, a patient with HIV sued his hospital after his doctor and the hospital allowed a newspaper to photograph him while he was being treated for his illness. The photographer had promised the doctor that the patient would be unrecognizable in the publication. However, members of the man's family were able to recognize him based on the newspaper's photograph. The patient sued and won a judgment against both the hospital and the doctor. The doctor and the hospital, in turn, sued the newspaper for breach of contract, causing a breach of the doctor-patient privilege and negligence, among other things. The court ruled that the First Amendment did not shield the newspaper from liability because requiring the press to comply with its own promise did not infringe upon the freedom of the press.[66]

In 2008, in protest of the German government's shift toward the use of biometric information, the Chaos Computer Club, based in Germany, obtained the fingerprints of German Home Secretary Wolfgang Schäuble. The Club then published the fingerprints in their club magazine, *Die Datenschleuder*. Along with a copy of Schauble's fingerprints, the magazine also contained a film with Schauble's print, allowing readers to use his fingerprint as their own.[67] This is an example of yet another potential medium, "fingerprint film." The nature of this medium allowed anyone to repeatedly intrude on Schauble's privacy and actually use his own fingerprints.

In 2009, Max Mosley, head of Formula One auto racing, sued a United Kingdom newspaper for invasion of his privacy. The newspaper reported that Mosley had participated in a Nazi themed sex party. Mosley sued the newspaper after it posted a secretly recorded video on its Web site. The video showed Mosley at the party with two women, who had secretly recorded the party. Mosley admitted that German language was used and that there were sadomasochistic overtones, but said there were no Nazi references. The court awarded Mosely a £60,000 judgment, holding that the newspaper had violated Mosley's privacy. The video depicted non-criminal private activity between consenting adults and its contents were therefore private.[68]

Found in the midst of a teenage feud gone crazy is an example of how online publishing has added to the media's ability to intrude.[69] Shana Sandler and Mia Calcagni were high school friends until their friendship soured and they began to spread rumors about the other. The tension escalated to the point where Calcagni painted swastikas on stop signs near the home of Sandler, who is Jewish. Calcagni was subsequently charged, tried and convicted of criminal mischief. Upset at the result, Calcagni, with the aid of her parents, published a book through an online publisher, which told Calcagni's version of the history between her and Sandler. An event that might normally have been handled in a high school counseling session escalated into federal litigation when Sandler sued under theories of libel, false light, and public disclosure of private facts, among other things. In discussing false light, the court held that privacy "must be relative to the customs of the time and place.... Complete privacy does not exist in this world except in a desert, and anyone who is not a hermit must expect and endure the ordinary incidents of the community life of which he is a part."[70] The court then dismissed the case. This is yet another example where embarrassing, invasive, and allegedly private facts were exposed, yet the private nature of those facts did not rise to the level of an actionable suit against the party who published them.

3. Broadcast

Until recently, the broadcast category, which includes television and radio, has been the general public's clear medium of choice for news and information. However, compared to print media, the impact of audio and visual cues on the public are higher and thus raise the risk of privacy intrusion, as revealed by the following examples.

The United Nations has urged regulators in the United Kingdom to curtail reality shows that feature children and teenagers. The UN fears that such shows may be exploitive and harmful to the children while violating their privacy.[71] Implicating content restriction in broadcast media, this issue begs the question: would the same story be restricted if it were printed?

A documentary film crew traveled to the scene of an accident with medical helicopter personnel. Arriving in the medical helicopter, the camera crew filmed the rescue and the medical care of the car accident victim both on the scene and within the helicopter. After being sued, the Court held that the film crew was not liable for invasion of privacy for the parts of the documentary that were filmed outside of the helicopter. According to the court, the general public could have viewed these scenes, and therefore the victim had no expectation of privacy when she was being treated at the scene of the accident.[72]

Next, a reporter from Fox News went undercover as a college student to research a story on campus cult activity. While on campus, the reporter met and became involved in a Bible study conducted by a woman who was the campus ministry leader for the local branch of an international church. As part of her investigation, the reporter expressed interest in joining the church, which involved a private Bible study at the ministry leader's home. While at the Bible study, the reporter secretly recorded the session, and later used excerpts of the video footage in a subsequent news broadcast. The federal district court ruled that there was no legal ramification for the intrusion due to the absence of any actual physical intrusion.[73] Even though legally valid, both the gathering of this information and its broadcast could be considered intrusive.

Next, two New Jersey policemen sued ABC news after the station ran a program using clips from a secret camera investigation. ABC, in order to investigate racial profiling, had equipped a car with hidden cameras and had three young, black males drive the car on the New Jersey highway. The two officers stopped this particular car for a minor traffic violation. Yet, although a minor traffic stop, the officers made the passengers exit the vehicle while they conducted a search of the car. The car's hidden cameras recorded the entire process. ABC then used the footage interspersed with commentary from a law professor concerning the legality of the search, in a documentary it aired. The officers claimed that ABC committed defamation and fraud, and violated the New Jersey wiretapping statute. The court held that although ABC may have committed defamation, the officers could not recover under the wiretapping statute because they had no reasonable expectation of privacy in the car that they were searching. Further, the officers could not recover for fraudulent newsgathering because ABC recorded public officials in performance of their public duties, and not a private act.[74]

4. Internet

The newest medium for disseminating news and information is the Internet. It has a reach far more broad and wide than any other medium. It has the potential to spread information instantly and globally. As a mode of delivering information it encompasses all the previous mediums (can deliver data in written words, audio, or video format) and streamlines their delivery. Consequently, its potential for abuse is vast.

The story of Shirley Sherrod perhaps offers the most striking example of the reach, nature and effect that new media has on privacy. On the morning of July 19, 2010, a blogger posted a video excerpt of a public speech made by Department of Agriculture official Shirley Sherrod. The blogger, Andrew Breitbart, stated on his blog that Sherrod had racially discriminated against a white farmer in distributing funds. The blogger used the edited video to support his assertion. The blog and video spread like wildfire on the Internet and was quickly picked up by the mainstream media. Within a day of the video being posted, Ms. Sherrod was forced to resign. However, it was later revealed that the widely disseminated video was merely a clip from a longer video, which the NAACP posted in full the following day. After viewing the entire video, and less than 24 hours after forcing Sherrod to resign, the Obama administration realized that the edited video took Sherrod's comments out of context and apologized. Although apologies were issued, the damage to Sherrod had been done. New media had intruded with frightening speed and devastating impact. The speed, lack of verification for inaccuracies, wide dissemination and instant mob mentality that represent Sherrod's experience are all part of the new media reality.[75] This example also illustrates the toxic combination of new media's lightning quick delivery of information, which may be false, and the perceived legitimacy that attaches to it when traditional media re-publishes the info.

WikiLeaks, as discussed above, offers an example real tension between a desire to expose corruption, fraud and secrecy but a need to protect national security. In 2008, Republican vice-presidential candidate Sarah Palin's e-mail account was hacked and screenshots of the contents were posted on WikiLeaks. Hackers gained access using Yahoo!Mail's password reset function. The emails were then sent to WikiLeaks where they were posted as news. Interestingly enough, the Associated Press refused a request by the Secret Service for copies of the leaked e-mails.[76]

An additional consequence of technology is the ability of the Internet to circumvent and frustrate judicial remedies. In May 2011, Ryan Giggs, a British soccer star, sought an injunction to stop U.K. tabloids from publishing rumors that he was having an affair with TV star Imogen Thomas.[77] Giggs goal was to prevent the press from publishing this embarrassing information. The injunction Giggs sought, called a super-injunction, would suppress both the information (i.e. his affair) and the very fact that he was seeking the injunction through (1) service on non-parties to the underlying suit; (2) anonymous proceedings; (3) limited access to court records; and (4) prohibition on the disclosure or existence of the order and its proceedings.[78] However, although the media was bound by the ruling and could not report on it, individuals who found out about it were not. Unfortunately for Giggs, individuals did find out and posted to Twitter, where the information spread globally, virally and quickly. Thus, although Giggs was successful in prohibiting the tabloid paper from publishing the information, he was not successful in his ultimate goal of keeping the information secret. The super-injunction failed mainly due to the new revelation with the Internet that every individual now has the power and the resources to be a member of the media.

Similarly, in 2008, a New Zealand judge issued a gag order preventing the publication of the names of two defendants in a murder case. However, the names of these defendants were posted to the Internet from sources found to be overseas and therefore outside the court's jurisdiction.[79] Like the super-injunction and Giggs, this example reveals the Internet's frustration of the privacy remedy implemented by the court. This example also reveals the complex issue of press—privacy disputes that cross international borders.

The Internet creates unparalleled opportunities, for publication that are also unparalleled opportunities to intrude. The Internet allows and facilitates anonymous bloggers and "forum posting."[80] In 2008, the court determined that an individual who posted otherwise libelous information on a blog was protected because the location of the blog was a place where hyperbole was expected.[81] The California court set a dangerous precedent by relying on the rationale that the nature of the blog was informal, and thus readers of the blog would take messages posted there less seriously.[82] This methodology, however, is not followed by all courts, as seen in a New York Trial Court order that held the exact opposite. In finding that the blogger could be held liable for defamatory statements on his blog, the New York court focused on the actual statements published, and not on the medium of disclosure.[83]

Anonymous blogging also raises questions in the enforcement of privacy remedies. Although an anonymous blogger's ability to speak without recourse does further the tenants of the freedom of speech doctrine, it also reveals the lack of accountability and remedies that exist on the Internet when speech amounts to a privacy intrusion. If the individual who disclosed information is allowed to remain anonymous, then it is impossible to seek a legal remedy against them. For example, the City of Memphis sought to identify an anonymous blogger who criticized the city and its police department. The City never obtained the blogger's identity and only recently dropped a subpoena seeking that information.[84] In this case, we are sympathetic to a critic of government and the law would likely protect the identity of the critic as part of free speech. Anonymity is an important freedom as well as a potential source for abuses and lack of accountability.

Conclusion

Technology facilitates collection and publication of information in previously unthought-of ways. A smart phone can record an image of an event and send it to a global audience. The political impact can be immense and positive. The images of government abuses turned global opinion in the Arab Spring of 2011 and fostered opinion within those countries. What if such technologies had been available to alert the public of horrors of earlier times-such as the Holocaust? The benefit of modern technology in using information to promote democratic principles is unarguable. We must protect the political speech new technologies and the "new media" publish. Protecting the identity of the individual "reporter" who sends images of government atrocities to the world is critical.

Nevertheless, the harm fostered and made possible by new technologies cannot be ignored. The new media and old media can most certainly behave badly and they should be held accountable. The law continues to struggle with the facts and the evolving law of very new situations. The challenge is to maintain free speech and to protect the individual right to privacy and to be let alone from intrusion. The job of balancing these interests will only grow more complex and more difficult as technology continues to evolve.

THE INSTITUTIONAL PRESS, THE INTERNET, AND THE PARADOX OF THE PRESS CLAUSE

*William D. Araiza**

I. The Problem

What is "the press"? This question matters for legal doctrine when one considers the possibility that "the press," however defined, is entitled to special legal protections, whether as a matter of legislative grace, common tradition, or constitutional right. The question has special resonance in the American context, given the Constitution's express protection for "freedom ... of the press."[1] Despite this seemingly clear mandate for protection of the press, scholars and commentators have been unable to reach a consensus on even the preliminary question of whether, independent of the United States Constitution's Speech Clause, the Press Clause protects particular conduct or a particular group.[2]

This question is particularly relevant to a discussion of how technology relates to free expression. It has been a generation since Justice White, writing for the Supreme Court in *Branzburg v. Hayes*, expressed the view that the Press Clause protected "the lonely pamphleteer" as much as the (then) modern newspaper.[3] Since then, the Court has had to consider the difficult definitional prob-

* Professor of Law, Brooklyn Law School. Thanks to participants in the Free Speech Discussion Forum held in London in June 2012, and in the discussion group held at the 2012 meeting of the Southeastern Association of Law Schools, for stimulating discussion and helpful comments on this issue. Thanks also to Kristie LaSalle for fine research assistance. The author wishes to acknowledge the financial support provided by the Brooklyn Law School Dean's Summer Research Stipend Program.

lems associated with the Press Clause. The problem is seemingly straightforward: if the Press Clause provides more, or different, protection than the Speech Clause, it becomes necessary to define who enjoys that protection and in what context. Since much of the argument about such supplemental protection for the press has centered on claims for special privileges—whether exemptions from generally applicable laws[4] or special access to government facilities,[5] documents,[6] or decision-making proceedings[7]—the definitional question requires an answer unless anyone who plausibly claims to be the press can avail themselves of those privileges. Indeed, even if the Clause itself does not require this line-drawing, legislative and common-law courts' decisions to grant such privileges do so. The Press Clause might be implicated, albeit indirectly, if the grant of such privileges by legislature and courts reflects principles drawn from the Press Clause.[8] These sub-constitutional decisions might also implicate the Clause in a very different way, if legislative and common-law distinctions discriminate among particular members of "the press" in a way the Clause prohibits.[9]

The need to define the press, already salient when the world included both major newspapers and "the lonely pamphleteer who uses carbon paper or a mimeograph,"[10] is even more critical today, when that colorful (no pun intended) image has been supplanted by the extraordinary variety of types and formats of communication online. The Internet has affected the debate in at least two different, though related, ways. First, it has expanded into infinity the number of potential members of the press, at least if "the press" is defined simply by reference to the technical ability to amplify one's expression beyond hearing range.[11] This development raises serious questions about the workability of claims for special press privileges. In the past, when only a small group of persons possessed the means of voice amplification, a technological definition of the press was consistent with the grant of special privileges to "the press," as so defined. No more. Today, a technological definition of "the press" means that everyone is the press. But if everyone is the press, the notion of special privileges loses its meaning conceptually and becomes, to say the least, problematic to implement practically.[12]

Second, this expansion of the universe of information disseminators requires a fundamental rethinking of what it means to be the press. At least since the Supreme Court accepted First Amendment protection for cinema in 1952 and hedged with regard to the question whether cinema constituted "speech" or "the press" or both,[13] as a formal matter "the press" has been understood to mean potentially more than the traditional institutional press. Nevertheless, claims of special protection for the press have generally emanated from persons playing a recognizable role as members of the institutional press.[14] Occupying such a role included (professed) adherence to a set of journalistic norms that set them apart from others and supported their claims to special legal protections.[15] Indeed, it is perhaps not a historical accident that the mid-twentieth century Court's enthusiastic embrace of a specific freedom of the press, distinct from freedom of speech, roughly coincided with the maturation of the institutional press as a major component of American society.[16] It is an interesting question whether this correlation has a causal element—that is, whether the oligopolistic quality of the traditional newspaper industry[17] *created* the conditions in which guild-like professional standards could flower.[18] But for our purposes the causation issue need not detain us. Rather, the relevant point is that those possessing access to speech amplification technologies became, at least more or less, the group that adhered (or espoused adherence) to professional norms.

Today, when anyone with an Internet connection has access to speech amplification, that connection is broken. With the increase in would-be press members comes the dilution of any discernible criteria distinguishing press members from others based on their social role and professional norms. Of course, an institutional press is still identifiable, but it is no longer perfectly— or even approximately—coterminous with the group of speakers with access to means of mass communication.[19] This decoupling matters for Press Clause purposes because the existence of those norms suggested a particular role for the press—as a generally trustworthy source of relevant, objective information needed for democratic self-governance—that, in turn, strengthened the structural argument for press protection. If those norms are not practiced— even ostensibly—by those who can otherwise claim status as members of the press, then the argument for press privileges becomes significantly more problematic, apart from the sheer numerousness of the claimants. Moreover, if those norms are practiced by some members of the *new* media, then an identification challenge arises that was either not present or not as difficult when the Press Clause came into full flower at the Court.[20]

II. The Modern Debate

Recently, a lively debate has broken out over various aspects of this issue. Eugene Volokh has argued that the original meaning of "the press" referred to what he calls the "press-as-technology" rather than the "press-as-industry."[21] His article provoked responses. Patrick Charles and Kevin O'Neill have challenged Professor Volokh's methodology, though not all of his conclusions.[22] They argue that the intellectual history of the framers' understanding of "the freedom of the press" reveals at least some awareness of the press's distinctive role in the process of democratic self-governance.[23] Randall Bezanson has also challenged Volokh's technology-versus-industry schema and repeating his own earlier-developed view that defines the press by reference to its function of providing the public with truthful information relevant to self-government, filtered through professional, independent judgment.[24]

Meanwhile, Sonja West has confronted the practical difficulty of defining the press as part of her argument that the Press Clause should be understood to provide the press with special privileges.[25] She notes that legislatures and courts, in providing and construing press privileges of non-constitutional stature, have had to define the press. West suggests that those definitions provide the starting point for a definition of the press for explicitly constitutional purposes. In doing so, she engages earlier scholarship by another prominent scholar, David Anderson. Anderson has expressed concern about granting such special privileges, exactly because their existence would provide non-beneficiaries with a constitutional claim of deprivation of that same right.[26] Thus, while West argues for such privileges, and offers criteria for determining who should get them, Anderson worries that recognizing such privileges will trigger constitutional challenges by those who are denied them.[27] In an Internet world, where far more persons have a plausible claim to performing press functions, the prospect of such challenges is daunting.

Recognizing this difficulty, Adam Cohen takes a more radical position.[28] He argues that new forms of journalism—what he calls the "Fifth Estate" in contrast to the traditional press's identity as the "Fourth Estate"—have come to supplement traditional journalism to such a degree that they deserve equal status with their traditional counterparts. Given the difficulty of drawing lines demarcating these new news reporters[29]—and the likely futility of such lines, given the pace of the Web's technological and social evolution—he argues that this equal status should take the form of generally-applicable rights of access and participation in government, unbounded by definitional exclusions.

These different positions suggest very different answers to the problem posed by the Internet's challenge to traditional journalism. This brief essay cannot hope to resolve these issues. Instead, it aspires to make some preliminary observations about these various approaches, and to suggest tentative conclusions pointing the way toward further research. The scope of this discussion is also limited in another way. There may well be important attributes of the definition of the press, or of the protection it should enjoy, which are not directly relevant to the challenges posed by the Internet. Those factors may well be crucial for purposes of the Press Clause more generally, but are not relevant here. This essay confines itself to considering how the Internet affects questions about the press's constitutional status.

III. The Numerousness Challenge

How does the Internet's vast expansion of mass communicators impact debates about the Press Clause? An obvious preliminary answer is that it raises questions about the logical coherence and workability of any special treatment the press should enjoy. As to coherence: if everyone becomes the press, how can we say that the press enjoys special privileges? As to workability: if everyone becomes the press, how can special privileges be allocated in any practically workable way?

An analogue from the pre-Internet era illustrates the point. In *Jersawitz v. Hanberry*,[30] the Eleventh Circuit Court of Appeals considered a claim by Jersawitz, a self-styled "independent journalist," for access to a jail in order to interview an inmate. Jersawitz was in some ways a perfect forerunner of Internet-based media: he broadcast a public affairs show from a local access channel on a cable network that did not exercise any editorial control over the content,[31] and whose public access studio facilities were allegedly open to any citizen. He argued that federal prison regulations governing inmates' press access, which defined the press "as … persons whose principal employment is to gather or report news for … a radio or television news program of a station holding a Federal Communications license," constituted discrimination in violation of the Press Clause.[32]

The court had no difficulty rejecting his First Amendment claim, but only because of Supreme Court doctrine that denied the press special access privileges to jails.[33] With the press enjoying no special access rights,[34] discrimination in favor of professionally-affiliated journalists raised no First Amendment issue. The point, of course, is that if members of the press *did* enjoy special access privileges, then Jersawitz's denial of access would presumably have created a more difficult First Amendment problem.[35] If Jersawitz had a colorable constitutional claim in 1986, based on his citizen-journalist status on public-access cable, then presumably anyone using the Internet's far more accessible and powerful version of public-access broadcasting would have such a claim today.

The Supreme Court's most recent statements on government's power to discriminate between members of the press suggest that this problem may not be insurmountable—the Court has recently given legislatures discretion to discriminate as long as they do not do so on the basis of content.[36] This permissive attitude likely explains the continued existence of state laws that distinguish among press members for purposes of granting privileges.[37] But once again the Internet puts pressure on this idea, at least to the extent that the difference between traditional and non-traditional media correlates to a substantive difference in perspective, and thus a difference in content.[38] Thus, for example, to the extent commentators suggest that the press can be distinguished by adherence to professional norms, those suggestions might be vulnerable to claims that such distinctions amount to a preference for a certain perspective on the news,[39] or even for certain news content.[40] The Internet adds force to this claim, given its (theoretically) complete accessibility to anyone who wishes to disseminate information.

IV. Norms and the Challenge to the Identity of the Press

1. The Problem

The sheer number of would-be press members in turn generates the second problem—the breakdown of our intuitive sense of who constitutes "the press." The flowering of the Internet over the last decade has definitively—and presumably permanently—marked the end of the era in which, as Professor Anderson states, "the identity of the press seemed self-evident."[41] Growing out of, but distinct from, the numerousness challenge, what we can call "the identity challenge" forces us to consider basic questions about the Press Clause.

If we assume that the Clause is more than a value-neutral confirmation that the protections of the Speech Clause extend to speech carried out by mechanical amplification,[42] then we need criteria distinguishing "the press" from other media.[43] This was an easier task earlier in our history—at least during the mid-20th century when First Amendment law took its roughly modern shape. During that era, marked by smaller locally-owned newspapers and large, press-focused corporations[44] (the "large metropolitan publisher" noted in *Branzburg*[45] and radio and television networks and their affiliates), an observer could identify, if not precisely, at least the archetype of a press organ.[46] It was this social reality that made possible Justice Stewart's famous argument that the Press Clause protected an institutional press—the press that only emerged in full flower in the 20th century.[47]

Today we are witnessing an erosion of that reality, in favor of a more cacophonous and diverse "media" environment.[48] At its most extreme, this cacophony takes the form of technological developments that allow information consumers to tailor the material they receive. This development erases, or at the very least severely erodes, the editorial judgment that marks traditional journalism.[49] At the other end of the spectrum but with the same effect, the infinite space available online allows entities like Wikileaks simply to "dump" information, leaving it to the reader to search and sift to find the information that interests him.

Leave aside these more dramatic developments and assume the continuation in some form of the model where speakers decide what they want to say, and listeners receive that filtered content. Still, the rise of diverse online information sources poses squarely the question whether the speaker's acceptance of a set of professional norms should constitute one — or even the main — criterion of the modern press. For example, Bezanson argues that the press as a constitutional category is defined in part by its commitment to a truth-seeking process.[50] Others have also recognized the importance of such norms,[51] and have called for participants in that new environment to self-police and voluntarily institute norms that exist as a matter of professional status in traditional media.[52] However, the very nature of many new media participants as diverse and alternative information sources suggests the difficulty of such a proposal. The realization that new media may not fully accept these norms means that the rise of the Internet will require some hard decisions about who merits the status of "the press."

2. The Possibilities of a New Professional Press

Some commentators suggest that the definitional problem is solvable. In a recent article, Sonja West points to the variety of definitional distinctions sub-constitutional law makes when providing privileges to the press, and suggests that those distinctions can form the basis of judge-made constitutional distinctions.[53] Writing several years before West, Linda Berger argued for a "functional" definition of the press, focusing on the would-be press member's track record of gathering and disseminating useful and truthful information and employment of a process designed to verify the truth of information it uncovered.[54] In their jointly-authored paper earlier in this book, Russ Weaver, Clive Walker and Geoffrey Bennett note that a number of new media outlets have become respected journalistic sources.[55] When these arguments are combined, it becomes at least possible to envision a rational system of distinctions between press and non-press speakers, which are both workable as a matter of judicial decision-making and reflective of the values underlying the Press Clause.

Still, caution is in order. First, to the extent the distinctions West finds in sub-constitutional law are based on common law or legislation, they raise questions about courts' and legislatures' competence to draw the granular and policy-heavy distinctions necessary for realistic categorization. Judicial decision-making in this area — especially when it takes the form of first-instance decision-making, rather than review of legislative action — requires courts to both articulate and apply criteria definite enough to allow them to decide which members of the media merit the protection of the Press Clause. With regard to legislatures, the dynamism of the Internet suggests that statutory definitions would need to be both clear enough to avoid the vagueness that might allow decision-makers to play favorites based on inappropriate criteria, but also capacious enough to account for technological change. These challenges present tall orders to both sets of decision-makers.[56]

Second, definitions based on journalists' performance of traditional journalistic functions such as the dissemination of fact-checked information[57] may become harder to apply if traditional journalists themselves begin playing more diverse roles. Consider the announcement in May 2012 that the New Orleans *Times-Picayune* was ceasing every-day publication and moving to a predominantly Web-based presence.[58] That announcement was accompanied by reports that heretofore traditional reporters were going to be expected to blog throughout the day. Conversely, the online news source *The Huffington Post*, which has been sharply criticized as being nothing but a news aggregator,[59] was recently awarded a Pulitzer Prize for national reporting.[60] In addition, old and new media entities are cooperating in ways that blur the boundaries between the two.[61] These developments suggest that seemingly straightforward inquiries into the functions performed by claimants of a privilege might become substantially more intricate in the future.[62] Even before the advent of the Internet it was becoming clear that the merger of news and entertainment was making it hard to isolate the former for protected status. The Internet has muddied the waters even further by adding a new category of information dissemination — news and commentary that fulfills some but not all the criteria of traditional journalism, or that fulfills them sometimes but not always.[63]

Third, even if such distinctions could be drawn, the question remains whether any such line-drawing would inevitably risk the type of favoritism the Press Clause was designed to prevent. This consideration complicates the line-drawing exercise even more, by introducing into the set of functional factors offered by scholars such as West and Berger the additional requirement that such distinctions not violate the basic premise of the Press Clause itself. Indeed, it may be that, to paraphrase Marshall McLuhan, the profession is at least part of the message.[64] In particular, using professionalism criteria to identify the press may risk discrimination based on the perspective of the would-be journalist.[65] In *Jersawitz*, the seemingly-straightforward case rejecting the citizen-journalist's prison access claim,[66] the court had to go out of its way to reject the plaintiff's claim that the prison's discrimination in favor of professionally-affiliated journalists was based on the prison's "decision whether or not a newsman would report fairly and objectively."[67] The court's explicit rejection of that argument implies the plausibility of a concern that professionalism criteria could mask a government preference for a particular type of content, or at least a particular perspective on the news. In a world where non-professional journalists played, at most, a peripheral role in mass information dissemination, this concern may not have been as salient, since only professionally-normed journalists enjoyed the capability of amplifying their voices.[68] That simplifying fact no longer exists. Consequently, today we are forced to confront the implications of relying on professionalism norms as a criterion for protection.

Some theorists, such as Bezanson, would likely not be concerned by the prospect of drawing lines between the press and others based on commitments to professionalism. For them, the press is, quite literally, defined by a professional concern for disseminating accurate information useful for democratic self-government.[69] If this understanding of the press prevails, then discrimination based on professionalism criteria would pose no constitutional problem, as long as we understood such a distinction as an appropriate exception to the Speech Clause's more general rule against identity or content-based speech restrictions.[70] Moreover, as scholars have noted, excluding persons from the status of "the press" would still leave them with the significant communication protections offered by the Speech Clause.

Other scholars might be troubled by the privileging of such criteria. Indeed, the focus on professionalism may be problematic in light of claims that such very professionalization has distorted the information provided to the public. Even if these latter commentators are not pleased with the current day's completely market-driven approach to the value of information,[71] the flaws of traditional journalism[72] may tempt us to reject professionalism as a criterion for bestowing whatever constitutional protection the Press Clause might provide. Stated more positively, non-professional journalists may play at least some useful role in fostering democratic debate.[73] Surely, for example, an amateur journalist who goes to Tahrir Square or Occupy Wall Street's encampment and seeks out protesters to interview and posts the interviews online plays some role beyond that of a mere information aggregator. Would they enjoy no rights under the Press Clause because they did not go to journalism school? Because they did not have an editor? Would we be content with those results if the amateur journalist continued to enjoy protections under the Speech Clause?

V. Preliminary Lessons

This short chapter cannot comprehensively analyze how the Internet affects coverage issues under the Press Clause. However, the observations above suggest some tentative conclusions.

1. Special Press Protection Requires Conscious Inclusion/Exclusion Decisions

If there was ever a time when it was easy to determine who constituted the press, that time is over. The Internet ensures that the ability to project one's voice now belongs to everyone. Thus, if the press is identified as comprising persons with the capability of amplification[74] that category is limitless, at least in the United States and other developed nations. Even if the press is defined as those with both the capability and the regular habit of doing so, the number is quite large.

This obvious fact leads to another, only slightly less obvious, insight: not everyone who could qualify as the press under even the more limited of the two definitions above can enjoy significant special protections. The brute fact is that special protections cease to be special when everyone, or a large group, enjoys them. If such protections are to follow from the status of press organ, then decisions will have to be made excluding from the press at least some individuals who regularly disseminate information to a broad public. Even if the press enjoys no special constitutional protections, it remains necessary to define the press in some way in order to decide claims of discrimination within the press.[75] Those definitional decisions may be based on a deeper theory of who *really* constitutes "the press"—for example, a theory that focuses on independent editorial judgment based on a concern for the public interest.[76] But such a theory would still require difficult inclusion/exclusion decisions.[77] Choices have to be made.

2. Exclusion Decisions Are Probably Best Made by Legislatures

Such choices are probably best made by legislatures. As a general matter, legislatures are superior to courts in drawing lines that are to some degree arbitrary, in the sense that they could just as defensibly be drawn elsewhere.[78] In our case, the criteria that would distinguish press members from non-press speakers are sufficiently indefinite that courts would find it exceptionally difficult to make distinctions with any credibility.[79] Indeed, to the extent those criteria themselves derived from vague principles flowing from the Press Clause,[80] they would be doubly ambiguous.[81] Judicial attempts to draw such lines would be subject to the criticism that they create unprincipled results that arbitrarily distinguish between similarly-situated journalists. By contrast, the nature of legislative power is such that such "arbitrary" line-drawing is both commonplace and accepted.[82] Thus, legislatures' superiority at what Anderson calls "fine-tuning"[83] access and other press-related rights justifies a primary focus on statutory, rather than judicial, recognition of press rights.

This tentative call for legislative implementation of the Press Clause echoes scholars' recognition in other contexts that legislative action may be best suited for implementing often-vague constitutional provisions.[84] As in those other areas, the ambiguity implicit in the Press Clause's open-ended language justifies legislative action, not just because of the institutional competence concerns noted above, but also because those concerns may lead courts to under-enforce constitutional rights.[85] In the press area, concerns about judicial competence are exacerbated by the fast-changing nature of the press-media landscape. The dynamism of that environment both makes credible line-drawing difficult at any given moment and renders decisions subject to quick obsolescence. Both of these factors militate in favor of legislative action, rather than action by courts. Concededly, the difficulty inherent in enacting or amending legislation suggests that legislatures may not be as quick as one might wish in responding to technological change.[86] But this disadvantage may well be outweighed by the problem facing courts in making principled decisions that require either granular distinctions between different actors[87] or, at the other extreme, rough categorizations that would appear arbitrary if coming from courts but that might appear defensible as inevitable legislative line-drawing.[88]

Furthermore, judicial decision-making is likely to be *post hoc*, at least in many circumstances, as plaintiffs mount press freedom claims that are not clearly governed by prior caselaw. The post-hoc nature of those decisions may render them less useful for vindicating underlying Press Clause values, if the unpredictability of those decisions either chills newsgathering or delays resolution of the claim until the newsworthy event has passed from public attention. This concern suggests the usefulness of *ex ante* rules. Given the difficulties courts would likely face in providing such rules, the practicalities of press protection seem to favor legislative action.

3. A Judicial Role Remains in Reviewing the Distinctions Made by Legislatures

This preference for legislative line-drawing does not mean that courts lack any role in these decisions. Distinguishing among speakers for the purpose of allocating special press benefits carries its own risks, which require some level of judicial oversight.[89] As a matter of standard constitutional doctrine, classifications based on speaker identity and speech content are presumptively unconstitutional.[90] Even if one accepts that the press enjoys special protection, therefore requiring identification of the entities that constitute the press, basing such identification on the content of the speech produced carries the risk of the sort of discrimination the Court has found to violate both the Press and the Speech Clauses.[91] Judicial review of such decisions may be necessary to guard against inappropriate discrimination.

Anderson argues that such distinctions need not concern courts greatly if they are based on non-constitutional grounds rather on the favored group's status as the press.[92] The theory seems to be that if the Press Clause does not grant any rights, then any favored treatment a legislature might grant is, by definition, not based on any constitutionally-favored status as "the press." But this argument presupposes that such protection is truly non-constitutional. That assumption may not be fully warranted. To the extent that one can understand such protections as prophylactic legislation enforcing an otherwise under-enforced Press Clause,[93] such legislation could be seen as resting on values underpinning the Press Clause. If the Press Clause does in fact contain such values, then legislation of this type could encounter the objection that it actually violates those values, and hence, the Clause itself.[94] This prospect warrants a judicial role—not to grant or deny "press" status in the first instance, but to review legislative grants of that status, at least for reasonableness and conformance with an appropriate non-discrimination requirement.[95]

Of course, sometimes the legislature may not act, or its legislation may not address every situation where a press freedom claim is made. In such cases, courts may be required to fill the gap and determine an individual's press status as a first-order matter. Such cases may present courts with difficult issues, even if they start with the assumption that their relative lack of institutional competence prevents them from protecting press actors to the full measure envisioned by the Press Clause. Perhaps the best that we can say about their responsibility to decide those cases is that those decisions should be understood as constitutional common law, susceptible to legislative overruling with the caveat that such legislative action should then itself be subject to some relatively deferential but still meaningful level of judicial review.

The template for such an approach may be *Katzenbach v. Morgan*,[96] the 1966 case where the Court upheld, as legislation enforcing the Fourteenth Amendment, a federal law banning certain literacy tests for voting, despite a previous Court decision refusing to find literacy tests *per se* unconstitutional. In *Morgan* the Court both recognized broad congressional power to make determinations relevant to constitutional questions when the judiciary lacked such competence, yet reviewed the legislation to ensure that it did not itself violate the right it sought to vindicate. Since *Morgan*, the Court, jealous about guarding its own supremacy in constitutional interpretation, has not looked kindly upon congressional attempts to fill in constitutional meaning in ways that appeared to supersede the Court's own decisions, even when those decisions appear to be motivated by concerns over its competence to do more.[97] Perhaps new confrontations with the Press Clause will lead it in a different direction.

4. Appropriate Identification of the Press May Turn on the Particular Rights at Issue, and Vice-Versa

At first blush this suggestion is counter-intuitive: one might think that the identification of the press poses a question logically on the determination of a particular set of rights the press enjoys. But the problem posed by the large number of parties with a plausible claim on the status of prior to, and independent of, "the press" is such that one can't decide who enjoys the protection of the Press Clause until we understand what rights that status actually bestows. This is true as a practical matter because, as noted earlier, not everyone can be "the press" if the press enjoys significant special rights.

But it is also true in a deeper sense. What the Internet proves (if it wasn't already clear) is that no natural category of individuals or institutions called "the press" exists. Rather, we need to choose which individuals enjoy that title for constitutional purposes. In turn, making that choice with open eyes requires us to understand the relevant identifying criteria. Those criteria could derive from a variety of sources: framing-era understandings, a modern theory of how the Press Clause fits within our democratic system, or other criteria entirely. Finally, in a move that creates a feedback loop, the criteria we select will influence the rights enjoyed by whoever we decide merits the title, "the press." For example, if we choose to identify the press by reference to its historical practice of assisting democratic self-government by providing reliable information about public matters free of government influence, then presumably that criterion will influence our understanding of what protection it should receive.[98]

Conclusion

The Internet has unsettled our perhaps too-comfortable assumptions about who constitutes the press. Given the Web's dynamism, no reason exists to think that a new conventional wisdom will arise anytime soon. This fact suggests caution about attempts to define for all time and as a constitutional mandate a set of rigid and detailed criteria for defining the press. But this insight in turn creates a paradox. If the press's role is to be independent of government, and if invidious non-discrimination between members of the press is the bare minimum principle of any press guarantee, then legislative definitions of the press—seemingly the obvious alternative to judicial definitions based solely on the sparse language of the Press Clause—are also potentially troubling.

Writing a decade ago, Professor Anderson observed that technological and business changes were rendering obsolete our ability to rely on formats as a non-controversial proxy for determining who constituted the press.[99] Those changes have, if anything, accelerated since then. The consequence is that *somebody* will have to decide who constitutes "the press." As sketched out above, answers are possible. But the task should be one jointly undertaken by courts and legislatures, each adding their distinctive competencies and checking the other. The result is likely to be messy, not fully satisfactory, and continually unstable as communications technology and business models evolve. But such a state of affairs is likely inevitable in a world where, otherwise, we all have a plausible claim to the protections of the Press Clause.

4

Does The Internet Require Rethinking First Amendment Theory?

Arnold H. Loewy[*]

One clear First Amendment principle is that each medium seems to have its own law. So, there is a law of movies,[1] a law of live entertainment,[2] a law of billboards,[3] a law of sound trucks,[4] a law of leaflets,[5] and a law of picketing.[6] For the most part, these different rules are predicated on the non-speech harm that each form of these media inflicts.[7] For example, live entertainment can involve indecent exposure[8] or excessive noise.[9] Billboards can distract drivers, sound trucks can be noisy, leaflets can be litter,[10] and picketing can involve trespass.[11]

The Internet, to be sure, has its own capacity for harm. Lies, half-truths, vicious rumors, and urban legends spread faster on the Internet than ever before. Citizens, who have to worry about real fraudulent schemes, may start worrying about schemes made up on the Internet. Frankly, many seem believable enough to concern otherwise careful people. The website, Snopes, has tracked down some that are false,[12] but in the meantime people believe them. These false emails include false stories of criminal methodology, as well as false statements of presidential intelligence. Of course in some cases, particularly in the eyes of those who don't like the demeaned president's politics, there may be just enough appearance of truth to be believed.

One thing that should be apparent is that these harms are directly related to speech. Consequently, they cannot be regulated because of the "plus" character that justifies the regulation of other media. If they can be regulated, it is only because to some extent pure speech can be regulated.

---

[*] George Killam Professor of Criminal Law, Texas Tech School of Law.

For good or ill, the United States Supreme Court has held that obscenity is not protected speech.[13] Consequently, anything on the Internet that is obscene is subject to prosecution. Of course, in recent years, little if any of what Justice Stewart used to know when he saw it[14] as obscenity would be obscene today. Consequently, that category, though nominally on the books, is essentially illusory. Of course, the display of exploited children in a pornographic way is subject to punishment whether it appears on the Internet or elsewhere.[15]

Beyond that, we are left with the Internet's capacity to proliferate lies. Should that concern us? Well, in the context of false statements about people, our libel jurisprudence should suffice.[16] To be sure, one can hardly imagine a president suing about a false claim of his low I.Q. And, it may be that few libel suits will be successful, or even worth bringing. That was true before the Internet, but I doubt that the Internet's added capacity changes the position.

One possible difference is what Russell Weaver terms: "The absence of gatekeepers."[17] At least before the era of the Internet, an irresponsible journalist had to get past the editorial board of a newspaper or a publisher of a book. No more. All he/she needs to do is post on the Internet in blog or even direct form. Neither intelligence nor honesty is a criterion for entry.

This distinction should not matter as far as libel is concerned. *New York Times v. Sullivan*[18] and its progeny have hammered out a relatively clear law in the area, and nothing about the Internet that warrants a different result.

What about out-and-out lies about things like phony scams and other such devices that can frighten the populace? The answer is indicated in the recent case, *United States v. Alvarez*.[19] Alvarez himself was not an Internet liar. Rather he told his lies the old fashioned way—at a public meeting. Specifically, he lied about his military record, claiming it was stellar when in fact it was nonexistent. He was convicted of violating the Stolen Valor Act,[20] which conviction was overturned by the 9th circuit. At issue in the Supreme Court is whether naked lies are punishable. The Supreme Court affirmed the 9th Circuit and struck down the Act[21]—and rightly so. Why? Well first of all, lies that do real harm, such as libel (under limited circumstances) and fraud are punishable. Naked lies classically have not been. As Judge Kozinski noted in refusing an *en banc* hearing, people lie all of the time.[22]

There is another reason for not punishing lies, which is that it gives government the power to declare the truth. While that may not seem like so much of a problem in *Alvarez*, what about punishment for misstating historical truths, such as the Holocaust denier? Although in America, it seems probable that such a prosecution would not be permissible,[23] the same cannot always be said for Europe.[24] So, by disallowing punishment for naked lies, the Court would avoid the problem that so besets some jurisdictions in Europe of having government declared truths.

Even after the judgment in *Alvarez*, is there not a difference in Internet lies given the possibility of detrimental reliance? For example, consider one message of fear spread on the Internet: "Do not lock your car with a remote key fob because thieves are able to intercept the code and unlock your door." Let us assume that this is false, but nevertheless a great many people refrain from locking their car with a key fob and others worry when they do it. Is this something that should concern us? The answer should be "no" for many reasons. First, a person can usually check the truth or falsity of the email on Snopes.com or elsewhere. Second, if the person is unaware of Snopes or chooses not to make any inquiries anywhere, the harm is relatively minimal. Third, the harm of government-declared truth is almost surely greater.

On that last point, consider the issue of litigating truth. Suppose the original poster, assuming that she could be found, establishes that there was an incident of intercepting the code from a key fob, and that person stole the contents of the car. Would that preclude the statement from being false even though the magnitude of the problem was grossly exaggerated? For sure, I cannot imagine the courts wanting to deal with that type of problem.[25]

So, it does not appear that there is anything about the Internet that requires special First Amendment rules. Obscenity and libel rules, such as they are, are already in place. Perhaps some limitation on juvenile access would be appropriate, although, as the Court said so many years ago: "[We cannot] reduce the adult population ... to reading only what is fit for children ..."[26]

The only remaining problem concerns lies that inconvenience or mislead people. In the light of the decision in *Alvarez* where four Justices took the view that false statements are not, by reason of their falsity, beyond from the First Amendment. Thus, a special Internet rule would be needed if we are to punish Internet lies.

In my judgment, no such special rule is warranted. The reason is simple. As Justice Jackson reminded us nearly seventy years ago: "It cannot be the duty because it is not the right of the state to protect the public against false doctrine. The very purpose of the First Amendment is to foreclose public authority from assuming a guardianship of the public mind through regulating the press, speech, and religion. In this field every person must be his own watchman for truth, because the forefathers did not trust any government to separate the true from the false for us ... Nor would I."[27] That was good law in the pen and paper age, and should remain good law in the Internet age.

5

The Promise and Peril of Protesting in the Internet Era

Christina E. Wells[*]

Introduction

There is much to criticize regarding government regulation of protestors these days. Pictures of crackdowns against largely peaceful protestors littered the news during the Middle East uprisings in 2011.[1] In 2012, Russia reportedly passed a law penalizing anyone protesting without official permission.[2] Western democracies fare little better despite their ostensibly strong free speech traditions. In 2012, after months of protests opposing university tuition increases, lawmakers in Quebec restricted protests, which eventually resulted in mass arrests.[3] In the United States, officials have also restricted protest activities in recent years, including caging protestors at presidential conventions,[4] using free speech zones at universities,[5] establishing large no-protest zones around funerals,[6] imposing restrictive permitting requirements on protestors,[7] and aggressively policing protestors, including the recent Occupy movement.[8] Such tactics, observers note, "represent a movement toward a perfect geometry of control over just the sort of speech [that we] ought to protect—that which challenges authority, offends sensibilities, or otherwise 'disturbs the complacent.'"[9]

Some of this desire to control protestors occurs in countries where free speech traditions are neither politically nor legally rooted. But even in coun-

* Enoch H. Crowder Professor of Law, University of Missouri School of Law. Special thanks go to Paul Vaughan for research assistance and comments on this essay. The participants in the First Amendment Discussion Forum in Notre Dame University, London also provided valuable insights and comments on earlier versions of this essay.

tries with arguably strong constitutional protection of free expression, such as the United States, there is still great room for censorship of protestors. Scholars have exposed the extent to which the United States Supreme Court's existing doctrine allows officials to control protests. For example, the Court's classification of government property into different kinds of expressive "forums"[10] significantly under-protects speech.[11] Similarly, the Court's use of a deferential balancing test to judge restrictions of protestors favors the government. Observers have called the test superficial, thoughtless and "untethered [from] the purposes that it is actually serving."[12]

This essay examines the effect of evolving technology and communication methods on protestors and the judicial treatment of them. Such technologies can have the pragmatic and liberating effect of allowing protestors to work around current restrictive practices that existing law condones. For example, rather than attempt to access public property directly (leaving themselves open to repressive physical tactics or inhospitable legal rules), protestors can organize online as they did earlier this year in response to the proposed Stop Online Piracy Act.[13] Similarly, the availability of social media and other electronic communication allows social movements to sustain themselves in the face of repressive tactics that otherwise affect individuals' abilities to associate for expressive purposes.[14] Ultimately, such use of Internet technologies may inform courts, perhaps giving protestors greater protection under the Court's existing doctrine.

Evolving technologies, however, come with a price for protestors. Individuals and groups' increased presence online brings increased vulnerability to different forms of repression. Government officials can more easily engage in surveillance of protestors over the Internet. Such surveillance has few legal restrictions and gives officials tactical advantages as they attempt to curtail traditional protests.[15] Protestors' reliance on Internet communications makes them similarly vulnerable to government attempts to control or limit communication when used to facilitate protests, as the Arab Spring protests illustrate.[16] Furthermore, Internet access and content decisions often lie in the hands of private decision-makers,[17] an evolution that sits uneasily within the Court's doctrine.

I. The Legal Landscape Relevant to Protestors

The United States Supreme Court has developed a relatively stable, if highly criticized, doctrine applicable to most protests. That doctrine focuses on protestors as physically-present actors whose desired use of property must be balanced against others' conflicting uses. There are three primary results from this focus. First, the Court determines the type of property to which protestors seek access; government officials and private property owners then have great latitude to claim that most property is inappropriate for protesting. Second, the Court allows officials to control negative effects and conflicting uses of protests via neutral permitting requirements. Third, the Court allows officials and legislatures to impose neutral time, place and manner restrictions that zone or otherwise restrict protestors.

1. The Rules

When and where protestors can assemble for expressive purposes depends largely on the type of property they attempt to access. Protestors effectively have no right of access to another's private property for expressive purposes.[18] As a result, publicly owned property is often the only available space in which protest groups of any size can gather.[19] The Supreme Court recognizes that assembly in certain public spaces—such as streets, parks and sidewalks—"has, from ancient times, been a part of the privileges, immunities, rights, and liberties of the citizens."[20] Categorizing such spaces as "traditional public forums," the Court has declared that "the government may not prohibit all communicative activity."[21] On the other hand the government may regulate expressive activity in traditional public forums "in the interest of all," subordinating free speech rights to "the general comfort and convenience" or "peace and good order" if necessary.[22]

In determining whether government officials may subordinate speech rights in a traditional public forum, courts focus first on whether a restriction is content-based or content-neutral. The Court's doctrine highly disfavors content-based regulations, subjecting them to strict scrutiny, which usually results in their demise.[23] However, it subjects content-neutral regulations to much lesser, intermediate scrutiny and often upholds them if they are deemed reasonable time, place and manner regulations of speech. Such regulations essentially take two forms—laws imposing restrictions on protests or permitting schemes requiring protestors to apply for permission prior to protesting.

When the Court scrutinizes a content-neutral law, such as a law excluding all protestors from certain streets and sidewalks near hospitals, churches or cemeteries,[24] it applies "intermediate scrutiny," which requires that the law be "narrowly tailored to serve a significant government interest, and … leave open ample alternative channels for communication of information."[25] This test is far more lenient than the Court's presumptive hostility to content-based regulations and the Court frequently upholds content-neutral regulations of speech.[26]

The Court's approach to permitting schemes is similar, subject to an added twist. Because licensing schemes require advance permission to speak in a traditional public forum they are potentially "prior restraints" of speech. Permitting schemes that vest unfettered discretion in officials are invalid because the lack of standards may hide content discrimination and cause speakers to self-censor.[27] The Court, however, recognizes that permit requirements can aid government efforts to accommodate both government interests and protestors' rights in traditional public forums. In fact, the primary purpose of such regimes is to "assure the safety and convenience" of people using public property and to "maintain[] public order" without "abridging the right of assembly."[28] Permitting schemes are constitutional as long as they apply clear, neutral standards that rely only on "considerations of time, place and manner so as to preserve the public convenience."[29]

Protestors often seek access to public property other than the streets, parks and sidewalks that constitute traditional public forums. But the Court is far less willing to recognize speakers' rights of access to such property. Thus, the Court recognizes "designated public forums," which include property, such as public meeting facilities, that government officials have "opened for use by the public as a place for expressive activity."[30] Such forums are created only through "purposeful government action" showing an intent to open the forum for speech purposes.[31] Although the government need not open such forums, once it does, it is bound by the same rules as in traditional public forums.[32] The last forum—the "nonpublic forum"—includes most remaining government property. Such property is "not ... by tradition or designation a forum for public communication" and government officials, like private property owners, are entitled to reserve the property for its intended purpose.[33] Because robust expression is incompatible with other uses of nonpublic forums, the government may control access to the property as long as its rules are reasonable and not aimed at suppressing viewpoints.[34]

2. The Critics

Commentators have not been kind to these rules. Observers criticize the very creation of the forum categories, especially the nonpublic forum, noting that the Court's doctrine closes off huge swaths of government property, effectively making such areas "free speech zones."[35] Only streets, parks and sidewalks remain areas of obvious access for protestors and only then because they have "traditionally" been so. Such a result, critics argue, fails to account for the many kinds of property—e.g., courthouse lawns, transportation hubs— that are similar to traditional public forums and which might be reasonable gathering places for speakers.[36] Furthermore, exclusion of protestors from most public property fails to account for the role that "place" may have to protestors' message.[37]

Scholars similarly criticize the Court's approach to the traditional public forum, the most generous of the Court's categories. Intermediate scrutiny's balancing of state interests and free speech rights is easily manipulated.[38] As a result, government officials can engage in repressive tactics and surreptitious content discrimination while arguably acting in accordance with the Court's doctrine. Many scholars criticize courts' failure to scrutinize the state's interest with any rigor, noting that officials wield "security" or "public disorder" as state interests with near impunity.[39] Once courts accept such interests, they usually apply the narrow tailoring requirements so loosely as to defer to the government's own "reasonable determination" of how to achieve its interests.[40] Thus, the caging or penning of protestors, the establishment of no-protest zones (places where speech is excluded from a public forum) or free speech zones (places where speech is allowed), or the heavy-handed policing of protestors are all tactics courts have considered narrowly-tailored to meet the government's interests in preserving security and preventing disorder.[41]

Such deference has significant negative implications for protestors. Despite the evident neutrality of the balancing metaphor, state interests such as security and disorder often mask content discrimination. Officials positing national security concerns to justify protestor "pens" or "cages" at presidential conventions inevitably raise them only against persons protesting candidate platforms; persons supporting candidates are rarely subjected to such indignities.[42] This is not to say that officials consciously discriminate based on content but simply that protestors who seek change seem threatening; officials are more likely to see them as source of disorder.[43] Accordingly, where protestors "are placed depends in substantial part on what [they] have to say."[44] Similarly, intermediate scrutiny allows restrictions that interfere with protestors' messages. By creating large bubble zones around an audience or caging protestors away from that audience, officials impede protestors' communication with their intended audience.[45] Furthermore, the point of many protests *is* disruption of the existing social or political order. "That message is suppressed entirely when [protestors] are herded into pens, cages, gazebos, and speech zones."[46]

Application of arguably neutral permitting schemes raises similar concerns. Critics observe that permit requirements effectively prevent "spontaneous or leaderless marches" and the natural, evolving messages that the protestors attempt to convey.[47] Furthermore, officials apparently assume that large groups of protestors or mass demonstrations pose an inherent threat of disruption.[48] Thus, they can deny permits if they believe a large protest will be unsafe or disruptive[49]—a consequence that is all too easy for administrators to envision.[50] Law enforcement officials supervising permitted protests operate on a similar assumption, increasingly using aggressive and violent tactics to quell "disorderly" protests that evidence suggests were simply large with isolated incidents of disorder.[51] The deference granted to police arresting protestors under disorderly conduct statutes often leaves protestors with little recourse when challenging their arrests.[52]

Ultimately, the Court's doctrine applicable to protestors, though ostensibly neutral, aids in promoting the commonly held view of them as "irrational, fickle, violent, undirected, and contagious."[53] Such a view undermines long traditions of public assembly and the power of group messages.

II. The Promise of Internet Technologies as Applied to Protestors

The advent of the Internet, and especially technologies involving social media such as Facebook, Twitter, and Flickr, as well as mobile Internet technology,[54] gives protestors alternatives to the traditional legal paradigm described above. Some of these alternatives are simply work-arounds, enabling traditional protestors to sustain their protests in the face of hostile government officials or unaccommodating doctrine. Others involve different forms of protest altogether.

1. Sustaining Traditional Protests

Internet technology gives leaders of social movements access to a broad array of organizational and communicative tools. As people increasingly use the Internet to communicate, both individually and through community discussion groups, protest organizers can easily and cheaply disseminate plans and organize events.[55] The protests in Egypt during the 2010–11 uprisings were partially organized through Facebook, as were protests in other countries.[56] Similarly, the Occupy movement in the United States uses a webpage to communicate information about planned protests and other events regarding the movement.[57] Such technology is useful not only for communicating with existing and potential members, it can also aid in working with officials while negotiating protest permits as it may facilitate faster, easier and better planning of protests.

Internet technology also helps sustain protests in the face of repressive tactics or inhospitable legal rules. Smartphone technology allowed protestors in

Tunisia and Egypt to photograph and videotape the repressive response to protests and post that material to various social media websites, eventually spurring further protests.[58] Similarly, the mainstream media largely ignored the Occupy movement until a video of police officers pepper spraying apparently peaceful protestors was posted online.[59] Subsequently, traditional media coverage and public support for the protestors increased.[60] Accordingly, self-reporting of protest events through Internet technologies aids in avoiding both "hard" censorship of government officials and the "soft censorship of the mainstream media."[61] The latter is especially important as the mainstream media, considered to be a primary check on government misconduct, often accepts (knowingly or not) the traditional portrait of protestors as "irrational, fickle, violent, undirected, and contagious." Internet technology forces that media to take seriously a group of people that it otherwise dismissed as a lunatic fringe.

In addition, self-reporting (and concomitant mainstream media coverage) can inform legal issues. Such coverage provides important factual information about protestors' actions and officials' response. Contrary to the prevailing presumption that mass demonstrations are inherently violent and disorderly, video footage and photos often reveal relatively peaceful protests.[62] Such evidence may be invaluable in lawsuits involving protestors. Videos posted on YouTube and elsewhere may be relevant to pending lawsuits challenging the arrests of Occupy protestors in various cities.[63] Video and photographic documentation of such events could also force courts to rethink their strong deference to the security and public order rationales used to justify restrictions under intermediate scrutiny. If protestors are largely peaceful, courts should require proof of necessity before allowing repressive caging tactics or other restrictions. Similarly, footage of largely peaceful protests suggests that the increasing militarization of policing since 9/11 is unnecessary, counterproductive, and based on a flawed view of the inherently disruptive nature of mass demonstrations.[64]

2. Mounting New Forms of Protest

Internet technologies can also produce new avenues of protest. Some avenues look familiar. For example, the website Change.org seeks to empower individual citizens and promote social change through the use of on-line petitions.[65] In this sense, the founders of Change.org took a new technology and applied it to one of the oldest and most important forms of collective First Amendment activity—the right to petition government for redress of grievances.[66] But the ability to organize and reach millions of people quickly through online communication methods reinvigorated this form of collective action.

Other on-line protests take less traditional forms. In January 2012, a series of coordinated online actions occurred as a protest to two pending laws, the Stop Online Piracy Act (SOPA) and the Protect IP Act (PIPA), both of which were designed to protect against foreign copyright infringement. Numerous sources criticized the bills, however, because of their potential to curtail Internet expression. Specifically, critics argued that the bills would allow courts to dismantle or blacklist entire Internet sites based upon bare allegations of infringement or because a site merely linked to a single infringing item.[67] Such penalties could chill Internet speech, especially user-generated content, such as blogs and most forms of social media that are central to traditional forms of protest.[68] When it appeared that the bills would become law, opponents began organizing on the Internet, including communicating about the bills and possible protests via Twitter and Tumblr, contacting their congressional representatives via email, and signing online petitions.[69] On January 18, 2012, over 115,000 web sites participated in a coordinated protest against the bills.[70] The protests usually involved a banner or message on the website or, in the case of Wikipedia, a purposeful day without access to Wikipedia's English language website. Persons accessing the Wikipedia website saw a darkened screen with a brief explanation and the phrase "Imagine a World Without Free Knowledge."[71]

The SOPA/PIPA protests were apparently successful, ultimately resulting in congressional postponement of the bills.[72] Thus, their organizers managed to engage in a powerful, widely-covered protest with almost none of the physical constraints associated with traditional protests in public forums. They were able to do so because they were highly organized, maintained their own websites and because the topic was especially relevant to the Internet. But their actions further suggest that the traditional paradigm associated with protesting is too narrow.[73] As a pragmatic matter, protests need not involve the classic paradigm of groups occupying valuable physical space. As a legal matter, the Internet allows protestors to circumvent onerous permitting requirements and repressive policing tactics that can interfere with spontaneity and the protestors' message.

The website WikiLeaks and one of its founders, Julian Assange, further exemplify the Internet as a possible source of new and unique forms of protest. Assange and others created WikiLeaks in 2006 to "expose corrupt and oppressive regimes throughout the world."[74] Since then it has posted hundreds of thousands of pages of generally accurate "raw source material," much of it confidential or classified government information about the United States, that its operators receive from anonymous informants.[75] For many people, WikiLeaks' actions pose a significant threat to national security.[76] Thus, people have likened Assange to a "high-tech" terrorist, argued that he should be indicted under the Espionage Act,[77] or that he should be killed.[78] Others, however, argue that the publication of classified information is protected journalism much like when the *New York Times* and *Washington Post* published the Pentagon Papers decades ago.[79] Most of the debate about Assange and WikiLeaks revolves around whether he is a journalist and whether the Espionage Act allows prosecution for publication even so.[80] Yet Assange also perceives WikiLeaks as a form of "radical resistance" to unjust regimes[81] and his actions fit within any general definition of protest.[82] They also serve the accountability-forcing function integral to much free speech theory.[83]

If a court viewed Assange's online publications as a protest, it might approach a prosecution of him differently than if it viewed his actions as the current debate frames them. The Supreme Court has given little direction regarding the constitutionality of criminal sanctions under the Espionage Act and the lower courts have applied a malleable test asking whether a defendant has knowingly published "closely held" information (i.e., information the government wanted to keep secret) that could potentially harm the United States.[84] If Assange attempts to assert a First Amendment defense under this standard, he will almost surely lose given the negative picture the media and government have painted of him.[85] Considering the WikiLeaks publications as protests, however, might counterbalance those negative assumptions. Speech criticizing government action is at the core of First Amendment protections.[86] Furthermore, the Espionage Act is a content-based law. Any prosecution must explain in detailed terms the government's justifications for suppressing political protests. Although such an approach might not change the ultimate outcome if national security is at issue, it should at least ensure that the national security rationale is real.

III. The Perils of Internet Technologies as Applied to Protestors

The Internet presents significant dangers for protestors as well. Some of these dangers pose pragmatic or legal hurdles for traditional protestors. Others may affect new forms of online protest.

First, although Internet technologies bring more organizing tools to protest movements, they also allow government officials greater access to the inner workings of those movements.[87] Protestors' increased presence online allows electronic surveillance of various social media, blogs, and other forms of organizing. Such surveillance is generally not illegal.[88] But there is widespread concern that officials use it to target and counter peaceful protestors. Accordingly, law enforcement officials have thwarted protests after using online surveillance to gather information about the protests.[89] Similarly, officials have collected organization's membership information, using it to facilitate pretextual arrests and additional information-gathering through individual questioning.[90] Furthermore, the ability to store information about protestors in searchable databases and to share it among law enforcement agencies exacerbates flawed data and assessments about protest movements.[91] Surveillance and subsequent actions of this sort are likely to chill protestors, or at least control them so as to diminish their ability to express dissent.

Second, the emergence of the Internet "as a dominant development in the technology of communications,"[92] may detract from the importance of traditional protests. The Internet's accessibility and widespread presence, along with the low cost of disseminating information, make it an attractive form of communication. Even the Supreme Court has noted that the Internet provides "relatively unlimited, low-cost capacity for communication of all kinds ... [A]ny person with a phone line can become the town crier with a voice that resonates further than it could from any soapbox."[93] There is concern that judges, who have been relatively hostile to large demonstrations in the face of security concerns, will consider communicating on the Internet a viable alternative to traditional protests.[94] Although the Internet supplements traditional protests, it is not a substitute for them. As one commentator notes, the history of protest in this country is largely "the history of *places*. The Mall, the Lincoln Memorial, Central Park, Selma; these are integral aspects of our social and political heritage. Cyberplaces do not retain or conjure lessons, meanings or memories in a like manner."[95] Given the amount of time we spend online, some Internet protests—e.g., Wikipedia's protest of SOPA—are likely to have significant meaning. Nevertheless, we would lose a great deal without the ability to gather physically in groups. Each medium of expression has its own benefits and no court should consider another form of expression as an adequate substitute for the ability to protest in person.

Third, increased dependence on Internet communications and organizations makes traditional protestors vulnerable to government control over Internet access. During the Middle East uprising in the Spring of 2011, officials in Egypt simply cut off access to the Internet altogether.[96] Thus, protestors who had depended on Twitter, Facebook, and mobile Internet technology to communicate found themselves unable to do so. Ultimately they managed to maneuver around these problems and government officials faced an enormous backlash for their actions.[97] But government control over Internet access is a significant potential problem for protestors in all countries. In 2011 the Bay Area Rapid Transit System ("BART") shut down its underground wireless system to stifle protests on its underground subway platforms in response to a shooting death that had occurred there.[98] BART officials argued that the protestors coordinated their protests using cell phones and attempted to halt train service although earlier protests had not done so.[99] Critics accused BART "of the kind of government intrusion employed by Middle East dictators."[100] The FCC launched an investigation but this is a murky area of the law. At the federal level Congress has discussed giving executive officials a similar "kill switch" for national security purposes.[101] To date, the First Amendment implications of this specific issue—i.e., whether a government entity can temporarily halt access to a portion of its network services to stop communications it believes are disruptive—are largely unexplored.

If traditional protestors are vulnerable to government control of the Internet, non-traditional protestors are more so. Inability to access the Internet prevents using it to protest. Thus, all protestors should be concerned with recent discussions regarding the government's ability to control access to the Internet even if officials execute such control primarily for national security emergencies.[102] Our experience with National Security Letters and the NSA's surveillance suggests that executive officials have little ability to constrain their actions taken in the name of national security.[103] Furthermore, if officials view traditional protestors as posing an inherent threat of disruption, they are likely to view online protests even more suspiciously given the view of the Internet as necessary to protect other critical infrastructure.[104] To be sure, it is unclear whether proposed legislation actually provides officials with unconstrained control over the Internet—as opposed to allowing officials to disconnect a power plant infected with a computer virus from computer networks. But the lack of clarity concerns free speech advocates.[105] Executive officials with power to shut off access to the Internet are likely to use it in a manner that sweeps broadly and views any protest as a possible threat.

Finally, those who engage in online protests can be subject to "indirect" censorship via non-government entities. Increasingly, government actors have enlisted the aid of private companies or triggered their actions denying individuals the ability to use the Internet.[106] Thus, after a public appeal by Senator Joe Lieberman, Chair of the Senate Homeland Security Committee, several commercial organizations denied hosting or payment services to WikiLeaks.[107] Although service providers may not have coordinated their actions with government officials, their willingness to respond to informal pleas "enabled the government to circumvent normal constitutional protections to crack down on critics who use the networked public sphere."[108] Bills such as SOPA and PIPA would have similar effects. By threatening substantial penalties for merely linking to a potentially copyright infringing website, a blogger or individual who maintains a Facebook page risks losing the entire enterprise. Individuals maintaining such websites have every reason to steer clear of people that have been labeled as undesirable (even if wrongly so). Government officials can successfully create private censorship on the Internet simply by stigmatizing an individual.[109]

Conclusion

The Internet presents opportunities and pitfalls to protestors. Although it can aid in sustaining protestors in the face of repressive tactics and inhospitable legal rules, it can also aid officials who want to control protestors via surveillance or access to the Internet. Similarly, the Internet has opened up new avenues of protest, allowing various forms of online protest. These new forms of protest can potentially destabilize the Court's existing narrow paradigm involving protestors. On the other hand, the very newness of these forms of protest can frighten regulators causing them to overreact and overregulate.

6

ADVANCING TECHNOLOGY & AGING DEMOCRACY

*Joseph A. Tomain**

Introduction

In 1964, Marshall McLuhan published his book *Understanding Media: The Extension of Man*.[1] After quoting General David Sarnoff for the view that too often people "make technological instruments the scapegoats for the sins of those who wield them,"[2] McLuhan rejects this view, or at least does not fully embrace it. Instead, McLuhan posits that the increased scale of technology affects us in ways that too often go unnoticed. McLuhan raises the Psalmist warning that "we become what we behold."[3] If society does not pay attention to the ways that advancing technology affects the human individual and culture, then this "somnambulism" could result in unintended and undesirable consequences for humanity.[4] In other words, the implications of advancing technology for democracy are filled with both threats and opportunities for societal and individual improvement. It is up to us to decide the acceptable uses of technology in our lives and society.

So, the question ought to be asked: What are the implications of an aging democracy confronted with technology that is advancing with greater speed than any other time in history? Are twenty-first century Americans up to the challenge of reflecting upon and confronting the implications of rapidly advancing technology on our ancestors' eighteenth century grand experiment of democracy? Or will we, as citizens of a self-governing society, sleep at the wheel and

* Assistant Professor of Law, Florida Coastal School of Law. Thank you to Russell Weaver and everyone at the Free Speech Forum London 2012, Brian Foley, Amanda Reid, and my father, Joseph P. Tomain, for their time and helpful comments. All errors are mine.

go so far down the road before we realize what freedoms we have lost due to uses of technology, uses with detrimental effects on individual liberty, as well as our ability to organize social structures in a more egalitarian and person-oriented design?

I barely know what Instagram is,[5] but I know a couple of individuals recently sold it for one billion dollars to Facebook.[6] I also know that not all of Instagram's current users are happy about this acquisition.[7] Facebook and Google are readily accessible examples of technology as both a threat to privacy and an opportunity for greater connections among individuals.[8] They exemplify McLuhan's warning that the scale of technological development has affected the individual and culture in ways that society at large is not recognizing, or not recognizing quickly enough to stem the tide of change. We are becoming what we behold and do not even realize the transformation.

Most law schools teach a course commonly titled Cyberlaw.[9] Lawrence Lessig has stated that not only does studying cyberlaw provide an opportunity to analyze whether and how existing law should apply to cyberspace, but also to reflect on how well existing laws are working in the offline world.[10] What follows are four categories of law to consider in that light, both in real space and cyberspace: (1) net neutrality; (2) electoral reform; (3) privacy; and (4) intellectual property. The specific areas were chosen because they involve considerations of democratic participation and individual rights that advancing technology puts at risk.

I. Net Neutrality

A precise definition of net neutrality is elusive.[11] A basic definition is: "Net Neutrality means that Internet service providers may not discriminate between different kinds of online content and apps. It guarantees a level playing field for all websites and Internet technologies."[12] The purpose of net neutrality is to protect the "simple but brilliant 'end-to-end' design of the Internet that has made it such a powerful force for economic and social good: All of the intelligence and control is held by producers and users, not the networks that connect them."[13] In other words, net neutrality theory holds that individual freedom and innovation is best served through protecting the ability for individual and collaborative creation by limiting the ability of gatekeepers (meaning, those that provide connectivity to broadband technology) from interfering with end users based on political, economic, or social biases.

Common carriage analogies provide a helpful framework for understanding the importance of net neutrality or protecting the internet's generative nature.[14] Consider the electric grid. The electric company does not have the authority to charge an end user more or less based on whether the use of electricity is for a television or a toaster, or based on the brand of the particular product being used. Nor is a person who creates a new invention that uses electricity required to seek permission from the electric company before connecting it to the electric grid. Another analogy is the public roads system.[15] If preferred status on the public roads system were granted to say, Ford owners, that prioritization of road use leads to unfair discrimination against drivers of other manufacturers' vehicles and creates unfair competition among car manufacturers. There is individual, social and economic value in allowing all drivers the same road access, regardless of the manufacturers of their respective vehicles.

Net neutrality applies similar common carriage principles to the internet. These protections are important because they prevent internet service providers from leveraging their control of the "transmission lines" to unfairly compete in the underlying markets that use broadband technology.[16] The underlying markets and uses of broadband technology are virtually limitless; and, humans (at least in developed nations) are increasingly dependent on it for daily social interactions and business transactions.

The threat to net neutrality is concentrated private power and its capture of government power. Despite the trope by opponents that net neutrality is a "solution in search of problem," there is a documented problem of internet service providers preventing customers from accessing the content and applications of their choice. A glaring example is Comcast's intentional and deceptive interference with its customers' use of a peer-to-peer file sharing protocol. The Federal Communications Commission (FCC) issued an order denouncing Comcast's actions and constantly changing positions throughout the investigation, and imposed certain requirements on Comcast going forward.[17] This administrative agency order, however, was overturned by a federal appellate court based on a finding that the FCC lacked the authority to impose these requirements.[18] Subsequently, the FCC issued a Report and Order that set forth limited net neutrality rules.[19] One of the key flaws in the FCC's rules is that discrimination on mobile broadband connections is permitted, whereas such discrimination is not allowed on fixed broadband connections.[20] While net neutrality proponents continue to push for more holistic net neutrality protection, internet service providers are challenging these watered-down rules as unauthorized, too restrictive and purportedly a violation of an internet service provider's First Amendment rights.[21]

Only a handful of corporations provide broadband connectivity. Verizon, AT&T, TimeWarner and Comcast are dominant players. Comcast is particularly concerning because it owns a controlling share of NBC and all its properties, and is America's largest cable and residential internet service provider.[22] It is a classic example of vertical integration. While vertical integration is not an inherently problematic concept in the abstract, there are inherent concerns when communication markets are vertically integrated because of tendencies to concentrate power in the hands of few owners and to shut out independent voices and new market entrants.[23] One need not reach moral judgments about Comcast to have concerns about this vertical integration. One need only recognize that Comcast has natural business incentives that conflict with the public interest in the free flow of information. For example, Comcast has the natural business incentive to discriminate against content and providers that compete with its NBC properties. The Comcast-NBC merger, approved by a 4–1 vote of the FCC Commissioners, was hotly contested by lobbyists on both sides of the issue.

An anecdote of regulatory capture, and one that is subject to difference of opinion, involves former FCC Commissioner Meredith Attwell Baker. Within four months after voting to approve this controversial merger, she announced that she would leave the FCC when her term expired to accept a position with Comcast.[24] At Comcast, she serves as senior vice president for government affairs for NBC Universal. Now, this is not proof of a quid pro quo, but would she have received the job offer had she voted against the merger? Did this prospect influence her decision making process? Most importantly, is the Comcast-NBC merger in the public interest? This anecdote is but one example of the golden revolving door between industry and the government actors that are supposed to carry out the will of the people, not the highest bidder.

While one might respond that the seeming unlimited nature of the internet reduces the need to worry about control of gatekeepers, Tim Wu explains that the intrusion of gatekeepers routinely occurs when new information technologies disrupt existing ones.[25] The internet is simply the most recent disruptive technology. Without robust net neutrality protection, the promise of the internet as a democratizing opportunity for society is greatly reduced. Because of the economic incentives of those that provide connectivity to the internet and their lobbying influence over government actors, it is important for citizens to make their voices heard that net neutrality must be a fundamental principle of our digital world. Without net neutrality, gatekeepers will continue to compartmentalize and control online communications with detrimental consequences to free speech, individual freedom and ground-up community-based innovation.

II. Electoral Reform

Advancing technology holds a variety of opportunities for improving the core activity in a democracy: voting. Two related considerations are, first, that vote-swapping is protected First Amendment activity and, second, that perhaps it is time to institute a national popular vote for presidential elections.

1. Vote-Swapping Is Constitutional

In 2007, the Ninth Circuit Court of Appeals held that vote-swapping is a constitutionally protected activity.[26] *Porter v. Bowen* dates to the 2000 presidential election when citizens formed a vote-swapping website. The purpose was to have the Green Party candidate, Ralph Nader, receive five percent of the national popular vote, without hurting Al Gore's chances of winning the Electoral College. If the Green Party received five percent of the national popular vote, it would qualify for federal funding in the next election.

Voters in "safe" states—states that would certainly go for Gore or certainly go for George W. Bush—could swap their votes with voters in swing states. For example, a voter in the swing state of Ohio who wanted to vote for Nader would vote for Gore, while swapping her vote with a voter who would vote for Nader in say, Alabama (a safe state for Bush) or Massachusetts (a safe state for Gore). Shortly after this vote-swapping website began, at least one other website was created that allowed voters to swap votes for any third-party candidates with either Bush or Gore, thus expanding vote-swapping beyond Nader-Gore swaps to swaps between any third-party candidate and either majority party candidate.

The California Secretary of State asserted that this activity violated both the state election laws and criminal laws. The Ninth Circuit disagreed and held that the First Amendment protected vote-swapping. Thus, one opportunity that advancing technology provides is the ability to strategically vote for the president and to empower third-parties. At least in 2000, citizens of our aging democracy did not sleepwalk through this opportunity. There is, however, a more sensible and direct solution than vote-swapping.

2. The Electoral College Is an Anachronism

Technology allows information to spread across the country instantaneously, let alone the world. This exponential advancement in the state of technology materially changes the democratic process from that existing at the time of the Framers of the Constitution. Why should we acquiesce to an electoral process where candidates and "unaffiliated" SuperPACs focus virtually all of their time and energy on a few swing states? An "every town counts" presidential campaign slogan and strategy in 2012 merely meant "some towns in some swing states."[27] More specifically, it meant a five-day bus tour through a handful of small towns in six of the fifty United States.[28] The slogan that "every towns counts" is inspiring and democratic in a candidate for national office, but is betrayed by only visiting twelve percent of the states for less than one week.

Digital communications technology makes a national popular vote system more practical than it would have been in the late eighteenth century. Whether one is in Wyoming or Washington D.C., real-time information is available through broadband, not to mention cable and radio. Is it not better for candidates to have an incentive to campaign in all fifty states by making every citizen's vote count in the final tally? It is no defense of the Electoral College to say it protects small states. Whether large or small, the current system leads campaign strategists to ignore states that do not swing, including California, New York and Texas.[29] Is it likely that voters on the losing end in a safe state might be more motivated to actually vote if they know it's not in vain? Studies show that voter turnout is depressed in "safe" states because voters know that their vote is essentially meaningless.[30] While a constitutional amendment abrogating the Electoral College would be the most direct method of moving to a national popular vote, another method of instituting this legal reform may be possible.

There is an organized movement for instituting a national popular vote.[31] The national popular vote plan involves a legislative pact among states to provide all of a state's electoral votes to the national popular vote winner, regardless of which candidate received the most votes in that state.[32] By its terms, the plan will only be implemented once enough states have enacted this legislative pact to provide the national popular vote winner with the sufficient amount of Electoral College votes to win the election.[33] Eight states and Washington D.C., possessing forty-nine percent of the electoral votes needed to deliver an Electoral College victory, have enacted such legislation.[34]

Technological advancement allows a more direct democracy, one more truly reflective of the will of the people. After all, if there were no Electoral College, there would be no need to engage in vote-swapping. While it's hard not to forget that Gore won the national popular vote in 2000 but lost the election,[35] it's also worth noting that Obama's "landslide" victory in 2008 was not so large when considering the national popular vote margin. Obama won 67.8% of the Electoral College (365 to 173), but only 53% of the national popular vote.[36]

As the creative vote-swapping strategy shows, digital communications technology provides new opportunities for individuals to play a greater role in our self-governing society. Technological advancement, however, offers more than an opportunity to manipulate the Electoral College. It provides the opportunity to reflect on whether the Electoral College remains desirable in the twenty-first century.[37] In any case, some improvement to our presidential election process is normatively desirable in light of the shallow, widespread and false overgeneralization that we live in a two-tone country of red and blue states.[38]

III. Privacy

Technological advancement holds little, if any, promise for privacy these days. Advancing technology brings mostly threats, potential and realized, to privacy interests, from apps collecting data in address books to employers asking for Facebook passwords and much more. That's not a cellphone in your pocket; it's a "tracking device."[39] But existing law does hold some promise and these threats provide the opportunity to reconsider existing law in both the real world and cyberspace, just as the technology that allows vote-swapping provides the opportunity to reconsider whether the Electoral College is an anachronism.

1. Intrusion Upon Seclusion

Louis Brandies and Samuel Warren's famous 1890 article, *The Right to Privacy*,[40] was a reaction to then-new developments in photographic technology, as well as the expansion of press coverage into private affairs. In 1960, William Prosser categorized the right to privacy as four separate torts, including intrusion upon seclusion.[41] Intrusion upon seclusion is based on the way information is gathered. If the method of gathering private information is highly offensive to a reasonable person, then there is a tort claim. Similar to Brandeis and Warren's development of a new legal theory of privacy in light of technological changes in the late nineteenth century, a couple of scholars have recently suggested that the intrusion upon seclusion claim could provide a remedy and legal deterrent for certain online data collection practices.[42] The secretive and intrusive nature of data collection makes intrusion upon seclusion a viable claim in the digital age. But, in many cases, there may be an impediment to this tort claim: "consent."

2. Contract Law

Did I consent to data collection because I clicked "I agree" to a voluminous, vague and broadly written set of terms and conditions … that I did not read?

Did I agree to data collection merely by continuing to visit a website or use an app with a term that states my continued use is an expression of my consent to terms I did not read and cannot change?[43] Formalistic, mechanical application of contract law recognizes such actions as consent. Such an approach to consent theory is legal fiction.[44] Thus, here we see an opportunity to reconsider what it means to consent to the terms of an agreement.

"Theories are problem-solving devices."[45] Current consent theory relies heavily on "manifested" consent.[46] Manifested consent is not subjective assent to the specific terms, but an objective outward manifestation signaling agreement to legal enforcement of those terms, as well as to default rules when disputes arise that the terms do not address.[47] A signature at the end of a written contract, or clicking, "I agree," in an online transaction is generally a sufficient manifestation of assent for courts to find that a party has agreed to the terms of the contract, regardless of whether a party understood or read the terms. Put another way, a party's outward conduct manifests consent to the assumption of the risk of a bad deal, or a license for a court or legislature to provide interpretations and default rules that might not reflect either party's intentions.[48]

This objective version of consent theory places too much weight on a signature or click of a button, especially when the agreement is an adhesion contract.[49] Because of imbalances in power and lack of alternatives that form the landscape of twenty-first century American society, the "manifested" consent theory is faulty. Concerns about enforcement of adhesion contracts predate the digital era.[50] Online transactions, however, are particularly troublesome because they raise new concerns about privacy and the commodification of people themselves through data collection and trade.[51] While it is reasonable to find that a consumer consented to the allowable minutes and monthly payment for her new mobile device, the same cannot be said for the myriad boilerplate terms that the telecommunications companies had sophisticated and expensive lawyers draft. The problem of fictional consent via the manifestation theory is exacerbated in a pluralistic society where individuals have different worldviews, let alone legal sophistication and access to legal representation in their transactions, especially seemingly mundane ones.[52] With the advent of new policy concerns regarding privacy and data collection, the theory that, at least some, boilerplate terms should be presumptively unenforceable deserves greater attention.[53]

Modern society is not a world where parties of relatively equal bargaining power negotiate and agree to the terms of a contract, especially when considering transactions between individuals and corporate entities. Yet, the law continues to ignore reality and holds consumers (whom I prefer to call citizens, or people) to unfavorable terms when they cannot really be said to have meaningfully consented to all the terms of an adhesion contract. Once again, technological developments help illuminate not only how law should be applied to new technologies, but also to reconsider whether existing law needs to be rethought in the offline world, as well as in cyberspace.

3. State Action Doctrine Revisited

Generally and broadly speaking, the state action doctrine holds that constitutional rights only apply against government actors, not private actors. A criticism of the doctrine is that it rests on the "illusory hope" that the line between public and private actors is a workable dichotomy.[54] The space between public and private grows increasingly blurry in the twenty-first century.

In violation of the Fourth Amendment and the Foreign Intelligence Surveillance Act (FISA), the George W. Bush Administration engaged in widespread illegal warrantless wiretapping on Americans' emails and phone calls.[55] The government enlisted the help of telecommunications companies to conduct this surveillance. After disclosure of this program, Congress considered legislation to expand the scope of government authority to engage in such surveillance going forward, as well as to provide retroactive immunity to the telecommunications companies that assisted in the prior illegal surveillance.

During the 2008 primary campaign, Senator Obama (as he was then) vowed to filibuster any FISA amendment that included retroactive immunity for telecommunications companies that assisted in the illegal warrantless wiretapping of Americans emails and telephones.[56] In July 2008, he failed to live up to his word.[57] Obama voted in favor of the FISA amendment bill that contained retroactive immunity and also expanded the authority for government surveillance of Americans' communications. Utilizing a page on Obama's own social networking site, tens of thousands of his supporters urged him to return to his original opposition to retroactive immunity. This vignette illustrates how advancing technology can improve the ability for individuals to participate in democratic processes through collective action. It also raises concerns about just how much the government is monitoring citizens' communications and what role private companies are playing in this data collection. The concern about disclosure by private companies at the request of government actors persists and grows.[58]

We should rethink the state action doctrine. More accurately stated, we should continue to rethink the state action doctrine.[59] Should constitutional rights apply against private actors in some instances? The Bill of Rights did not always apply to the states. It had to be incorporated by the Fourteenth Amendment and court interpretation of law. Private actors regularly breach individuals' online privacy through the surreptitious collection and exchange of data, placement of cookies on computers and use of location tracking devices, to name just a few concerns. Such spying would be offensive to most Americans if it were conducted by the government. The mere fact that a private actor is engaging in similar intrusions into the lives of citizens does not ameliorate the invasion, regardless of whether the private actor shares the information with the government. Large institutional actors, both public and private, threaten individual liberty interests of the people.

The U.S. Supreme Court has already applied constitutional rights against private actors. In *Marsh v. Alabama*,[60] for example, the Court held that a town owned by a private company violated a citizen's First Amendment rights when it arrested her for criminal trespass. The citizen had the right to stand on a sidewalk in the business district and distribute religious literature, regardless of whether the town was owned by a private company. *Marsh* was the high watermark of the extension of individual citizens' rights against private entities pursuant to U.S. constitutional protections because the shopping mall line of cases pullback on the application of First Amendment rights to restrict private corporate behavior.[61] But, shopping malls are not fundamental means of mass communication, and the Court's 1994 *Turner Broadcasting* opinion makes clear that the First Amendment allows government regulation of private actors to protect the openness of critical pathways of communication.[62] Thus, it would not be breaking totally new ground for courts or Congress to establish that a citizen's constitutionally enumerated rights apply against abuses of concentrated power, whether public or private.[63]

Of course, one ought to ask what policy considerations underlie the rights set forth in the Constitution. Why did our ancestors (figuratively speaking for most Americans) leave England? Did they seek to flee from any sense of government power, or from *abuse* of government power? Why didn't they have equal outrage and motivation to cross the Atlantic Ocean because of abuses of concentrated private power? Because concentration of private power did not exist then in the way it does today. The corporate form of the twenty-first century is dramatically different from the time the Framers.

The abuse of concentrated power is an affront to individual liberty. That liberty interest should be protected by our founding document, regardless of whether the abuse of power is public or private. The Ninth Amendment is a possible source of authority to apply against invasions of privacy by private power: "The enumeration in the Constitution, of certain rights, shall not be construed to deny or disparage others retained by the people."[64] The Framers of the Constitution could not have foreseen the technological world of the twenty-first century. Now is the appropriate time to engage in extended discourse about some of those unenumerated rights whose importance could be clearly seen only in our digital age, such as a right protecting against surreptitious data collection by broadband service providers, websites, apps and government actors. Data is being collected almost reflexively in greater degrees and kinds than in the past. Data will continue to be collected and used in ways that we do not anticipate. These dramatic changes in public and private data collection call for reflection on individual rights that may have been taken for granted in the past.

Moreover, the state action doctrine might not be an impediment. The Ninth Amendment protects unenumerated rights, rights that conceivably may exist against private actors.[65] While the Ninth Amendment is not a likely a source of law to rest a case upon, you may say I'm a dreamer.[66] The political feasibility of an idea is not a dispositive test of the worth of its exploration.[67] With the enormous and often opaque, if not secret, intrusion into the privacy and movements of people, further exploration on the unenumerated rights protected by the Constitution is warranted as our world that creeps closer to George Orwell's *Nineteen Eighty-Four*.

IV. Intellectual Property

As James Boyle has noted, the changes in intellectual property law have only gone one way: providing more and more protection to rights holders.[68] In large part, this enclosure movement is a result of legislative capture.[69] But for the confluence of interests from new technology companies in Silicon Valley combined with grassroots and netroots activism on the left and right, the Stop Online Privacy Act (SOPA) and Protect IP Act would probably have sailed through Congress.[70] The recent controversy regarding SOPA and the Protect IP Act bring into sharp relief the struggle to balance the protection of intellectual property rights with the public's ability to make use of others' works. There are legitimate interests on both sides.

Creators of content need the incentive to create works or the public loses the benefits of new creative works. The concerns of content creators are legitimately heightened because of how advancing technology makes copying so easy today. Citizens desire and exercise (if not need) the ability to use, access and build upon existing works as part of culture and maybe even the human condition. Before balancing these competing interests, pausing for a moment to recall the purpose of the Copyright and Patent Clause is helpful.

The purpose of the Copyright and Patent Clause of the Constitution is to protect the public interest in the creation of new inventions and creative works.[71] For how long must a monopoly be granted to incentivize a person to create a new work? Thomas Jefferson noted that this is not an easy question to answer, but that exclusive rights to inventions are not natural rights and are only worth the public embarrassment of monopoly to the extent necessary to preserve the incentive to create.[72] Today, United States law provides copyright protection for life of the author plus 70 years after death.[73] Under the Copyright Act of 1790, the first duration of copyright protection was 14 years, with a possible renewal period for another 14 years, *if* the author remained alive.[74] Although Jefferson is correct that determining what deserves monopoly protection and for how long are not simple questions, life of the author plus 70 years is excessive and not worth the public embarrassment.

In light of how easy it is to copy in the digital age, our seemingly boundless amount of content and our "attention deficit disorder" culture, it is time to reduce the duration of copyright. As long as the current excessive copyright duration remains law, children will be outlaws because they will "pirate" works.[75] This is harmful not only to the copyright holder, but also to the value of law in our society. Our legal system works because it is respected. Once we have a culture that overwhelmingly does not respect the rule of law, we all lose. Thus, to balance the competing interests of copyright holders and those that make use of copyrighted works, perhaps we should return to the original duration of copyright, 14 years.[76]

If the duration of copyright were only 14 years instead of life plus 70 years, then perhaps *some* of the draconian provisions of SOPA and the Protect IP Act would be tolerable for that short time period. Maybe some of the strong protections provided by SOPA or the Protect IP Act are reasonably necessary in light of the easy ability to copy in the digital age, but only if those protections are counterbalanced by a much shorter duration than life plus 70 years.[77] After that, the work would become part of the public domain and "free as the air to common use."[78] Indeed, even *more* creative works may result because of the ability to legally utilize recent works.

Conclusion

Through brief forays into intellectual property, privacy, election law, and net neutrality, this chapter helps show that free speech in the internet era is a topic of broad scope and there is much to resolve. This essay also raises the question about whether citizens in our aging democracy are able to rise to the challenge to curtail or avoid the speech-threatening developments that technology supplies to those with the power and incentive to expand. Or, will American citizens sleepwalk through these changes before it is too late (or at least significantly more difficult) to reverse.

Making net neutrality a primary concern is a critical step to protecting free speech in the internet era because without a neutral or generative internet, the ability to communicate on countless topics or create new uses of this continuously, rapidly developing technology will be severely limited. Not only is net neutrality normatively important for maintaining free speech in the internet era, it provides a pragmatic opportunity for a successful collective action because it brings together diverse and strange bedfellows, as did the opposition to SOPA and the Protect IP Act.

In 2008, the Christian Coalition's Vice President of Communications provided Congressional testimony in support of net neutrality.[79] As an example of anti-neutrality behavior by a mobile telecommunications provider, she cited Verizon's blocking of a pro-choice organization's text messages that were being sent to recipients that requested such messages. The Christian Coalition representative did not cite this example because pro-choice reflects the values of the organization; quite the contrary. She cited Verizon's blocking of pro-choice text messages because she appreciated the risk posed to everyone by gatekeepers. This testimony exemplifies the importance of free speech in society and the realistic possibility that net neutrality can be restored because it is an issue that has the ability to bring together diverse and often antagonistic groups to support the common cause of free speech of human beings in the internet era.

If individuals and organizations of diverse interests join together to restore net neutrality, as they did to at least stall SOPA and the Protect IP Act,[80] it will help establish limits on the ability of internet gatekeepers to control and censor online communications. A likely consequence of such a result is the ability for more robust discourse on other threats and opportunities discussed in this chapter and beyond because the creativity and collaboration of individuals will be unimpeded by the few large faceless entities that provide connectivity to broadband access.

THE DIFFERENCE BETWEEN ONLINE AND OFFLINE COMMUNICATION AS A FACTOR IN THE BALANCING OF INTERESTS WITH FREEDOM OF SPEECH

Indra Spiecker genannt Döhmann[*]

I. The Conflict between Freedom of Speech and Protection of Data/Protection of Privacy

Freedom of speech belongs to the essential fundamental rights granted in all western constitutions. Maybe it can even be called *the* fundamental right, as it is at the core of any democratic state as imagined in western societies inseparable from fundamental rights and a state governed by the rule of law.

Freedom of Speech is almost always linked to an identifiable person: the expression of an opinion is generally connected to an individual. It identifies Julia Timoshenko who is kept in prison for addressing corruption in the Ukraine; it identifies Chen Guangchen who was held under arrest for criticizing the Chinese government; it identified the Scholl siblings who were beheaded by the Nazi Regime for distributing leaflets addressing the cruel crimes against humanity

* Prof. Dr. iur. Indra Spiecker genannt Döhmann, LL.M. (Georgetown Univ.), holds the chair of Public and Administrative Law, Information Law, Environmental Law and Legal Theory at Goethe University Frankfurt a. Main, Germany. She is also Director of the Research Institute on Data Protection. Thanks go to Clive Walker, Felix Kübler and Daniel Burke for their input and to my colleague Thomas Dreier as well as the group of the Free Speech Discussion Forum 2012 for helpful comments.

and the Jews which were being committed. The means that these persons use for distributing their opinions often engage the functions of media and particularly of the press as the oldest instrument of media, but nevertheless, on the most basic level, it is an individual person who makes use of the freedom of speech.

The freedom of speech's prominent position in fundamental rights is often linked to being the backbone of a functioning democratic society. If individuals do not practice free discourse, a reliable election as a reasonable and educated choice between different candidates and political opinions cannot be expected. The idea of democracy itself, it is often argued, can only function if freedom of opinion is guaranteed. It is through this function that freedom of speech and freedom of the press are closely linked, since the press as a distributing organ fulfills an important role in securing the freedom of speech's impact. Therefore, for the purposes of this chapter, freedom of speech and freedom of the press will be considered to be two sides of one coin. A differentiation—that is necessary in other regards—will therefore not be made in this paper unless explicitly stated.

But there is more to freedom of speech than its importance for democracy. It also protects the possibility of individuals to express themselves. Holding an opinion, stating an argument, expressing one's agreement or disagreement with a societal, technological or any other development is always a communication of personality. The protection of freedom of speech then is part of the protection of personality and thus of great importance to the development and existence of individuality itself.

Freedom of speech, however, is only one element of how a person's individuality is constituted. Consequently, freedom of speech does not completely protect a person. Individuality is also closely linked to the protection of privacy and personal data, without being identical. Information about a person triggers data protection. The German Constitutional Court stated in its groundbreaking *census* decision in 1985,[1] that data protection is defined as the right of the individual to know who knows what about herself and thus be able to predict another person's evaluation of one's own. Therefore, the German constitutional data protection right is called the "Right to informational self-determination."[2] Data protection in the European sense does not start with the distribution of information, but begins already with the transfer of the information from the person to whom this information is assigned to any other person or institution.[3] One could say that the change of informational sphere is what triggers data protection. The very moment information leaves the sphere of the originating person (the person who is described by this information and to whom it is attributed), this data can potentially be misused. Therefore, a data protection oriented view on the world is an explicitly negative one: the pure threat of misuse that is aligned to the change of sphere is sufficient for the legal consequence of an infringement of the right to self-determination.

Together with issues like data protection, freedom of speech is part of a protection of individuality and personality that is assisted by other rights. Looking at the fundamental rights in this bundle, it seems that freedom of speech and data protection/protection of privacy both guard an individual in elementary informational settings. While freedom of speech concentrates more on the particular content—opinion—, data protection more concentrates on the outer shell of information—data. Therefore, freedom of speech may vary depending on the particular content, while data protection protects all types of information alike.[4]

There is one additional and legally relevant difference, however: freedom of speech is linked necessarily to publicity, to a communicative act, as any expression of opinion or information requires at least one potential recipient. Therefore, freedom of speech always involves an outgoing of information. Data protection and privacy, on the contrary, are not linked to communicative acts. Rather, they protect particularly those wishing to refrain from dissemination of information, from communication and socializing. Freedom of speech is therefore a fundamental right in public, freedom of privacy a fundamental right in privacy. Looking at it from an informational point of view, freedom of speech (and freedom of the press) both represent the interest to divulge information about a(nother) person, while data and privacy protection aim at precluding others from noticing information. Protected is the interest to divulge information versus the interest to confine information.

This leads to an inevitable problem. It is not a rare event that these individual rights collide, that data protection, personal life and privacy on the one hand, and the freedom of speech/freedom of the press on the other have to be balanced against each other. This conflict is obvious for the freedom of the press versus data protection: that the interests of a free press may infringe on the rights of an individual to protect ones data and privacy can be observed as a day-to-day collision of the interests of journalists. In many cases, it is even the essence of their business. Thus, tabloids, particularly the yellow press, concentrate on the dissemination of personal information of prominent people and have created a significant market for photos and information about these people and thus created the existence of a profession of paparazzi. But also "serious" press documentation e.g. of a politician's private life in the midst of an election campaign necessarily involves an interest in his or her personal data.

The conflict is not a new one. The law has established rules on how to balance interests and how to give both freedom of speech and data protection and the Right to Privacy its place in society. European Law therefore includes pro-visions in order to protect privacy and data protection and the freedom of speech and freedom of the press, with a particular focus on the Freedom of the press. For example, Art 9 of the European Data Protection Directive of 1995 regulating the gathering and use of personal information explicitly al-lows for national exemptions for press activities ("journalistic purposes") from most of the regulations within the Directive. One of the recent verdicts of the European Court of Justice has strengthened this predominance of the freedom of the press, when the Court extended the application of this exemption to services concentrating on the distribution of information rather than on the commenting element of press activity. In *Satamedia*,[5] a Finnish company col-lected the freely available information about individual tax payments of com-panies and private persons and distributed these in an electronic letter via an SMS to its customers. The Court held that the Finnish company acted under the privilege of media and therefore was exempt under the Data Protection Directive. This ruling has been criticized as it extends the freedom of the press privileges in a dramatic way: anyone who collects information and distributes it would be now protected with this very high standard. The journalistic input into the collection and distribution of information that was so far considered to be required as an add-on under *Satamedia* is not necessary anymore. Even if this high standard of protection of the freedom of the press does not guar-antee its absolute prevalence over data protection, it clears the way for a dis-regard of privacy rights, particularly data protection. And it creates a considerable additional uncertainty about the relevant law. If the Press Exemption applies, then the Data Protection Directive will not apply any more. Each company claiming freedom of speech/Freedom of Media will now have to establish its own standard how to balance their interests with the interests of those individuals reported about.

Satamedia already hints at a new development given that the medium of SMS was used and the information distributed collected by automated systems of the Finnish company. However, neither the European Court nor the dis-cussants of this verdict and related incidents of conflict between these two rights have paid much attention to the particular situation of the Internet as a very special media with very special consequences for the distribution, col-lection and use of private and personal information.

II. The Difference between Online and Offline Communication

The natural conflict between freedom of the press/freedom of speech, on the one hand, and data protection/protection of privacy, on the other hand, has reached a new dimension with the Internet, an information technology nowadays broadly available and widely made use of. The Internet enables worldwide accessibility of information; its existence and use stresses the importance of the dissemination of information as such. One could call the Internet the medium of the knowledge society. Thus, Internet applications and services sharpen the conflict between those who believe in free accessibility of any information and those who believe in restricted accessibility of some information. This general dispute—catalyzed in Internet events like Wikileaks, Google Books or Facebook—has effects on the conflict between freedom of speech/ freedom of media and data protection/protection of privacy as well. In regard to information-based rights—such as freedom of speech, data protection and privacy protection, the Internet can be considered as the origin of some relevant factors in evaluating potential infringements of rights and thus influences the balancing of interests in a most relevant way.

1. Attribution of Roles

It is not a new insight that telecommunication services have changed our daily world, our style of communication and our practical existence. It is also not a new insight that the Internet has increased these changes dramatically, maybe even to a qualitative and not just quantitative effect. However, the law still has not completely found satisfying, stringent and convincing answers to the many new problems caused or accentuated by the Internet.

One of the most dramatic changes can be observed in the development of products and services. In a traditional setting, the production of the value of goods and services allows for a clear distinction between producer and consumer. Legal rights adopt these differentiations and usually assign legal risks, duties and obligations according to these roles.

The value of many Internet services, however, derives from processes in which numerous parties are involved. Usually, these persons and entities operate unconnected to each other; often it is only the technical platform that connects them. Social networks and Internet platforms, blogs and evaluation fora, online libraries and even particular software could not have been developed if not for this open procedure. It is important to note, that their economic added value originates from a number of unconnected activities. Wikipedia serves as a prominent example, but also social networks like Facebook make well known use of such a structure. Likewise, the founders of Wikipedia constructed their own platform and the core governance structure, but its importance as the major online reference has been created by the many individuals contributing to the content and its control in many different ways, not restricted to authoring articles but including controlling, correcting, mediating or supervising. These tasks as a whole make the result so valuable and reliable. Looking at the result of Wikipedia, one can only express praise for the possibilities of the Internet. The medium has allowed the creation of a functioning worldwide community producing added value to their information by sharing it with an anonymous crowd regardless of economic rationale. The economic theory of Common Goods—already honored by a Nobel Prize— has once more gained new attention as a role model for producing and distributing non-private goods.

However, there are other considerations involved aside from distribution issues that allow for a more differentiated view on the merits and downsides of the Internet. Not the least is the problem who can be legally considered to be responsible for the service and its results. The typical attribution according to the role of entrepreneur, of producer, of organizer or of consumer is difficult to establish. Since often no single identifiable person or legal entity can be attributed with the added value, this typical means for attributing consecutive legal responsibility fails when looking at risks and damages. This aspect becomes particularly important if the violation of individual rights is systematically part of the Internet service, whether intentionally or as a side effect. Data protection is not the only case, Intellectual property is one more very prominent example in video, photo and music exchanges.

Closely linked to the difficulty of responsibility is the difficulty of attribution. The value of the service is created by many individuals, but its financial power is gained exclusively by the owner of the service platform. Mark Zuckerberg would not be a multi-billionaire today, if he had had to share the monetary fruits of Facebook with the users whose information his company exploits.

This insight addresses the question of power and its distribution. Legal rules often balance power between parties, such as between contractual partners. However, the traditional understanding of diversity and sometimes even separation of power does not function properly for many Internet services due to the many parties involved in its creating process. Even the role of the service operator changes. The more the value of a good is created together with others and even partially by the consumer himself, the less powerful a platform operator becomes as his major contribution remains the presentation of a technical tool together with the administration of general rules of use. Only if the platform operator manages to build a business model on top of the managing of the platform, can he turn the success of his technical invention into a societal and financial success. This is particularly the case with information. The accessibility of the 800+ million users of Facebook has turned Facebook into an economic success. This shift of power and the lack of clarity of attribution may therefore have a significant effect for the balancing of interests between freedom of speech and protection of data/protection of privacy in the Internet.

2. Effects of Globalization

It has already been stated many times that the Internet is in principle global and egalitarian. Potentially, everybody can gain access to, and make use of, the information, products and services offered in the Internet, and potentially everybody can offer information, products and services there. No central registration agency exists, and most sites available are not protected but are available and accessible for free and open for use to everyone. This had led to the claim that the Internet is a legally unbound sphere, that it is an open space in which legal rules neither restrict nor bind nor enable its participants. It is a restriction free zone in which everyone is equal and with equal rights. That this claim cannot be upheld has been shown many times, not in the least by the many restrictions of access to the Internet enacted by some states, and also by the obvious shifting of power between the big Internet players, the search engines, the access providers and so on.

In addition, national and international legislation has for quite some time begun to regulate the use of Internet in many ways—not the least often in the name of protection of individual rights such as intellectual property and data protection/protection of privacy by reacting to defamation and other misuses of freedom to the damage of others. One of the core arguments of the discussion around net neutrality on both sides of the Atlantic is the future of the equal opportunity to accessibility of the Internet.[6] It also remains an open question whether indeed the Internet would develop in the way it does if legal rules did not exist. Legal rules lurk in the background and thus form the structure of the Internet, but they also increasingly address the many contents of the Internet. Any Internet service that requires payment is in need of enforcing strategies, and most of these are offered by the existing legal regimes. Some of them have been designed for Internet purposes, but most have existed earlier in the offline world before.

Globalization changes the role of the natural and legal persons involved in creating and using the Internet. A change of role already takes place because of the different structure of many Internet services, as mentioned above. But globalization changes the relationship in another way, as well. The Internet's value is used and produced very often by private individual persons. They buy and sell, they communicate, and they contribute. As the Internet has become a huge marketplace with ever rising online activities, companies as professional actors are also major players. The Internet has become professionalized. But even in these areas, the added value of many platforms and services offered in and via the Internet often rely on the users' input. It is the easy, quick and inexpensive communication that makes the Internet such a driving force, and the medium is still very much the communication of private persons and private companies.

This view, concentrating on private persons and entities, leaves out one important player—the states. Not only do they themselves offer information and services via the Internet, particularly in democratic states with a high regard for transparency and accountability, but also states themselves make use of the Internet as a source of information. It is not only private entities that are interested in personal and business information made available freely via the Internet. States are interested in it too for a number of reasons, in democratic states at least closely linked to their public duties. Prevention of terror attacks and detection of criminality are only the obvious reasons. Discovery of tax evasion, spying on citizens or detecting potential opponents' activities in oppressive regimes are other motivations. But States have also more and more come to understand that there is potential harm involved in an unregulated Internet, and not only in economic aspects. In order to protect the participants of the Internet and to protect them from fraud, defamation, abuse or other downsides, many states have enacted Internet legislation. Such legal rules governing the Internet may be rules on the accountability of hosts of webpages for content distributed via their platforms. They may be rules, as mentioned above, to protect individual rights such as intellectual property or data protection. They may be rules to ensure information technology security by establishing standards of use and standards of technological equipment. This activity involves new legislation against specific Internet crimes as a new form of criminality and new rules of prosecution.

It can be observed that, at least in some situations, states tend to chose not national, but rather international approaches to solve a problem within the Internet, such as the Council of Europe's Cybercrime Convention.[7] This is clearly a reaction to the global structure of the Internet. Although it makes individual states less influential in national regulation, globalization of the Internet forces states to act together and on common grounds.

Globalization of the Internet therefore changes communication among all relevant actors. It changes the structures of communication by affecting power-relationships between producers and consumers, between individuals and companies, between states and privates and between states themselves.

3. Network Effects

The Internet's architecture is a network structure with different layers but which functions overall in the way of a network.

Economists have long developed a theory on networks.[8] Networks tend to develop into natural monopolies due to their effects on scale, density and scope. How far the Internet will turn into a monopolistic structure is difficult to predict. Many players that have been important in the founding years of the Internet have become insignificant now. However, it can clearly be observed that certain services in regard to the Internet or offered via the Internet have monopolistic structures, particularly social networks like Facebook. There is also some empirical evidence that monopolies in the Internet might be consecutive. Whether this observation is one to be proven or whether this effect continues, cannot be certain. What has become obvious is the fact that small and medium-size professional actors with a purely national span of activity have little influence on the development of the communication strategies in the Internet. If they do not reach into the globalism of the Internet and become international, they tend to disappear or become insignificant.

Therefore, any communication platform has to think "big," has to opt for the global Internet society and take up the economic lessons of the network theory. Regional differences tend to vanish. Globalization and network effects work hand in hand. Any threat, therefore, that is formulated against individual rights must be evaluated in the light of globalization—numerous people being potentially affected—and the network effects on the market: The tendency towards big players allows for little individuality and for little precaution and protection beyond generalised standards.

4. Anonymity

The effect of globalization and the different services offered online compared to offline lead to another aspect of the Internet that plays an important role as a distinct form of communication. As the Internet is accessible from almost any location in the world and as access to the Internet does not require any means of identification or registration, anonymity is commonplace. Although technicians claim that, with enough meta-information, almost anybody can be identified and real anonymity is therefore hard to achieve, they also agree that this result demands a lot of individualized effort. And even if this level of detection became more widespread, open access to the Internet via W-lan, hotspots or in Internet cafés could still serve anonymity to those who wish to remain unidentified.

Additionally—and even more importantly—the process of identification and/or verification of a given identity usually cannot be performed in quick time in the Internet, and the Internet usually does not allow for additional clues that are available in an offline communication. Internet communication allows for very little additional information about users. What is standard in eye-to-eye communication is therefore the exception in online communication. The social setting in which an individual acts is not generally detectable by the online communication partner, not even the general local attribution. Someone who shops in a small town in the United States will most probably have some connection to this town—the pure presence there already allows certain conclusions about the person. The outer appearance of that person gives additional information about social status, age and gender, possibly about individual preferences and statements made via fashion. A dialect or an accent gives regional reference as to the area of upbringing, maybe even about the social circumstances, as well. Accordingly, the interest of a person in guide-books for London in a local German bookstore says much more about that person than the same person's visit on the Amazon webpage looking for London guidebooks.

The effect of anonymity can be judged in various ways. If individuality is the goal of protection, anonymity may be interpreted in a positive and a negative way. On the one hand, anonymity allows protection against prosecution by public authorities or powerful private individuals. On the other hand, anonymity also hinders the identification of a person with the statement given. It is much easier to say something anonymously than to stand up for it. Thinking about the reasons for protecting freedom of speech, this ability to represent an opinion is an important facility. But there are other aspects to consider in judging anonymity, as will shortly be discussed.

That there is a great demand for information on particular, identifiable persons shows the immense success of Internet services like Facebook and Google. They have earned their influential position in the Internet by providing information about their users directly (Facebook) or to third parties (Facebook, Google). Their success has been furthered because they not only pass on information about their users, that is directly available through their statements or behavior, but also because they have used highly potential algorithms to group their users according to types of information on which specialized predictions can be made. This new information about users—that is interestingly not available to the users themselves—can be used for many different purposes and is accordingly very valuable.

5. Ineffectiveness of Legal Remedies

The currency of the Internet is information. The Internet has become a major means of communication.

This description immediately leads to problems of ownership and liability. It is generally understood that information cannot be considered as a property right as such, but that rather parts of it can be legally protected, such as by intellectual property, by data protection or by patent laws. The Internet has catalyzed the question of who may use information and who may not. One of the reasons for this catalyzing function is the wide accessibility of the information present in the Internet: whatever information is so presented there is available to a wide number of people for a wide number of purposes. A violation of information rights is therefore not a limited violation but always a most far-reaching and extensive one.

This general—and for the modern knowledge society decisive, but yet underestimated—problem is enhanced by the effect of anonymity and of globalization if one concentrates on possible violations of information rights. And it is very often the press that is considered to be a potential violator of such rights, especially data protection or protection of privacy.[9] Legal remedies against violations can easily fail in the Internet, and the knowledge of this weakness enables potential violators to circumvent existing borderlines and regulatory effects to hinder violations. Anonymity makes defamation and hate speech easier as it cannot be attributed to a person and legal remedies cannot be used.

In a world of globalization, persons and entities act differently than in a national business and communication environments. Reputation is of diminished value in a globalized world. In some markets, secondary reputation measures, i.e. information intermediaries, have been established such as Trip Advisor to allow for the judgment on hotels, allowing users to share their experiences and thus following classical economic theory on how to overcome information asymmetry in trust and experience goods.[10]

Therefore, classical legal remedies are of little effectiveness in the online world. It is often not clear which national law applies, and general international law rules are lacking. Even if laws exist, it is easily possible for potential violators to circumvent the law. For example, the European Data Protection Directive declared itself applicable only if the gathering or use of personal data took place within the E.U. territory. For all information that was provided by

E.U. users on the Internet and then used by someone located outside the E.U. and not having a local subsidiary within the E.U., European standards of data protection did not apply.[11] This limit, however, will be changed within the new E.U. Data Protection Regulation, proposed by the E.U. Commission in 2012. Under this regulation proposal, E.U. legal data protection standards apply if it is the information of an E.U. citizen that is collected and used.[12]

Even if the legal standard is clear, anonymity on the Internet and the lack of a duty to register allows potential wrongdoers to circumvent existing rules by relocation to a legal regime that does not enforce other regimes' legal rules. Certain countries are well known for being a haven for servers with doubtful information and doubtful attitudes towards individual rights. Even if the operator of an Internet service is detectable, many of the services are not provided directly by it, but in cooperation with individuals not known to it. The interdependency of roles, already mentioned,[13] does not automatically attribute a violation of rights within in the Internet to the service operator. It may offer the service, but not the content.

Given this situation, communication structures in the Internet allow for ways of expressing speech and distributing information that lack a significant factor typical of offline communication, so that stating opinions or information is no longer inseparable from the person issuing it. In this aspect, some of the goals of the protection of freedom of speech and of legal responsibility are contradictory to the goals of anonymity and the effects of globalization.

6. Accessible and Unforgettable Information on the Internet

The Internet's availability and easy accessibility has increased the information available about individuals, events and things. Archiving has become much easier to achieve;[14] information can be more easily stored, traced, retrieved and updated not to speak of the easy possibilities of recombination and comparison. Technical and individual means have improved access to information quickly, inexpensively and without any restraints in time, place or availability. Opening hours of archives, waiting periods or travelling to a place of storage are obstacles of the past once information has become available in the Internet. This change also means that information is indestructible. What sounds at first sight very appealing and as a cure to many problems, also had downsides: Wrong, manipulative or disputable information can also not be eliminated or often even challenged.

This situation also leads to another phenomenon: Whatever information about a person has reached the Internet can also be stored, traced, received and updated. And of course, it can also be combined with other available information, regrouped and recombined.[15] This observation does not contradict the earlier observation of increased anonymity in the Internet. Rather, the accessibility of information once present in the Internet depends on the possibility of identifying an individual. Once a person has been identified, she can easily be tracked and the diverse information about her collected from different sources and reorganized. New and easy services that offer identification by face or voice add to the probability of being detected in a public place.[16] This also means that changes in personality and character become much more difficult; different roles are more difficult to assume and unwanted and illegal information cannot readily be erased from the public memory of the Internet.[17]

Accessibility and the huge amount of information finally produce another problem important to the Internet that has a significant effect on assessing potential infringements of freedom of speech/ data protection/ protection of privacy: Since the Internet's architecture is egalitarian, all information is in principle considered to be equal. Search engines that assist in locating information and organizing services that assist in storing and retrieving information become important players. However, their organizing rules and algorithms decide on the importance and accessibility of information in many instances, and, by ranking the results of a search or an organizing process, they automatically influence the importance of the selected information. It is therefore the values and interests of these Internet operators that organize the information available. The very moment information has been ranked, the level of significance changes accordingly.

7. Group/Cohort Identification

Closely linked to the easy identification and recombination of information is another technology very evident in the Internet: group or cohort identification. It is already well practiced. It is used mainly in advertising and merchandising, but it can easily be extended to criminal prosecution, contractual conditions, insurance agreements or any other area of decision-making about an individual.

Cohort identification works with the increased information available on the Internet on the behavior of certain groups. We are not as individualized as we tend to believe. For instance, people above the age of 30 in general tend to view the changes due to information technology as less welcome than people under the age of 30. Blond women tend to buy at least once a year shampoo or hair cosmetics to lighten the color of their hair. European men tend to be interested in soccer. With probabilities attached and thus a likelihood attributed, our behavior can be predicted.

This is not done on an individualized level ("person A has always liked ice-cream and bought it many times."). Rather, algorithms perform a generalized, probability-based estimation—"person A is part of a group that likes fast food (91%), sun (86%), and outdoor activities (93%). With a probability of 90%, people who like these things—and are therefore part of this cohort—also like ice cream. Therefore, it is highly likely that person A likes ice-cream." On this probability assessment, decisions in regard to the individual can be taken. The more data about a group and an individual belonging to that group are available, the more precise the predictions which can be made. This raw data is easily available in the Internet, particularly with the changed mode of information outpouring by individuals. Facebook is just the tip of the iceberg producing this type of information.

In consequence, it is much easier possible to predict the behavior of individuals belonging to a particular cohort. This predictive activity may sound neutral. A general statement claims that hardly anyone minds receiving advertising that really serves our needs. But aside from the manipulative power of some advertising, the prediction of behavior on the basis of group information can have very serious effects on the individual. Individuality is no longer basis for a decision, but solely general information and whether it applies to the individual or not. Furthermore, the individual usually has no chance to alter the result of the algorithms applied because she usually does not have knowledge about this attribution of group information. Thus, an insurance company would not offer health insurance to a man above the age of 40 living in a certain area of town, being interested in Internet games and obviously spending his money mostly on Internet gadgets, if cohort information produces the information that typically, men of this type do not work regularly and have a tendency to be criminally active aside from being physically inactive and therefore prone to heart diseases. But maybe this person is a police officer who is very active in all sorts of athletics. Or it is possible to exclude a person from certain services and goods because she lives in a certain area in which a low pay rate is very high. Therefore, the individual pay-record of a person would not be able to overcome the generalized statistical information. Insurance companies and credit agencies already function with this method, but in European standards (and law) there is an obligation to include individualized information in such a decision, as well as an obligation that certain cohort information cannot be used.[18]

Information on the Internet about individuals is readily available. It is easily used not only to gather individualized information, but also to gather information about the type of group the individual belongs to—and then to use that information and other information in order to classify the individual. Open communication in the Internet therefore also can be used and misused by those interested in gathering this type of information. Any spreading of information via the Internet therefore is also addressed at these third parties, whether their oversight is wanted or not.[19]

8. Mass Infringements

The Internet is considered to be a mass medium. Even if no clear definition exists as to what constitutes a mass medium and with which consequences, it is generally agreed, that free accessibility by large numbers of users are constituent.

Although the decentralized structure of the Internet allows for many sub-groups, and as there are many services within the Internet some are used only by a very limited number of people, nevertheless, it is the possibility of access that clearly argues for a mass medium. This is only possible because the services on the Internet are usually open to everyone interested in receiving them. Consequently, Internet communication rarely takes place in a secure and private environment. It is therefore a mass communication especially as many people may be on-lookers of a communication deemed at least personal, maybe even private, by the active communicators. As the technical way of communication does not show who observes it, often protective measures of the communication parties are not taken. And the service provider always has access to the communication and its content.

This possibility of being observed and the information then being used by numerous other, not individually known, identifiable persons, programs and entities, causes another effect which is highly important for the estimation of infringements of individual rights. Any infringement on rights by the government, any misuse of power by service providers, any measure taken by other users usually affects masses. Due to the technical structures behind such infringements, it is not an individual problem but a structural one. Thus, if a service provider collects information about the origin of its users, this might be a minor informational infringement against the individual user. But this action also constitutes infringements against all users and therefore on a considerable scale of impact and seriousness.[20]

That a seemingly small infringement can turn into a heavy default shows the possibility of recombination of information. As information searches are much easier via the digitalized means of the Internet, information from many sources can quickly be reassembled. Seemingly uninteresting information—being an alumnus of a particular school—may be used together with other information—attendance of a party last weekend—and allow for a phishing attack using fake email-contacts from former classmates referring to small-talk at that party about having been classmates. Therefore, protective measures have to begin with the small infringement due to its potential to be recombined.

Conclusion and Outlook

As freedom of speech may collide with other fundamental individual rights in regard to opinion and information such as protection of privacy or data protection, a balancing of interests is often necessary. Balancing of interests, however, requires a determination of the intensity in which interests are hindered and rights infringed and in what way protection is necessary. Otherwise, a weighing is impossible. Both sides of the balancing of interests can be influenced by the means in which freedom of speech is expressed and by the dangers and misuses possible, and both influences have to be taken into account.

The Internet produces contradictory effects. It allows for more freedom of information, for easily, quickly, inexpensively access to information with little restrictions for time, space and other resources. However, it also changes the impact of communication considerably. Therefore, some of the effects almost unnoticed and of little importance in the offline world become a major factor in an online surrounding.

When having to perform the difficult task of balancing the interests of those involved in the typical conflicts between freedom of speech / freedom of the press on the one hand and data protection / protection of privacy on the other hand, it has to be tested whether the positive or the negative outcomes play a role and how far this influence goes. It cannot be neglected that the informational effects of distribution via the Internet have a much different impact than the typical media used in offline communication. They pose a considerable threat to personality, privacy and personal information and can influence behavior in ways often not anticipated.

The Internet poses new challenges and new questions. But often, it asks us some of the old questions again. We should not be afraid to find new answers and to allow for a differentiation between the offline and the online world.

8

DEFAMATION AND THE NET: ANONYMITY, MEANING AND ISPS

Eric Barendt*

Introduction

This subject of this chapter has recently been tackled by the Joint Committee of the House of Lords and Commons in its Report on the United Kingdom government's Draft Defamation Bill, which had been issued in March 2011.[1] Indeed, its consideration of defamation law in the context of communication on the Internet provides, as it were, a foundational text for the themes of this chapter. The Committee pointed out that the Internet has fundamentally changed the way in which we communicate by creating a new world in which everyone can effectively share information and engage in debate, potentially with vast numbers of their fellow citizens and indeed with many people around the world. That is to be welcomed. But the Committee went on to point out a drawback or disadvantage with this means of communicating information and ideas. The Internet is a platform from which it is all too easy to destroy reputations (and also for that matter infringe privacy and damage fair trial rights by publishing prejudicial material).[2]

This chapter discusses how some aspects of defamation law should be applied to the Net, and how far it is realistic to apply without modification principles which have been developed in the contexts of book and pamphlet publication and of communication through the traditional mass media of the press and broadcasting. Alternatively, of course, principles or aspects of defama-

---

* Emeritus Professor, University College, London.

tion law might be reconsidered in the light of experience of how they are, or should be, applied in the Internet context. These questions are of course not confined to defamation law; we may also need to ask how, say, the principles of obscenity law should be applied to communications on the Net. An examination of defamation (or obscenity) issues can be used as a basis for broader reflections on how to treat speech on the Net: should it be regarded in the same way as mass media expression?

The chapter looks in particular at three aspects of Internet communication and libel law. First is the significance of anonymous speech, or the use of a pseudonym or alias which is very common for bloggers and contributors to online discussion; secondly, how communications on the Net are, or should be, interpreted or understood; and thirdly, there is the issue of the responsibilities of ISPs and other intermediaries who provide platforms for speech on the Net—the extent to which they should be held responsible for defamatory messages on their platforms or services. This chapter does not tackle other important aspects of defamation law and the Internet, especially the question of which court has jurisdiction to hear libel actions. This is, of course, a crucial issue in the context of the Net; it is a real problem whether the courts of each state where recipients may read the allegations is entitled to hear a libel action brought in that state; and if it does, whether other states' courts should enforce its judgments. As is well known, it is an issue on which the media, authors, and lawyers in the United States have expressed strong critical views about English libel law and the practice of our courts in exercising jurisdiction over defamation actions brought against American publishers. Rather than revisit this controversial territory—well covered by practitioner and academic literature—this chapter examines other issues that have been rather less fully covered, at least in English legal writing.

I. Some General Points

A few general points will set the background for the more detailed discussion that follows. First, it may well be that the Internet has indeed transformed the exercise of the rights to freedom of speech (or freedom of expression, if the term in the European Human Rights Convention is preferred). For the first time, communication to a community—whether national or wider—is not the prerogative of newspaper editors and correspondents, political figures, and those who enjoy privileged access to radio or television. Anyone with access to the Net and appropriate technical assistance can participate in discussion groups, or set up a website or blog, so that their views are accessible to the world, or to at least that part of it which enjoys unlimited access to the World Wide Web. As an American judge in a leading United States case has said, the Net provides "the most participatory form of mass speech yet developed."[3] Secondly, communications on the Internet are not subject to any form of editorial or legal control before they are dispatched round cyberspace. There is no editor judging the appropriateness or relevance of the message, nor is there a lawyer advising the blogger or website operator that his remarks are defamatory, infringe privacy, or contravene other legal provisions. In short, the Net provides a system of communication without gatekeepers.

But a third introductory point is that, though some used to argue otherwise,[4] the Internet is not, and should not be, a law-free zone. It is all very well to talk about cyberspace or the virtual world created by the Internet. We must recognise that communications on the Net may have a significant impact in the real world, by, for example, damaging an individual's reputation or infringing her privacy. Further, it has often been said that the law should be technology-neutral—that it would be wrong to adapt or reform the common law to suit a particular technology or means of communication. First, as Kirby J said in his fascinating judgement in the famous *Dow Jones v Gutnick* case in the High Court of Australia,[5] any special rule devised for the Net is likely to be outdated very soon—technologies change. A second reason for reluctance to change the law to suit any particular media is that there is intense competition between the different branches of the media—not only between newspapers themselves, but between the press on the one hand, and bloggers and citizen journalists on the other. If the law appeared to favour the latter, there is no doubt that the press would have a legitimate source of complaint.

These principles were accepted by the Joint Committee in its Report on the United Kingdom government's Defamation Bill. It said that defamation law should apply in the same way to Internet publications as it does to the more traditional forms of media, and that the Internet should not be exempt from legal regulation. Nevertheless, the law needed to take account of the new challenges posed by the Internet.[6] The question then becomes whether the law can do this, without infringing any principle of technology-neutrality, by appearing to confer advantages on those who communicate on the Net in comparison with those using the print media or radio or television.

II. Anonymous Speech

Anonymous speech long antedates the Net, and even now is not confined to it. In the eighteenth century the anonymous *Letters of Junius*, attacking the policy of George III's government in handling the rebellion of the American colonies, were influential in bringing down Lord North's administration. Their author has never been identified to this day. The *Federalist Papers*, outlining the principles of the United States constitution, were written principally by James Madison and Alexander Hamilton with the use of pseudonyms. Until the late 1950s every article in *The Times* (London) used to be written anonymously,[7] and that remains the practice with the *Economist* magazine. Strangely, anonymity is in these contexts apparently considered to reinforce the authority of the authors' articles—the news or opinion is brought down to us, as it were, from on high. The views cannot be challenged on the grounds that they emanate from a reporter well known for her eccentricity or the peculiarity of her political stance. But it is surely reasonable to be interested in the identity of the author when determining how much respect to accord to a publication. We are much more likely to think that pseudonyms are adopted largely to protect individual journalists from legal action, and that their use weakens, rather than strengthens, the authority of their articles.

The Internet has now given anonymity and the use of pseudonyms a new dimension. Blogs are often written under a false name—for example, the most famous, right wing blogger in England, Paul Staines, writes under the name, *Guido Fawkes*, a variant of the Guy Fawkes who attempted to blow up the Houses of Parliament in 1605.[8] Anonymity and the adoption of false names has become part of the informal tradition of Netspeak, together with bad language, sloppy grammar, and emoticons. The practice creates real problems for the enforcement of defamation law. A claimant may find it difficult to identity the author of the allegations about which she wishes to complain and perhaps eventually to bring proceedings. Her problem is even more acute, if she is unable to bring separate proceedings against the ISP, which has hosted or carried the defamatory message (discussed later in this chapter). For the moment I am concerned with the problems there may be in identifying the original author.

This difficulty caused some concern to members of the Joint Committee on the Defamation Bill, when they heard evidence from representatives of the ISPs, Yahoo, and computer law experts. The evidence was that complete anonymity is unobtainable. A court order in civil proceedings, or the police in a criminal case, can compel an ISP to identify the subscriber from whose computer the message was sent. The courts in England have rejected the argument that an ISP may refuse to identify its subscriber because it has the same privilege as a journalist not to disclose its source.[9] In *Totalise v Motley Fool*,[10] it was held by Owen J that an ISP or website operator does not take responsibility for the publications it transmits or hosts, so it does not enjoy the same privilege as an editor of a newspaper or magazine not to identify the subscribers whose information it carries. Courts instead have discretion to order an ISP or website operator to disclose the identity of someone who has posted a defamatory allegation, or at least to reveal her email address. But it was conceded by one of the witnesses to the Joint Committee that, though it is always possible to identify the computer and Internet Protocol address from which a message is sent, that does not mean that one can necessarily identify the exact individual who made that posting. There are real problems, where there is a shared computer in a household or messages are sent from an Internet café.[11] Quite apart from that situation, authors can also make it difficult, if not impossible, for them to be identified by using special software programmes.

In exercising their discretion to make an order compelling an ISP to disclose the identity of the author, courts must take a number of factors into account, among them the strength of the claimant's libel case, the seriousness of the allegations, and the fact that the author is sheltering behind a screen of anonymity when blogging or contributing to a discussion board.[12] However, the Court of Appeal in *Totalise* said that it may sometimes be legitimate to protect an anonymous speaker's identity, and that it might be right for a website operator to inform the speaker and so give him the chance to produce reasons to the claimant and the court for preserving his anonymity.[13]

These problems are even more acute in the United States, where the courts have recognised a First Amendment right to speak anonymously. The justification for this line of decisions is that otherwise some people might be deterred from speaking their mind, because they are worried about the consequence their speech may attract,[14] though some Supreme Court judges have recognised the drawbacks to recognising a right to speak anonymously: that it encourages the making of fraudulent or false claims and makes more likely the coarsening of political debate.[15]

To protect the anonymity right in the context of defamation actions, United States courts require claimants to satisfy a threshold test before they are willing to compel an ISP to reveal the identity of the subscriber from whose computer a defamatory message has been sent. The usual test is that the claimant must show a prima facie case of defamation, and further she must satisfy under a balancing standard that her interest in discovery of the author's identity outweighs the defendant's right to speak anonymously.[16] The claimant must produce sufficient evidence to support each element of the defamation case, for otherwise the *prima facie* requirement offers the defendant no protection at all; further, in applying the balancing standard, the court takes account of the character of the defendant's speech, so the author of anonymous *political* speech is more likely to be immune from unmasking than the author of a defamatory *commercial* allegation or of slurs on private individuals' sexual lives. To give an example of the latter, in one recent case a federal District Court compelled an ISP to identify subscribers to its service who had posted scandalous comments under a pseudonym about the sexuality and sexual behaviour of female law students at Yale University;[17] it was rightly unimpressed by the case for anonymity, when the subscribers had made seriously defamatory remarks of little or no free speech value.

One interesting point in this Yale student case is that the District Court judge rejected an argument that bloggers had an expectation of privacy when they posted anonymously. It was clear from the ISP policy to which they had agreed that AT&T would comply with any court order or subpoena to identify its subscribes. In an interesting case three years ago, an English judge also rejected the privacy argument, holding that blogging is intrinsically a public activity, so he declined to grant the author of a blog, known as "Night Jack," an interim injunction to stop Times Newspapers from revealing his identity.[18] This decision can be criticised, for undervaluing both the freedom of expression and the privacy arguments for protecting the anonymity of the blogger;[19] it is doubtful, however, whether another court in England would take a different approach. Indeed, as will be discussed in section 4 of this chapter, the recent report of the Joint Committee recommends a change in Internet culture and in the respect given to anonymous blogging and other user-generated comment. Whatever the strength of the arguments for a right to speak anonymously, the use of anonymity and pseudonyms undeniably makes more difficult the enforcement of defamation law in the context of the Internet; moreover, the practice may affect the interpretation of defamatory communications on the Net, the topic to which the chapter now turns.

III. The Interpretation of Communications on the Net

The meaning of language is often critical in defamation law. Indeed, the Faulks Committee, reviewing the reform of English libel law in 1975, described it as the single most important factor in defamation litigation.[20] It is crucial to deciding whether the allegations are defamatory, whether they amount to an allegation of fact or are rather an expression of opinion, and whether the defendant has proved the truth of any factual allegations for the purposes of a defence of justification or as the basis for a fair comment defence.[21] In principle the same general approach is taken to the understanding of allegations whether they are made in a newspaper, on a television or radio programme, or over the Internet. The court, sometimes the jury, tries to determine, or ascribe, a single meaning to the language—did it, for example, make a particular defamatory allegation against the claimant, or was it just mere abuse or an insult, which is not actionable?

But meaning is to be determined in context, and courts may take account of the fact that a message has been communicated on the Net in characterising it as defamatory or not. This practice is shown in several United States cases where courts have emphasized that defamatory allegations are to be understood and interpreted within the context in which they were delivered. So according to the California Court of Appeal in a leading case,[22] it is relevant that the remarks were made anonymously on a financial message board; the informality of Internet message boards made speech there more like gossip than accurate reporting. In the court's view, hyberbole and exaggeration on the Net are common,[23] so it is unlikely that readers will take such messages seriously. Posts calling the claimant and other corporate officers of a Florida company "boobs, losers and crooks," and purporting to outline the sexual fantasies of the Corporation's Legal Officer about the female claimant were therefore characterised as opinion rather than as asserting objective facts. The posts were rude, childish, and offensive, but were not to be treated as defamatory. In another case,[24] a federal District Court emphasized that the posts were put on an Internet message board where Yahoo! had placed a disclaimer ("These messages are only the opinion of the poster, are no substitute for your own research, and should not be relied on....") so suggesting that they should be treated as opinion, rather than as allegations of fact. Distinctions should be drawn, however, between different types of Internet communication. In a leading case, the Supreme Court of Delaware said that Internet chat-rooms and blogs are not as reliable as the *Wall Street Journal Online;* they were not generally treated as sources of facts or data on which reasonable persons rely.[25] The clear implication, of course, is that it would be right to treat remarks in an online newspaper in exactly the same way as comparable material in the printed version.

In at least two English cases a similar approach has been taken to the interpretation of defamatory communications on the Net. In *Smith v ADVFN plc* Eady J upheld a stay of 37 libel proceedings brought by the claimant in respect of comments on bulletin boards that were highly critical, indeed abusive, with regard to his behaviour in trying to coordinate a shareholders' action group. The judge drew attention to the character of bulletin board communications, which are "rather like contributions to a casual conversation ... are often uninhibited, casual and ill thought out; those who participate know this, and expect a certain amount of repartee, or 'give and take.'"[26] It was relevant, in his view, that the participants mostly used pseudonyms—moreover, they did not take others' contributions literally or seriously and construed them merely as abuse. It is often obvious, he added, that people are saying the first thing that comes into their heads, and remarks are not intended to be taken seriously. In the case itself many of the remarks of which the claimant complained were themselves prompted by what he had written himself. So it would be a waste of court time to consider them. Admittedly, Eady J said he was not suggesting that blogging can never form the basis for a libel action. But these claims were wholly without merit.

In the second case, the character of postings on a football club supporters' website was taken into account in deciding whether to compel the website operator to disclose the identity of the posters; a disclosure order should only be made in respect of the more serious, non trivial allegations, where the claimants' reputation rights—they were the directors of Sheffield Wednesday FC—outweighed the right of the authors to maintain their anonymity.[27] On the other hand, the authors of mere saloon bar grumbling about the management of the club or other abuse should not be identified under a court order.

The Joint Committee of the House of Lords and House of Commons approved this judicial approach to online defamatory allegations. It concluded that " … many derogatory and mocking statements on blogs and social networking sites may be read casually, remain fleeting in their impact and be given limited credence by readers when compared, for example, to material published by reputable media organizations."[28] These considerations should be given appropriate weight when courts determine whether the publication of defamatory allegations is likely to cause serious harm to the claimant's reputation—a new requirement for a successful action under clause 1 of the Defamation Bill, which has just been introduced by the United Kingdom Coalition government.[29]

What should be made of this approach? One question is whether it is compatible with the general principle that the law, including defamation law, should be technology neutral, so that in principle an allegation treated as defamatory, if printed in a newspaper or made in the course of a radio interview, should also provide the basis for an action if made over the Net. That would suggest that it is irrelevant to the interpretation of remarks that they are communicated on the Net, rather than in the traditional mass media. But it is of course also a familiar principle of English libel law that the meaning of any statement, which, it is alleged, defames the claimant, should be determined by looking at its context, as well as at its explicit language. That principle was applied in an English case to treat as a humorous joke, words in a parody, or spoof version, of Elton John's Diary published in *The Guardian Weekend* section of the Saturday newspaper, which, on a literal interpretation, alleged the celebrity had hosted a lavish Ball as a self-promotion event.[30] The judge suggested that a reader would have taken the words more seriously, if they had been published in a news section of the chapter.

So it is surely right to take account of the conventions of Internet speech and the undoubted fact that much of it is spontaneous, off the cuff, and probably not intended to be taken seriously. For some commentators this provides one reason why defamation law should be applied more leniently to blogs than to comparable commentary in the press and on the broadcasting channels; "... the lack of the voice of authority is a characteristic of the blogosphere."[31] On the other hand there is some indication that at least in England Internet users place greater trust in the Net than they do in other media, particularly newspapers.[32] Whether warranted or not, reliance on information on the Net can have significant consequences, and bloggers should be accountable for them.[33] In the libel, and perhaps other contexts, courts should, as the United States District Court judge did in *SPX Corporation v John Doe*,[34] distinguish between different types of Internet communications. Some blogs and certainly most online publications should be taken as seriously as articles in the broadsheet press or on a television channel. In appropriate cases their reports should be treated as providing information and therefore as potentially making defamatory allegations of fact. In contrast other communications, particularly reader comments on blogs, may be more easily dismissed as too trivial to provide the basis for a libel action. Similar distinctions can be drawn between different types of publication within the traditional mass media, or even within the pages of a particular newspaper as the Elton John case shows.[35] It is unclear, however, how relevant it should be whether a communication is sent anonymously or by an identified author. The courts in *Smith*[36] and *SPX*[37] certainly considered this relevant; in their view a communication sent anonymously or with the use of a pseudonym is less likely to carry a clear defamatory meaning, and should generally be understood as mere abuse or the expression of an opinion. The difficulty with this approach is that it may encourage the use of pseudonyms by authors who will appreciate their messages are less likely as a result to be interpreted as carrying a defamatory meaning. A final point is that, experience of speech on the Net might exercise some influence on the future development of defamation law; courts may now be more willing than they have been to interpret allegations as too trivial to cause substantial harm to the claimant's reputation.[38]

IV. The Legal Responsibilities of ISPs and Other Platform Providers

The third aspect of defamation law explored in this chapter involves the legal responsibilities of intermediaries who provide platforms for Internet speech—ISPs, website operators, the moderators of online discussion groups, and bloggers whose sites carry comments from readers. Can defamation actions be taken against them as well as, or as an alternative to, proceedings against the original author(s) of the defamatory allegations? The discussion focuses on English law, for in the United States it is clear that ISPs and others who re-publish speech are entirely immune from liability. Section 230 of the Communications Decency Act of 1996 states: "[n]o provider or user of an interactive computer service shall be treated as the publisher or speaker of any information provided by another information content provider." That means in effect that no defamation action can be brought against an ISP or website operator. The provision has the laudable aims of encouraging self-regulation by ISPs and promoting freedom of speech on the Net, but it does this at the cost of reputation rights, which may become virtually unenforceable if the original author, perhaps sheltering behind a pseudonym, cannot be traced. That leads to grotesque results, as evidenced by the infamous decision in *Zeran v America Online*,[39] where the claimant's life had been ruined after it had been falsely alleged online that he was responsible for the bombing of federal buildings in Oklahoma City. Because of the provision in the 1996 statute, he was unable to take libel proceedings against AOL which had been very slow in taking down the defamatory postings made anonymously by an untraceable subscriber to its service.

In England, the position has been that a website operator or an ISP, as well as the original author, can be treated as the publisher of a defamatory allegation. That is in conformity with the usual principles of English defamation law. The editor of a newspaper, its distributor, and indeed, individual newsagents and vendors, are publishers of defamatory material, just as the journalist or other author is, so on this point a standard principle is applied to the Internet. However, in an important decision, Eady J did rule as a matter of law that an ISP which performed no more than a passive role in facilitating postings on the Net could not be regarded as a publisher of those postings.[40] But that would probably not cover ISPs and others involved in publishing communications on the Net, once they have been given notice that they are hosting, or even merely carrying, a defamatory allegation. In that event they are to be regarded as publishers, so it seems after notification by a claimant to that effect, they must remove the defamatory remark, unless they are prepared to run the risk of a libel action.[41]

However, ISPs and other secondary publishers have defences under section 1 of the Defamation Act 1996, and under Regulations introduced in 2002 to give effect to the EU Directive on Electronic Commerce.[42] The Regulations, unlike the Defamation Act, were framed specifically to deal with the legal problems arising from Internet communications, and they provide broader defences than the United Kingdom legislation. The Regulations distinguish between the position of ISPs who merely provide access to customers and that of hosting providers who store others' content online—whether websites or user generated content posted on a website. The former, known in the Regulations are "mere conduits," enjoy complete immunity from liability for damages or any criminal penalty as a result of their transmission of communications.[43] But, under Regulation 19, host providers are only not liable for the content they store, if they do not have actual knowledge of unlawful activity or information, and on acquiring such knowledge, if they act expeditiously to remove or disable access to the information.

The Internet Service Providers Association (ISPA) and groups campaigning for reform of English libel law[44] argued last year in their evidence to the Joint Committee on the government's draft Defamation Bill that current law creates in effect a "notice and take down" regime, under which ISPs, once notified by a potential claimant that they were hosting defamatory material, automatically removed it, even if it were not seriously damaging to the complainant, or its content was true or could be defended as fair comment. ISPs naturally tended to err on the side of caution in removing material alleged to be defamatory; unlike a newspaper editor or broadcasting channel controller, they have no interest in defending libel actions to preserve their reputation as good journalists. It is of course difficult for an Internet service provider to determine whether a message is defamatory and if so, whether it might have a good defence to a libel action; in this respect, defamation is much harder to detect and control than obscenity and child pornography. The ISPA argued that this system compelled them to act as judge and jury,[45] while a campaign group contended that it exercised a chilling effect on freedom of Internet speech.[46] They argued that a claimant should be required to obtain a court order before an obligation should be imposed on an ISP to remove allegedly defamatory material.

Ian Walden, a computer law specialist, argued that it is inevitable that one party or other would be at a disadvantage, if no court order is required to compel the removal of allegedly illegal material on the Net. In his view, while it was right for an ISP to remove content likely to be in breach of the criminal law, such as that proscribing child pornography, before a court decision, any risk of an error—what he termed an "error preference"—should be in favour of freedom of expression in the case of material, such as defamatory allegations, which might give rise to civil proceedings.[47] But he did not favour the total exemption of online interactive chat, on sites such as Twitter and Facebook, from any legal liability for libel, as that would be unfair to the victims of defamatory allegations and would discriminate against the traditional media.

The Joint Committee considering the draft Defamation Bill made a number of innovative recommendations in this area. They are designed to ensure that people defamed online have a quick and inexpensive remedy to protect their reputation, and at the same time to give greater protection for freedom of speech by reducing the pressures on hosts and service providers to take down material alleged to be defamatory. Further, the Committee intended to promote "a cultural shift towards a general recognition that unidentified [that is, anonymous] postings are not to be treated as true, reliable or trustworthy."[48] To achieve these ends, it proposed that the law should distinguish between the treatment of material sent by an identified author, and that sent anonymously by an unidentified person. A host or service provider would be required to publish any notice of complaint about allegedly defamatory material posted by an identified author alongside that material—the notice would reduce, the Committee thought, the sting of the libel without compelling the immediate take down of the material. A complainant could, however, opt to apply to a court for a take-down order, which would only be made *after* the judge had heard paper based arguments from both complainant and the author. The intention is that this would be decided quickly with minimum expense.

By contrast, an ISP host would be required to take down material written by an unidentified person, unless the author responded promptly to a request to identify herself, in which case the other procedure takes effect. It would be open to the host to apply to the court for a "leave up" order, where it believed that it was in the public interest for an anonymous posting by, say, a whistle-blower, to stay up on the Net. Otherwise, the ISP host would be exposed to defamation proceedings as a publisher. In the long term the Committee hoped that people will pay less attention to anonymous postings, and presumably that bloggers and contributors to discussion groups and online forums will be more willing to communicate using their real names, because otherwise they know that their posting will be taken down immediately there is a complaint.

These objectives are laudable, as the government agreed in its response to the Joint Committee Report.[49] It shared "the Committee's concern that anonymity should not be used as a cloak for making abusive or untrue statements without fear of any comeback."[50] But it thought there were significant practical and technical difficulties to the two-track system recommended by the Committee, so it would not be workable. The government proposed instead that an ISP or other intermediary should act as a liaison point between the complainant and the person who had posted the allegedly defamatory material, where her identity and contact details are not known to the complainant. Intermediaries are to be required to provide details of the author to the complainant who would have to take legal proceedings against her to secure removal of the material. A complaint could only sue an intermediary, if it was unwilling or unable to provide the author's details and also failed then to take down the material about which the complaint had been brought.[51] Regulations will be introduced to flesh out the skeletal provisions in the Bill. Intermediaries will, I think, be strongly encouraged to ensure that they host postings from identifiable persons, for that guarantees them immunity from defamation proceedings.

Conclusions

An obvious first conclusion is that *anonymous* postings, or rather in practice the standard use of *pseudonyms* to hide the real identify of the author, greatly complicate the operation of libel law in the context of the Net. Proposals to discourage the use of pseudonyms should be supported, as otherwise claimants find it difficult to enforce their reputation rights, which in English law are covered as a human right by Article 8 of the European Convention on Human Rights. Whether the cultural change that the Joint Committee hopes to achieve will really occur is another matter. The subtleties of defamation law, and the risks of a defamation action, may not greatly influence bloggers' decisions whether to use their real name or adopt a pseudonym.

Secondly, courts are right to curtail actions for what is really only vulgar abuse or offensive childish speech on the Net. They rightly recognise that the Net readily lends itself to hyperbole and exaggerated claims that nobody is likely to take seriously. But that is also almost certainly true of many allegations in the traditional mass media that have led in the past to libel actions before the courts. It is surely doubtful, for example, whether the allegations in *Berkoff v. Burchill*, that Steve Berkoff was "hideously ugly" would be regarded now, as they were by a majority of the Court of Appeal in 1997, as capable of being defamatory of the director-actor.[52] Internet speech is not special, even if it is recognised that it may be less likely than comparable expression in the mass media to carry a clear defamatory meaning.

But it would be wrong to go further. It would be misconceived to apply a more lenient libel law for the publication of defamatory allegations on the Net, because of the special nature of communications on the Internet, particularly anonymous speech. It has been argued that anonymous communications are never taken seriously and cannot cause harm.[53] That is surely an exaggerated claim. Anonymous rumours initiated by blogs can cause enormous financial loss or ruin someone's social standing.[54] There is no reason to think that the old adage, "There is no smoke without fire!" does not apply to the Net as much as it does to the spreading of rumours by more traditional means. Further, anonymous blogs may be taken up and reported by the mass media of the press and broadcasting, and there seems no justification in these circumstances for exposing those media to libel actions, but not the original author of serious defamatory allegations.

The last point is the most fundamental point. We cannot argue that the Net has transformed freedom of expression, giving ordinary individuals for the first time the ability to communicate their ideas effectively, and then at the same time claim that as readers they necessarily regard blogs and other Net communications as too silly to provide a basis for libel proceedings. If it is right, as it is, to take the claims to freedom of speech on the Net seriously, so we should take equally seriously arguments that its exercise may, and sometimes does, cause significant damage to reputation (and other) rights. There is no escape from detailed consideration of both claims in the context of the Net, as there is in other more traditional contexts.

Free Speech in the Internet Era: Developments "Online" in Defamation and Privacy Law — Brief Observations

Paul Tweed*

The purpose of this chapter is to offer a variety of media law related topics which have been encountered in legal practice. They range from superinjunctions, to the WikiLeaks scandal, pending British defamation legislation, and a recent British defamation decision. One common theme is the constant conflict between freedom of expression and protection of reputation evident in these areas.

I. Ryan Giggs Super-Injunction

One simple tweet naming Ryan Giggs as the professional footballer who had taken out a super injunction to conceal an extramarital affair did more not only to undermine the UK judicial system, but also to highlight the apparently insurmountable difficulties presented in any attempt to control online publications.

---

* Paul Tweed is a senior partner at Johnsons Law Firm, Belfast. He practices in the UK, Ireland and the US. He has been involved in many high profile defamation actions both for claimants and publishers. His experience also extends to breach of confidence and privacy and intellectual property. He has been a consistent advocate of mediation when appearing before the House of Commons Joint Committee on Defamation and several Ministry of Justice Panels.

Ryan Giggs' lawyers had moved quickly to seek an injunction, after an article was published in *The Sun* newspaper on April 14, 2011 revealing an account by the model Imogen Thomas of her ongoing sexual relationship with a famous yet un-named footballer, in 2010. The Manchester United Football Club mainstay, who would admit to involvement with the model throughout a short period in 2010, had received text messages from Miss Thomas asking for money, and a telephone call from the model's solicitors indicating that she had engaged the services of publicist, Max Clifford, in close proximity to the publication of *The Sun* article. The implication was clear; there was a genuine likelihood that Giggs would be named, and on the same day as the publication, an interim injunction was obtained at the High Court in London against News Group Newspapers to restrict publication of the footballer's identity. The question of issuing the injunction on a permanent basis was considered by the High Court in London on April 20, 2011, by Eady J—the Judge at the forefront of libel and privacy jurisprudence in England and Wales (and in turn, the United Kingdom)—and his reasons were published in a corresponding judgement of May 16, 2011.[1]

In granting the injunction, Eady J had rendered a careful and considered judgement, which addressed the core issue of whether the footballer's right to privacy under Article 8 of the European Convention on Human Rights (ECHR) would prevail over the newspaper's right to freedom of expression under Article 10 ECHR. In the first instance, it was held that the nature of the information so much as it concerned conduct of an intimate nature should allow Giggs to enjoy a reasonable expectation of privacy in respect of the information. Secondly the Court found that it was not in the public interest for the footballer's identity to be published, as the revelation would not contribute to a debate of general interest. Indeed, Eady J was noted[2] to have found that the balance would not usually favour the media in cases regarding information concerning individual's private and family life, or in cases involving "tittle tattle about the activites of footballer's wives and girlfriends"[3]—a "kiss and tell" story. The reputation and privacy of the superstar appeared to be safe.

The terms of the final injunction would prohibit any other party in the world from publishing these details, without risk of being found guilty of contempt of court. In finding that the Article 8 right to privacy under the European Convention would favour protecting the married superstar and his family from invasive press intrusion, the Court held that this injunction should apply *contra mundum* (against the rest of the world). It was a "super injunction," the zenith of the English Court's application of the law of privacy and the bane of the life of the tabloid journalist and their would-be philosophy of (in the words of the Duke of Wellington) "publish and be damned"!

In theory, this injunction would apply to any party and any publication, online or otherwise. However, by May 16, 2011, the publisher of the *The Sun* had applied to vary the terms of the injunction, so as to remove the anonymity granted to Giggs, purely on the basis that "many tens of thousands of people can, if they are sufficiently interested, find out who the Claimant is by making appropriate searches on the Internet.".[4] The identity of the footballer had been leaked and became widespread within the public domain, primarily via the social networking site, Twitter.

The Court, in refusing the request, had to produce a fairly sophisticated reason for doing so, namely that it would distinguish the degree of invasiveness and embarrassment that would occur if the disclosure was made public by way of press publication, as compared to the more "unofficial" source of *Twitter* and the Internet. This did not mean that the damage had not already been done in real terms—the social networking community had undermined the authority of the Courts. While each of the some 75,000 Twitter users would still technically be in contempt of court as a result, in practice there was little that could be done to prevent the news spreading. To add insult to injury, the footballer's identity was made the subject of a speech in Parliament by John Hemming MP, using parliamentary privilege to breach the injunction without any ramifications.[5]

II. Assange and Wikileaks

The problems of controlling free speech on the Internet were further highlighted by the WikiLeaks scandal, when Julian Assange became embroiled in a global controversy that demonstrated how the Internet could and was being used to actively flout any exposure to risk that would usually be associated with a breach of official secrets. Assange, the publisher and media entrepreneur had established his website, "WikiLeaks" as a base for the anonymous publication of otherwise sensitive, confidential, or "leaked" documents. Since 2006 the site had been involved in the publication of material documenting extrajudicial killings in Kenya, a report of toxic waste dumping on the coast of Côte d'Ivoire, Church of Scientology manuals, Guantanamo Bay procedures, the July 12, 2007 Baghdad airstrike video, and documents concerning the conduct of large banks such as Kaupthing and Julius Baer, amongst numerous other sensitive documents. The site allowed the disseminators of the material to remain completely anonymous, at the same time due to its being based in the U.S., serving as a safe haven against any legal action, in for example for breach of privacy, that may have been contemplated on foot of any of the site's more controversial "leaks," which may have caused instant damage to the organisation or individuals that had compiled or were the subject of the confidential documents.

It was in November 2010 when the site began to release some of the 251,000 American diplomatic cables that had fallen into its hands, of which over fifty three percent were listed as unclassified, forty percent as "Confidential" and just over six percent classified "Secret," that the U.S. Government suddenly realised that the protection of free speech had ramifications that had never been anticipated.

An initial investigation into the WikiLeaks scandal had been undertaken by the Australian Attorney-General, focusing on the activities of its Australian founder. The A-G had sanctioned the Federal Police to carry out this investigation, although their conclusion was only that Assange was not criminally liable for the leaks under Australian law. The United States Department of Justice then launched its own criminal investigation into the leak. While no formal charges were levied, on December 14, 2010 the U.S. Department of Justice issued a subpoena ordering Twitter to release information relating to Assange's account on the social networking site.[6] At around this time, Mastercard, Visa Inc. and Bank of America also halted their dealings with WikiLeaks,[7] while on December 6, 2011, the Swiss Bank, PostFinance had announced that it had frozen Assange's assets.

The responses to the leaks were varied, with former House Speaker Newt Gingrinch labelling the site's activities as "Information terrorism," which could "lead to people getting killed,"[8] following that with the view that "Julian Assange is engaged in terrorism. He should be treated as an enemy combatant."[9] In May 2010, Senate Minority Leader McConnell concluded that Assange had "done enormous damage to our country" and should be "prosecuted to the full extent of the law."[10] On the other side of the coin, the Sydney Peace Foundation had awarded Assange a gold medal for "exceptional courage and initiative in pursuit of human rights"![11]

The problem of policing online activity has been further compounded by the different levels of protection offered to Internet Service Providers (ISPs) on either side of the Atlantic, with many ISPs having now moved to seek the First Amendment and other protections offered in the United States, making enforcement against them virtually impossible, leaving those operating via these ISPs with the opportunity to "publish ... and never be damned!"

III. Defamation Bill 2012

The options available to the courts and legislators in dealing with this relatively new and rapidly developing problem are extremely limited. In reviewing the current UK Defamation Law, Lord Mawhinney's Joint Parliamentary

Committee[12] and the United Kingdom Government have been debating how best to tackle this new phenomenon in a practical way that would acknowledge one party's freedom of speech on the one hand, while protecting reputations and ensuring that the mainstream media are treated in the same way as their online competitors.

The proposals for reform have resulted in the draft Defamation Bill that was placed before Parliament on May 11, 2012, following a long consultation process. Several provisions in the Bill deal with the position of individuals who finds themselves in the position of having been the subject of an attack on their reputation online.

Operators of websites are dealt with under Clause 5 of the new Bill, which provides protection for a website provider in circumstances where they are not the author of the defamatory content on their site, the recent case of *Tamiz v. Google*[13] already establishing that a facilitator such as Google is not liable for defamatory postings.

The website facilitator could, however, still be liable if they fail to take action on being notified of a defamatory third party posting, with the onus on website operators to maintain increased vigilance in terms of website content, particularly for user forums. This may go some way to address the "hands off" approach taken by many web forum operators, who have been able to avoid liability on the basis that they take no part in regulation or monitoring of any user-generated content. Presumably, the implication would be that ISPs should become more willing to promptly disclose the unique IP addresses of their users on receipt of a complaint. However, this may also raise further issues in light of the current online landscape, where users of the Internet have developed an expectation that, if they so choose, they can contribute while remaining completely anonymous. It will remain to be seen how effective this regulation will be in terms of its implementation across the "wild west" of the Internet. However, any ISPs who are less willing to comply will lose the benefit of the defence in relation to any defamatory content appearing on their site.

It has been observed that Clause 5 was specifically intended to deliver a greater degree of protection against liability on the part of online intermediaries,[14] which, in relation to identifiable posts, is probably achieved in comparison to the existing defences available under section 1 of the Defamation Act 1996 and by way of the "conduit, caching and hosting" provisions of the Electronic Commerce Directive.[15] What has also been criticised is the degree of substantive clarification that is left to be added to the Bill by way of as yet unwritten secondary legislation, particularly with regard to the requirements for ISPs in a situation where a forum system allows posts to be made on a totally anonymous basis, which allows the defense to be defeated. This may place significantly on the back foot any ISPs which choose to allow anonymous posts or do not maintain a system for identifying their users, which may constitute a large section of the online community. The introduction of the defence is curious in light of the principle recently established in the *Tamiz v. Google* case. If it is a defence for an ISP to show that it was not the author of a posting, is there an implication that the *Tamiz* principle will have to be revisited.

In *Tamiz*, it was held that *Google Inc.* were not considered to be the publisher of any third party material posted on its "Blogger" website. However, if an ISP must now show that it was not the author of a third party posting, will further costly and prolonged litigation be required to provide clarification as to how the Bill would actually function alongside this common law principle? Aside from this, the actual meanings of the terms 'website,' or 'operator' would also stand to be challenged. For example, how would these definitions apply to individual profile pages on social networking sites such as Facebook or Twitter?[16] Further considerations include the extent to which the Claimant may be accepted as being able or unable to identify the author of particular content on a website. Does this assume that the Claimant has made a request for these details to the operator, even taking into account the prospect of applying for a *Norwich Pharmacal* Order?[17] This case already provides a mechanism to allow a potential claimant to apply to the Court for an order than an ISP intermediary compel disclosure of information, namely the identity of a third party who had posted potentially defamatory content, which may otherwise not be available from the website on its face.[18] It will need to be clarified whether these principles will be moulded around the new legislation.

The provision could therefore perhaps be expected to incentivise website operators to ensure that the identity of its users is as clear as possible. The more information is available on the face of a website as to the identity of third party contributors, the less risk there is for the ISP in terms of liability—they are in effect taken completely out of the frame. However, this could be expected to clash with the commercial character of some websites, such as free blogging sites.

The mechanism of Claimants giving notice of potentially defamatory material to a website operator resulting in the operator either disclosing contact details for the author, or removing the posts, could also perhaps be open to fairly arbitrary abuse—a factor that would undoubtedly be objectionable to privacy groups. For instance, the mechanism does not incorporate the possibility of considering defences to the defamatory posting (unless there is recourse to litigation), such as truth, honest opinion and responsible publication on matters of public interest.[19]

IV. Further Discussion and Conclusion

Legislative changes and the shifting and often inconsistent common law decisions still leave a totally unsatisfactory situation on any view, whereby the World Wide Web remains very much a law onto itself. While it is one thing to expose the sexual frolics of professional footballers, it is quite another to jeopardise the necessary confidentiality behind an injunction protecting children, suicide risks and victims of blackmail. Surely no civilised society should tolerate a situation where a disparate range of Internet service providers and their contributors should be allowed to appoint themselves as their own judge and jury?

Further, we are not just talking about confidentiality and privacy issues here. Recently an Irish international footballer, James McClean, was the subject to death threats on Twitter following his controversial decision to play for the Republic of Ireland as opposed to his native Northern Ireland team.[20] This is but one example of more sinister elements capitalising on the potential anonymity offered by many social networking sites, enabling those with their own, often warped, agendas to disseminate threats and unsavoury information at will.

However, given the different attitudes and approaches to freedom of speech by different governments, with the United States opting for a much more liberal approach under the First Amendment, compared to the stricter protection offered to the individual under UK law, the resultant diverging approaches would suggest that it is most unlikely that international agreement can be reached on a common approach dealing with the aforesaid conduct.

A particularly draconian example of Internet control can be found by examining the interface of the Google search engine with the online market in China, where initially the company's Chinese incumbent was subject to the Communist government's Internet censorship, which restricted a large number of its search results. In March 2010, Google however attempted to circumvent the censorship system by redirecting Google China search requests to its server in Hong Kong, where the same censorship did not apply.[21] In what was perceived as a backlash, China then implemented an apparent ban on accessing Google in China.[22] Although such a strategy would be repugnant to Western democracies, nonetheless it does provide a stark illustration of how the Internet can be policed in purely practical terms, which could perhaps be brought to the attention of those ISPs that have shown a total indifference to the rights and wellbeing of the private individual. Google Inc. nonetheless continued to cause controversy earlier this year on the release of its latest privacy policy, which suggested that personal information submitted into separate elements of the site by its users (e.g. GoogleMail, YouTube, Blogger, etc.) could be shared by the entire service, including the search engine itself.[23] The obvious application will relate to unwanted targeted advertising, although the principle will apply to the issue of how ISPs should be expected to handle and store a user's personal data, particularly now that in the UK they will be expected to be compliant to the provisions of the new Defamation Bill. On the other side of the Atlantic, President Obama's proposal for an Internet Consumer's Bill of Rights, to protect the privacy of information provided by online consumers,[24] may be monitored on the same theme.

Another interesting, and remarkable, case highlighting the curious interaction of the medium of online social media and the law concerning freedom of speech is the criminal prosecution against Paul Chambers. Chambers was arrested on January 10, 2010 after Tweeting to a friend that he intended to meet in Belfast, by way of flying from Doncaster, "... Robin Hood airport is closed. You've got a week and a bit to get [it] together otherwise I'm blowing the airport sky high!" Chambers was charged under the Communications Act 2003, section 127, after extensive searches were carried out of his home and personal computer, for having sent "by means of public electronic communications network a message or other matter that is grossly offensive or of an indecent, obscene or menacing character." The conviction under this charge was later overturned on the basis that this "Tweet" did not constitute or include a message of a menacing character,[25] but even its very prosecution, given the humorous and satirical nature of the Tweet, albeit that it was available to be seen by other users, marks this case as a bizarre overreaction by the state to a jibe that clearly would not have been intended to be taken seriously. The legislation used to convict Chambers was seldom used and had rarely been considered by the Courts.[26] Further, as should now be familiar, this case highlights that the spectre of the invisible global terrorist post 9/11 is clearly still active in overruling common sense. The DPP has since issued interim guidelines, setting out the approach prosecutors should take in cases involving communications sent via social media and attempting a distinction between communications which amount to credible threats of violence, a targeted campaign of harassment against an individual or which breach court orders on the one hand, and, on the other hand, other communications sent by social media that are grossly offensive but without these consequences.[27] The first group will be prosecuted robustly, whereas the second group will only be prosecuted if they cross a high threshold.

The next few years will therefore be very interesting indeed, and may no doubt be expected to serve as a yardstick, not only for the future development of regulation for online publication, but also for the harmonisation of privacy and freedom of speech laws and regulation of use of the Internet that may establish universal standards for future generations to come.

10

Now Trending: Loving the Internet Terrorist?

*Christopher J. Roederer**

"Love thy neighbor as thy self"[1] "Love you therefore the stranger"[2]

"Do unto others as you would have them do unto you"[3]

"God grant us the serenity to accept the things we cannot change, courage to change the things we can, and wisdom to know the difference."[4]

Nazis, Communists and Terrorists on the Internet:[5] "I want you, I need you, but there ain't no way I'm ever gonna love you"[6]

Introduction

While no one wants to give up the Internet, would the world not be better if a decade after 9/11 the terrorist would have gone the way of the communist, or at least, the Nazi? Wouldn't it be nice if the combination of these words, "Internet" and "terrorist" had little to no rhetorical weight? We allowed the word "terrorist" to define the last decade; we should not allow the phrase "Internet terrorists" to define the next. We need to reverse the trend.

* Professor of Law, Florida Coastal School of Law. The author would like to thank Rachael Soule, Amanda Isaacs, and Fernando Dutra for their research assistance and Christine Napoleon, his library liaison, for help in gathering sources. Thanks also go to Christina Wells who provided prior access to some of her forthcoming works, Julia McLaughlin, Jack Van Doren and Joe Tomain for their written feedback on earlier drafts of this work as well as to the organizers and participants of the London Free Speech Discussion Forum. The author would like to thank Florida Coastal School of Law for supporting this research through a summer research grant, the Fulbright Foundation for supporting his research in South Africa while finishing this chapter, and the University of the Witwatersrand School of Law for sponsoring him during the Fulbright Grant.

Although an overwhelming majority of United States political leaders and citizenry profess adherence to "the Book,"[7] and thereby to the fundamental tenants in the first two quotes above, the United States approach to terrorists, like the United States approach to Nazis and communists before them, is more accurately captured in the fourth quote above. Why is this so? Why can't we quit the terrorist? Why do we appear to have such a strong emotional need for this enemy? Why is there such a gulf between our ideals expressed in the first three quotes above and our practice in the last? Does the fourth quote aid us in bridging the gap or is it part of the problem? Have we too readily changed that which we can, in order to instantly satisfy base needs and desires, instead of recognizing this weakness and guarding against it?[8]

This chapter is largely about the bogeyman created by the United States in this thing we call the terrorist, particularly as amplified and rarified by the Internet. The argument is that it feeds our unhealthy needs and sustains our unhealthy fears. As it gets larger, we are diminished. We have let it undermine the rule of law, weaken our democracy, and diminish our human rights (including our First Amendment rights and freedoms, among others). It has hurt us morally and has cost us severely. Ultimately, it does not make us richer, happier or safer. How do we exercise our First Amendment rights, much less our civic duties, if we cannot talk or listen to those whose actions appear to be directing many of our domestic and international policy decisions, namely those we suspect of terrorist activities? Our abilities, in this regard, have been limited both personally and legally. How do we function as a democracy, if we keep ourselves willfully ignorant of our enemies, if our executive branch gets to keep its legal policies secret,[9] and if those in our legislative and judicial branches have washed their hands of the matter?

Part I of this chapter addresses our pathological need for enemies and some of the reasons why the Internet terrorist is so well suited to play this role. It also addresses why the threat of the terrorists working through the Internet succeeds so well in terms of the political needs of the executive branch of the United States government. This article demonstrates that terrorists, and Internet terrorists, in particular, fit these needs even better than the Nazis and Communists before them. Part I ends by concluding that because of the way we have characterized those who fall under this label, it is conceptually impossible to follow the commands and rules reflected in the quotes above. Part II uses game theory to demonstrate why it is neither strategically wise to follow the commandment or rule, nor wise to even sympathize with those who might. Game theory helps explain both why a minority group of this nature is subject to sanctions and ostracism, as well as why those who might try to sympathize or cooperate in any way with them are also likely to be ostracized or sanctioned. This in turn helps explain why we tend to reduce Internet terrorists to a radical minority. Part III addresses how the events on September 11, 2001 presented an opportunity for the United States to reflect on its role in the international community and to try to come to grips with what could have gone so wrong to allow such an event to take place. Rather than taking the opportunity to evaluate our own role in the international community, or to figure out how we in the United States may be responsible in some small way for the hatred that was taken out on us, the United States acted immediately to take revenge. In so doing, we, in the United States, disregarded the moral high ground, international law, and human rights. We shut down communication with the international community, except on our terms. We made it clear to the world that "you are either with us or against us." Part IV concludes the chapter by addressing the Serenity Prayer quoted in the beginning and notes that the problem is not that we lack the wisdom to know what we can and cannot change, but that we lack the wisdom to know what we should and should not change.

We have made numerous changes since 9/11, most of which have resulted in a less open and transparent government, fewer due process rights, and less freedom of expression (not to mention some costly wars). Because of our need for instant gratification, our need for a common enemy, our general lack of interest and knowledge about what our government does overseas, and the corresponding lack of checks and balances on what our executive does overseas, we have sat by and allowed this to happen. We allowed it because we thought it was all directed at "them" and was designed to protect "us." Unfortunately, this has been a costly mistake. We are all neighbors. That which was designed to hurt them, has in fact hurt us. Although we cannot eliminate our need for enmity, and it is highly unlikely that we will ever truly love our enemies, we would benefit from acknowledging this weakness and guarding against it. We would benefit from rational engagement and open communication.

I. We Want You, We Need You
[We Might Even Assassinate You]

We, in the United States, appear to want terrorists, and perhaps even need them,[10] be it to satisfy our own insecurities and needs,[11] or to serve the needs of political leaders to mobilize the electorate, expand executive power or service the military industrial complex.[12] A few years prior to 9/11, Kathleen Murray and Jason Meyers explored this issue in their article, *Do People Need Foreign Enemies? American Leaders' Beliefs after the Soviet Demise.*[13] Using data from the

Leadership Opinion Project from 1988–1992, they found that United States leaders had not satisfied their "need" for a new foreign enemy after the Soviet demise.[14] While they found support for the hypothesis that those who showed higher levels of suspicion of the Soviets before the fall would be more suspicious of other countries after the fall, they found no support for the hypothesis that one foreign enemy would need to be replaced by another.[15] They noted, however, in almost prophetic language, that their "analysis assumes the target for transference would be a country, but it is conceivable that the target is a more free-floating threat such as a fear of terrorism."[16] It is now trite news that the terrorists have taken over from the Communist and Nazi before them.

This is not to say that Communists, Nazis and terrorists have posed no threat, or that there was no need to adjust our policies, laws, and behavior in response to such the threats. Rather, it is important to appreciate the role they play in our personal and collective psyches. Not only do we need to worry about the actual threat that they pose, but we need to also worry about how our society, politicians and our media terrorize us with the very idea of them and how individuals allow themselves to be threatened by them. It is easy to both revel in the idea of a common arch enemy and to rally together in opposition to such enemies. Sadly, it is one of the strongest unifiers of our otherwise fragmented and divided nation.

In a perverse sense, the "war on terror" is a win-win situation.[17] By fighting fire with fire, the terrorists and the government simply add fuel to the fire for both sides of this war. Terror itself has won, in part, because we abandoned the moral high ground (of respecting human rights and fundamental liberties) and decided to go to the "dark side."[18] As Friedrich Nietzche once said, "If you gaze for long into an abyss, the abyss gazes also into you."[19] Our use of drone strikes,[20] the abuses at Abu-Graib, Guantanamo Bay, and other black sites (secret detention facilities), have not only created terror, they have also provided terrorists with a good recruiting tool, and have gone some way to providing legitimate justifications for their ongoing attacks against us.[21] As professors of peace and conflict studies, Funk and Said have asserted, "In any situation of intense conflict, there is a tendency among disputants to become trapped inside their own stories of threatened identity, justified fear, and unjustified suffering."[22] A Gallup World Poll indicates that majorities in every predominantly Muslim country surveyed view the United States as ruthless,[23] and nearly 80% do not believe that the United States cares about human rights in other countries.[24]

Our executive branch also appears to be winning, because a war on something as amorphous and scary as terror, has allowed this branch to increase its powers, both abroad and domestically.[25] It helped President George W. Bush secure a second term,[26] and, although many thought (hoped or feared) that the Obama administration would abandon the "war on terror," his failure to close GITMO,[27] his retreat from trying suspected terrorists in federal court,[28] his use of predator drones to kill, among others, American citizens suspected of terrorism,[29] his signing into law the National Defense Authorization Act, (which calls for our Nation's "homeland" to be treated as a "battlefield")[30] and the regular use of the state secrets privilege,[31] all indicate that President Obama is making full use of his expanded executive powers.[32] The vast amount of information we now have on potential terrorists has not resulted in an empowered citizenry, or even an empowered legislature. Rather, the response has been to abdicate our roles, wash our hands of this messy and overwhelmingly complicated situation, and to let the executive and its experts handle the situation—lest "we" get it wrong.[33]

The "war on terror" has crippled the United States economy,[34] and recent polls indicate that the economy is the most important thing on the list of potential voter's concerns,[35] with terrorism, ranked at number five.[36] Although the American people want their president to fix the economy, presidents have very little influence over the economy. If our focus is on the economy, most every president looks weak. Thus, presidents have a motive to shift the electorate's focus to those areas where the president can actually act—namely foreign affairs.

"We" want and need the terrorist, perhaps because we need a common enemy to give us purpose, to deflect our attention from our own failures and shortcomings or to make it look like our politicians are accomplishing things. We used to have Nazis and Communists to call our enemies, but today, to take these enemies seriously is very hard. It seems almost laughable that France and Germany still have such strong anti-Nazi laws[37] and that South Korea has prosecuted people satirizing communism.[38] Although there are still Neo-Nazis and even communists who commit serious crimes and engage in terrorist activities, they no longer pose an existential threat to the United States They no longer fill the role of national enemy. Communists were pitched as our mortal, evil enemy for forty some odd years, and they played this role well. They were depicted as standing in contrast to everything "we" value, including democracy, freedom and, of course, capitalism.[39] Since the end of the cold war, communism, particularly in its distorted state socialist form, is largely washed up. Terrorism is not new, but thanks in part to the cold war and its demise,[40] terrorism is perceived as important, and terrorists are a plentiful commodity, at least in theory. In many ways, the terrorist is an even better arch-enemy. While the communist was a rational product of modernity, the terrorist is depicted as fanatically irrational. Terrorists are depicted as not only hating our freedom, they purportedly hate modernity and everything our modern world stands for. They would probably take away our Internet on top of all the other horrible things they would subject us to. They have no concern for human rights or innocent civilians, and they cannot really be reasoned with due to their fanatical views. They are not a state or even one group. Rather, they are any number of designated groups and lone wolves.[41] Timothy Recuber argues that we have turned the terrorist into a folk devil and mass commodity, which is the product of a "mass-mediated moral panic."[42] He explains that, "Today, massmediated moral panics focus on certain vulnerable groups who are perceived as threats to social values or interests and are defined in a stylized and stereotypical manner as 'folk devils: visible reminders of what we should not be.'"[43]

Now that these "pre-modern" terrorists have discovered the power of the Internet, they are, in a sense, the perfect enemy. What do the two words "terrorist" and "Internet" invoke? The first word evokes fear, or at least it used to (the term has lost some of its zing since our airports have been on orange alert for over a decade).[44] The terrorist is someone who could strike any of us at any time with no concern for civilians, the innocent, the elderly, the young. In many respects, the terrorist represents an unknown and largely unknowable threat to our existence. Furthermore, the word Internet evokes many things, but when uttered alongside terrorist, the phrase "Internet terrorist" takes on a new dimension. The Internet is something of an abyss—an expansive interconnected universe with no core, no center, no fixed design, structure or configuration. Yet it connects virtually everything and everyone in our little world here in the United States The terrorist operating in this dimension can conspire from anywhere, strike from anywhere, incite from anywhere.

The Internet terrorist also fits our post-atomic age so much better than the communist. The cold war was a rather boring, drawn-out standoff between two giants with lots of complicated intractable proxy wars. By contrast, the Internet terrorist fits nicely into our habits and need for instant gratification for little cost (including through drones and video games).

By definition, to love this enemy is nearly impossible (except in the way that someone loves something so perfectly designed—or in the way that one loves to kill alien bad guys in video games).[45] How do you love something that is no more than a negation—the ultimate creator of negative emotion—not just fear—but terror? Of course, this thing, "the Internet terrorist," is our creation. As Nietzsche once said, "The Christian resolution to find the world ugly and bad has made the world ugly and bad."[46] This impulse to divide the world into Good and Evil, God and Devil, American and Terrorist, makes the command to love our enemies difficult, if not impossible.[47]

II. Commandment, Rule and a Prayer? Game Theory Explains It Better

At the start of this chapter, one will find an Old Testament commandment, the golden rule and a prayer. Although most Americans are presumably bound by the first two rules, given our purported religious views, they are not the type of rules that have been internalized and are rarely, if ever, invoked by our leaders in times of crisis. While they may represent our aspirations during good times, they do not represent our gut reactions in times of stress, nor are they articulated as our aspirations in times of crisis.[48] Most likely, only a minority of people share the first sentiment (love thy neighbor as thy self), even in good times, and only a rare human could live up to the rule in her or his daily life. As J.L. Mackie puts it, "[p]eople simply are not going to put the interests of all their 'neighbours' on an equal footing with their own interests ... and with the interests of those who are literally near to them."[49] This is not to say that we do not love some of our neighbors as ourselves, or that we do not treat some people the way that we would like to be treated. Nonetheless, without this sentiment of universal love, or at least universal respect for the inherent dignity of all human beings, it is very difficult for the second rule to get off the ground.

If we accept that we are immutably rational, self-interested, wealth or utility maximizers, as the law and economics scholars and game theorists suggest,[50] then it may be that we are incapable of truly loving our neighbors as we love ourselves. At the very least, this commandment and the golden rule are difficult to follow. The easier path is to turn to our prayer and find a way to change the things that we can change more easily, namely, the golden rule and commandment.[51] The easy fix is to water down the notion of "love thy neighbor" to some vague idea like "I will pray for your soul so it does not suffer eternal damnation and fire" or to narrow down that group of people we consider our neighbors.

If we view others as inherently and qualitatively different, then perhaps we do not really need to count them in our group of "neighbors" or circle of friends (even if they do live next door). If we follow the rational maximizing approach of the game theorist, then the above rules can be modified to something like, "treat others well if they are likely to be repeat players who treat you well and who will continue to treat you well if you treat them well." Repeat players are people with whom you will have continued interaction. There is little to be gained (in the rational self-interested sense) by being nice to those who will not return the favor. The strategy of a standard rational self-interested person is to be nice to repeat players because, if she or he is not nice, then those players will not be nice to her or him. On this view of the world, it is better to be able to take advantage of others than to treat them nicely, and the worst situation is when others take advantage of you when you are nice.[52] Although not ideal, from this perspective, being nice to everyone else is still better than for everyone to be mean to everyone. Therefore, as long as the group of people forms something like a stable community, there will be a tendency towards something like "loving your neighbors as yourself," or at least treating people the way that one would like to be treated.

If people get out of line within these communities, then the game strategy that is traditionally considered best is a tit-for-tat strategy, which scholars such as Paul Mahoney and Chris Sanchirico have described as "essentially the command to 'do unto others as they have just done unto you.'"[53] In other words, we might practice a form of tough love on those neighbors with whom we have continued interaction. These scholars go further, arguing that tit-for-tat does not impose a credible enough threat to ensure cooperation and that it misses an important element of normative behavior that should be taken into consideration. They provide the following example to illustrate the point:

> In a particular neighborhood, an informal understanding exists that all of the houses will be painted in light, neutral colors to preserve the historic feel of the neighborhood, of which all the residents are proud. One resident, Mr. Smith, decides to paint his house a very bright purple. Neighbors react by gossiping about Smith's poor taste and uncooperative nature. They also shun him by refusing to attend a party he throws after finishing the painting. But one neighbor, Mr. Jones, goes out of his way to praise Smith, attends the party, and extends him a reciprocal invitation. Neighbors will also react negatively to Jones. They may gossip about him to punish him for siding with the original transgressor.[54]

What this illustrates is that individuals not only sanction those who defect, but they sanction other individuals who fail to sanction defectors. Cooperation with defectors is often punished, based on the idea that if you are with them, you are against us. In religious circles this is often known a shunning.

This captures some very common sentiments, and explains, in part, the behavioral aspects of children on playgrounds, law students in study groups, partners in law firms and even professors on tenure committees. The extreme form of this is to cast out or exterminate, not only the bad neighbor, but also anyone who may be seen as a sympathizer. One of the most horrendous examples of this can be found in the 1994 hundred day genocide in Rwanda, where otherwise common Hutu citizens killed not only those they identified as ethnically Tutsi, but also Hutu moderates who showed sympathy for the Tutsi's plight.[55]

A similar sentiment was echoed by former President G. W. Bush after 9/11, when he stated, "[e]ither you are with us, or you are with the terrorists."[56] Sadly, Secretary of State Hillary Rodham Clinton made nearly the same comment at the time.[57] The "you are either with us or against us" mentality is also embodied in the Antiterrorism and Effective Death Penalty Act, which makes it a crime to provide "material support" to designated terrorists groups.[58] The United States government has defended the law on the ground that it only incidentally affects the right to association.[59] However, the law, as upheld by the United States Supreme Court in *Holder v. Humanitarian Law Project,* goes so far as to make it a crime for human rights organizations to give legal advice on human rights adherence to designated organizations.[60]

One would hope and expect that those in the United States who profess to be religious would not fall into this way of thinking. Unfortunately, many studies show that they do.[61] So, "why don't we practice what we preach?" Why do agnostics come closer to following the above commandment and golden rule than those who claim to be more religious?[62] Why is it that humanitarian values are largely expressed to in-group religious members but not to out-groups? While highly religious people are more likely to help family and friends, studies show that they are not more likely to help unidentified others.[63] These conclusions stem from a number of reasons, including the fact that our religious congregations have been, and remain, largely segregated.[64] As Martin Luther King Jr. stated back in 1963, "At 11 am Sunday morning ... we stand at the most segregated hour in this nation."[65] Strong religious in-group identity with members of one's own race promotes ethnocentrism.[66] The divine is often imbued with in-group attributes and religious groups tend to view their own religious beliefs as morally superior.[67] The corollary is that outside groups are seen as morally inferior.[68]

This also helps explain why our public perception of "the terrorist" tends to reduce the diverse world of those who have committed terrorist acts to the stereotype of a radical Middle Eastern Muslim. Muslims are a very small minority in the United States,[69] and it is virtually impossible to know how many people of Middle-Eastern decent live in the United States[70] Thus, it is both easier for "us" to identify bad things with them and to treat them as other.[71] Although Timothy McVeigh, who was raised Catholic, committed the most deadly terrorist attack on United States soil prior to 9/11,[72] and Irish Catholics have a well-documented history of terrorist attacks in the U.K.,[73] most Americans would never causally connect these things. There are probably far more Americans who think Anwar al-Awlaki is not an American than who think Timothy McVeigh was an Irish Catholic terrorist.

If we return to our game theory explanation above, it is relatively self-evident that the majority of Americans are not repeat players with people of Middle Eastern dissent, much less Muslims, much less radical Muslims. They do not go to church, service or Mosque with Muslims and otherwise rarely interact with them on anything more than a superficial level. Thus, for such individuals, there is little reason to "cooperate" with "them," or to even forgive any one of them if they "defect." There is little reason to try to understand or communicate with these larger groups that "we" suspect terrorists come from (people from the Middle East, Muslims or both) and even less reason to do so with those who in any way defect from "our" norms by denouncing our actions, calling for some kind of action against "us," or taking some kind of action against "us." This view of "the terrorist" not only makes it easy to defect from these groups, but it also makes it easy to defect from those who "we" consider to be engaging in unwarranted cooperation with them.

Most Americans, including six out of nine Justices on the United States Supreme Court, likely did not see much harm to our First Amendment freedoms when Congress passed a law that says that we cannot speak in coordination with foreign groups that we know our executive has designated as terrorist organizations.[74] It is probably quite difficult for the average American to understand why American Humanitarian organizations would want to give any legal advice to Kurdish and Sri Lankan terrorists/ separatists, unless they were somehow terrorist sympathizers. The average non lawyer, and perhaps few lawyers, saw no problem with the fact that Charles Swift, the Judge Advocate General lawyer for Salim Ahmed Hamdan (Ben Laden's driver), lost his job after successfully defending him at the Supreme Court in *Hamdan v. Rumsfeld*.[75] Winning a landmark case in front of the Supreme Court is not usually the kind of thing that gets one fired; however, there was little to no public outcry over the termination.

Viewing "the terrorist" as a dehumanized "other," rather than as a human being, one of us, is ultimately hurting "us." As will be argued below, until we can change this perception, stemming the tide of incursions on our democratic freedoms will be difficult.

III. September 11, 2001: Before and After

September 11, 2001 was pivotal moment in United States history. This catastrophic event, like most catastrophic events, presented an opportunity for serious reflection, a better understanding of our world, and potential growth. There is an urgent need to come to grips with such events, if only to avoid them, or at least mitigate or manage them in the future. So, what was "our" response when "our Country" was attacked on 9/11? Was it the kind of slap in the face that wakes one up? Did it bring us to our senses and force us to seriously explore why this happened? Or, rather, did it shut down our cognitive abilities and engage our basic survival instincts? After 9/11, one New Yorker stood up and asked the question, "why do they hate us so much?"[76]

Wasn't this an excellent question? But few, if any, took the question seriously. Rather than take the question seriously or ask what we may have done to provoke such an act, our response was to reduce the organizers and perpetrators to fanatical, irrational extremists who hate modernity and our freedom.[77] The immediate reaction by Congress (just three days after 9/11) was to pass the infamous Authorization For Military Force by a vote of 98–0 in the Senate, 420–1 in the House, which gives the President a virtual blank check to use any means necessary to go after those that the President determines planned, authorized, committed, or aided in the 9/11 attacks or harbored those who did.[78] The only dissenter was Representative Barbara Lee (D-Oakland) who voted against the legislation because of comments made earlier in the day by Nathan Baxter, then Dean of the National Cathedral in Washington, DC, who, when leading the nation in a National Day of Prayer and Remembrance, warned that "we must not become the evil we deplore."[79] Why was there no pause by the rest of Congress before seeking revenge? Why was there no attempt to see this as the outcome of a deeper set of problems that simple recourse to military force could not solve?

For most Americans, there is little knowledge of our affairs in Latin America[80] or the Middle East,[81] other than that we give so much aid to these countries and are always trying to do nice things. While there is no legitimate excuse or justification for 9/11, there are also no legitimate excuses or justifications for many of the things that we have done or supported since WWII. Although we used the Taliban and the likes of Bin Laden to fight our proxy war with the Soviets in Afghanistan, we did little to nothing to help them when that war was over.[82] Our positions on foreign affairs have a homeland impact that few Americans are aware of.

We have appeared to almost always side with Israel on very complicated and controversial issues involving human rights violations and the right to self-determination of everyone in Palestine. For instance, the United States House of Representatives, by a vote of 344 to 36, condemned the *Goldstone Report* created by the United Nations Fact Finding Mission on the Gaza Conflict, which found numerous violations of international humanitarian law by both Hamas and Israel during the 2008–2009 conflict.[83] Representative Dennis Kucinich (D-Ohio) had the following to say about the resolution:

Almost as serious as committing war crimes is covering up war crimes, pretending that war crimes were never committed and did not exist. Because behind every such deception is the nullification of humanity, the destruction of human dignity, the annihilation of the human spirit, the triumph of Orwellian thinking, the eternal prison of the dark heart of the totalitarian. The resolution before us today, which would reject all attempts of the Goldstone Report to fix responsibility of all parties to war crimes, including both Hamas and Israel, may as well be called the "Down is Up, Night is Day, Wrong is Right" resolution. Because if this Congress votes to condemn a report it has not read, concerning events it has totally ignored, about violations of law of which it is unaware, it will have brought shame to this great institution.... We will have peace only when the plight of both Palestinians and Israelis is brought before this House and given equal consideration in recognition of that principle that all people on this planet have a right to survive and thrive....[84]

Americans then, as now, remain woefully ignorant of how our actions overseas impact the lives of people throughout the world. Few Americans know that 9/11 came just two days after the United Nations *World Conference Against Racism* in Durban, South Africa had finished.[85] The United States and Israel did not want the Palestinian issue on the table, and when they could not block it completely, the United States delegates walked out.[86] As Tom Lantos reports, Secretary Powell met with the U.N. High Commissioner for Human Rights, Mary Robinson, on June 18 in Washington and told her that:

[T]he U.S. would not participate in the Durban conference if the language condemning Israel was not removed. He made clear to her that he expected her to take a leading role in asserting the principle that it was not appropriate to single out one country for criticism and one territorial dispute for discussion at Durban. Powell also asserted that, although the U.S. was willing to explore appropriate language to express regret for its involvement in the slave trade, we were not prepared to use the word "apology."[87]

Unsurprisingly, the United States did not get much help from our allies in the West, much less our allies in the Middle East, on this issue of changing the agenda of the conference.[88]

The United States wanted to go to a U.N. World Conference on Racism in South Africa, and we did not want to apologize for our involvement in the slave trade or talk about the issue of Apartheid-like practices in Israel. In fact, we did not want to talk about any particular problems, in any country concerning racism. Lantos went so far as to propose House Resolution 212, which, according to him, "specified 'that since racism, racial discrimination, xenophobia, and related intolerance exist to some extent in every region of the world, efforts to address these prejudices should occur within a global framework' … [that] should be constructed 'without reference to specific regions, countries or present-day conflicts.' "[89] The response from the U.N. High Commissioner was "that a majority of states felt that the situation in the Middle East, and Israel's settlement policies in the occupied territories, could not be ignored in the Durban discussions."[90] Once it became clear that we would not get our way at the conference, Lantos urged the Secretary of State, Colin Powell, "not to dignify the proceedings with his presence."[91] Our Secretary of State did not attend the conference. Instead, we sent a low-level "working-level" delegation.[92]

As this shows, prior to 9/11, the United States found talking with the world about issues in the Middle East, racism, or even the history of the slave trade, difficult. So, post 9/11, is there any chance of talking with suspected terrorists, much less listening to them,[93] those neighbors we consider our enemies or Muslims here and abroad who are our neighbors and not our enemies?[94] Have we demonized them, like the Jews purportedly demonized the Samaritans and Hitler demonized the Jews? President Obama was severely criticized during the 2008 campaign for suggesting that he might talk with some of our traditional enemies. As recently as July, 2011, Republican candidate, Mitt Romney, criticized President Obama, saying, "During his first year, President Obama said he 'was going to visit Kim Jong-Il and Ahmadinejad and Assad and Chavez—the worst actors in the world.' "[95] While it was no big surprise that President G. W. Bush boycotted the 2001 World Conference on Racism, it may be something of a surprise to learn that eight years later, the newly elected biracial United States President and his administration could not be seen dignifying the 2009 U.N. World Conference on racism.[96] The 2009 Conference was boycotted because the draft document adopted a reference to the 2001 Conference document which singled out Israel and arguably posed a threat to freedom of expression. Thus, our response was simply not to engage at all with the conference.[97] This might work if the United States does not need the support and cooperation of other nations, but if it does, and I would suggest that it does, then this is no way to be a good neighbor.

IV. Back to the Prayer: What Do We Really Need Wisdom For? Wait.

Whether or not one believes in prayers, there is something attractive about the words of wisdom contained in the Serenity Prayer quoted at the beginning of this chapter. Unfortunately, the prayer is somewhat misguided, in part because of what it asks, but more importantly, because of what it fails to ask. Humans and Americans, in particular, are amazing at adapting.

While the above prayer does call on a higher being to assist us in figuring out what we can and cannot do, this still leaves us woefully short in the practical wisdom department. What we need to know, is not just what we can and cannot do, but whether doing it, is itself a good idea, and whether it is worth the collateral damage that comes with it. In other words, do we really want to get to point C, and is it worth negotiating the obstacles in our path to get there?

So we should be asking for the wisdom to know what we should and should not change, before asking for the courage to do the changing. We do not appear to lack the courage of our convictions as much as the wisdom to guide those convictions, particularly in times of crisis. We appear to have an insatiable appetite for instant results and gratification. We used to wait for the phone to ring, the mail to come, or even for someone to come beckoning at the door. We even used to wait before rushing into war.[98] Radio connected us to the world beyond. Now we can check our email, Facebook, instant messages and twitter and find some external source to validate our existence on a near minute to minute basis. We can almost always find someone to comment on, or to at least, like, our most recent photo or even location.[99] We do not even need to be tied to a computer for this anymore. We can access all of this on our cell phones.[100]

One lesson that may be drawn from the Prayer at the beginning of this chapter is that it is not wise to believe that we can eliminate our need for enemies, nor that we will love them any time soon. However, it does not follow that we should simply give in to this pathological need. Rather, we should attempt to manage or mitigate it. While loving the terrorist is unrealistic, rational engagement is not. We might just start with the presumption that suspected terrorists are human beings, who, contrary to all the rhetoric, actually function in much the same way that we do in terms of needs, fears, hopes, and motivations. At the very least, it would be good if we could both speak and listen to them. Even if we had a functioning right to speak and listen to them,[101] our rhetoric surrounding "the terrorist" has made it very difficult to do so, without appearing to join them. Can one download the latest *Inspire* magazine without any fear that she or he might attract negative attention?[102] As noted above, we have allowed "the terrorist" to define our last decade. We have lost countless lives, spent billions of dollars, and "the terrorist" has been a watershed for laws and policies that radically affect our fundamental rights and liberties, the power of the executive branch and democratic transparency and accountability.

A great deal has been written about how globalization impacts and often overwhelms, if not undermines, democracy within nations.[103] Decisions, policies and laws that are made at the international level are often, at best, tangentially the product of truly democratic processes on the domestic level. Yet, these decisions, policies and laws are often as important and have as great or greater impact on the lives of those who live in a given country as those decisions, policies and laws that are created through domestic democratic processes. Decisions by the United States in the international arena have often had this effect on other countries. We have become accustomed to American exceptionalism in our foreign relations. We expect that we will, and should, have a larger than equal share in decisions effecting the world.[104] Yet "our" share is itself not the product of our normal democratic processes and checks and balances. While our executive has traditionally had very limited domestic powers, it has much more power to act within the sphere of international relations and in territories overseas.[105] The general public, the legislative branch and the judicial branch have often given the executive free reign overseas. It's complicated enough to keep an eye on local and national politics, much less to be seriously engaged with all our efforts abroad.

But now those expanded and largely unchecked powers, that have, for decades, distorted the domestic political processes of other countries, have come home to roost. Although the mechanisms are in place to put checks on the executive, our democratic institutions have atrophied; the legislative, and even judicial branches, have arguably abdicated these roles.[106] No-one wants to go soft on "the terrorist," in part, because no one wants to be blamed for the next attack. The fear is not a fear of the terrorist him or herself, but of the political and perhaps personal fallout that comes with erring on the side of rights.

However, if we cannot speak or listen to them, than how can we as a nation rationally assess what, if anything, should be changed in response to them?[107] As long as we remain in the grip of a moral panic,[108] we run the risk of doing further irreparable harm to our own freedom, safety and ideals. This is due in part to the fact that we have cultivated a react first, think later culture. It is also due to the fact that we have, for some time viewed what happens overseas as too alien, too complicated, too remote from our democratic concerns at home. We simply do not seem to care.[109] The result is that we fail to understand why events like 9/11 take place, fail to democratically engage in figuring out ways to prevent events like this from happening in the future. Rather than demanding a rational democratic response from our government, we have allowed the government to undermine our own liberties. We allowed this because our government was supposed to be targeting "them" the radical enemy, and protecting "us" the good guys. In part, we let this happen because we let our government, our media, ourselves, accept this depiction of "the enemy," rather than seeing "them" as human beings just like "us."

The commandment and golden rule quoted at the beginning of this article were not created as a reflection of our general tendencies, but as a counter to them. Their power, in part, draws on the idea that we are all created equally, be it in the eyes of a creator, or from the perspective of moral philosophy. Although the aspiration of seeing everyone as one's neighbor is out of reach, we can choose to either draw the world closer to us, or to push it away, to further alienate our enemies, or to attempt to bring them into the fold. This is something that we can change. The closer we are to the rest of the world, the easier it will be to see "others" as part of "our" community. The better we understand how connected we are, how our actions affect others and how this in turn has affected us, the easier it is to see why we should be seeking long term cooperation with the world.

Obscenity, Community and the Internet

*Kevin W. Saunders**

The United States and Europe have both taken into account differences among communities in making determinations regarding what materials may be held to be obscene. The cases establishing the role of community, on both sides of the Atlantic, were in an era prior to the development of the Internet. That new medium, a medium with no firm attachment to any particular geographic location, calls into question the earlier reliance on geographic community and requires an analysis of community in the Internet era.

I. Obscenity and Community before the Internet

1. The United States

The First Amendment to the Constitution of the United States provides: "Congress shall make no law ... abridging the freedom of speech, or of the press...." While the terms of the amendment speak to a limitation placed on Congress, the limits also apply to the states and local subdivisions thereof through the Due Process Clause of the 14th Amendment. The terms of the amendment also seem more absolute than they, in fact, are. The United States

---

* Professor of Law & The Charles Clarke Chair in Constitutional Law, Michigan State University College of Law. Professor Saunders' career has included clerking for the Honorable Kenneth Starr, U.S. Court of Appeals for the District of Columbia Circuit, and then various academic posts in the Universities of Arkansas, Oklahoma and Drake University prior to his current chair. Professor Saunders is the author of three major books on speech issues—*Violence as Obscenity: Limiting the Media's First Amendment Protection*; *Saving Our Children from the First Amendment*; *Degradation: What the History of Obscenity Tells Us about Hate Speech*

Supreme Court has recognized the existence, based primarily on history, of a number of exceptions to the protection afforded by the amendment.

The obscenity exception to the First Amendment was recognized in the companion cases *Roth v. United States* and *Alberts v. California*.[1] The Court pointed to statutes from the era of the framing of the Constitution that placed some limitations on expression and other statutes and case law providing "sufficiently contemporaneous evidence to show that obscenity, too, was outside the protection intended for speech and press."[2] The Court made it clear that not all sexual material is obscene. It is only material appealing to a prurient interest, a shameful or morbid interest, in sex.[3]

The *Roth* Court also mentioned community in its opinion. The mention was in the context of distinguishing an acceptable test for obscenity from that used in England. The English rule, derived from *Regina v. Hicklin*,[4] judged material based on its effect on particularly susceptible persons. The Court said that the *Hicklin* test presented too great a danger of allowing prosecution of material that actually treats sex in a legitimate manner. While rejecting that test, the Court spoke positively of decisions by lower courts in the United States using as a test "whether to the average person, applying contemporary community standards, the dominant theme of the material taken as a whole appeals to prurient interest."[5] The test was seen as an improvement over *Hicklin*, because of its use of the average person, rather than the most susceptible person, but the court did not provide any real explanation of its reliance on community.

After some evolution in the test for obscenity, the Court finally came to the current definition of obscenity in *Miller v. California*.[6] That test asks

> (a) whether "the average person, applying contemporary community standards" would find that the work, taken as a whole, appeals to the prurient interest; (b) whether the work depicts or describes, in a patently offensive way, sexual conduct specifically defined by the applicable state law; and (c) whether the work, taken as a whole, lacks serious literary, artistic, political, or scientific value.[7]

While the phrase "contemporary community standards" appears only in the first portion of the *Miller* test, the Court later made it clear that it also applies to the second portion as well, while the third factor is judged, instead, on a reasonable person basis.[8]

Importantly, for purposes here, the Court also discussed its reliance on community. In the Court's view, the size of the United States and variation among states made a national standard unworkable:

Under a National Constitution, fundamental First Amendment limitations on the powers of the States do not vary from community to community, but this does not mean that there are, or should or can be, fixed, uniform national standards of precisely what appeals to the "prurient interest" or is "patently offensive." These are essentially questions of fact, and our Nation is simply too big and too diverse for this Court to reasonably expect that such standards could be articulated for all 50 States in a single formulation, even assuming the prerequisite consensus exists.[9]

Furthermore, states should not have to live with decisions made by other states:

It is neither realistic nor constitutionally sound to read the First Amendment as requiring that the people of Maine or Mississippi accept public depiction of conduct found tolerable in Las Vegas, or New York City. People in different States vary in their tastes and attitudes, and this diversity is not to be strangled by the absolutism of imposed uniformity.[10]

It is clear that what concerned the Court was that the national standard would require more conservative communities to accept depictions based on acceptability in more liberal areas.

The issue of community came back to the Court in the case *Hamling v. United States*.[11] *Hamling* involve federal charges, based on the distribution by mail of obscene material. Among the many issues raised on appeal was whether or not federal obscenity charges require the use a national standard, in place of the community standards used in state cases. The Court concluded that the fact that a mailer of obscene materials may be subjected to different community standards in the various locations into which the materials were sent did not make a conviction unconstitutional.

The fact that distributors of allegedly obscene materials may be subjected to varying community standards in the various federal judicial districts into which they transmit the materials does not render a federal statute unconstitutional because of the failure of application of uniform national standards of obscenity. Those same distributors may be subjected to such varying degrees of criminal liability in prosecutions by the States for violations of state obscenity statutes; we see no constitutional impediment to a similar rule for federal prosecutions.[12]

In either a state or a federal prosecution, the mailer of obscene materials may be found in violation of obscenity law in the jurisdiction into which the materials were sent. It may be true that the mailer is not as familiar with community standards as a person residing in a particular community, but the mailer of materials does know to what communities the materials are sent. The mailer should familiarize himself with standards there.

A more recent, but still in an era before the real development of the Internet, relevant case from the United States Supreme Court is *Sable Communications v. Federal Communications Commission.*[13] The case involved a statutory prohibition on the commercial provision, by telephone, of indecent or obscene conversation, a service known as "dial-a-porn." The case is remembered, primarily, for its conclusion that FCC authority to regulate indecent material in the broadcast media does not carry over to telephonic service. The affirmative step required to access "dial-a-porn" conversations distinguished it from the ubiquity of radio or television. The child, since even before the ban there had to be measures in place to prevent access by children, and the unsuspecting listener were not likely to be exposed to objectionable material.

That part of the opinion relevant to this issue had to do with the prohibition not on indecent, but obscene, telephonic transmission. Sable Communications argued that the statute "creates an impermissible national standard of obscenity, and that it places message senders in a 'double bind' by compelling them to tailor all their messages to the least tolerant community."[14] The Court found no inconsistency with *Miller*'s "contemporary community standards" requirement. A federal statute addressing communications by telephone did not establish a national standard any more than did statutes prohibiting the mailing of obscene materials.

With regard to Sable's perceived "double bind," the Court said "Sable is free to tailor its messages, on a selective basis, if it so chooses, to the communities it chooses to serve."[15] The Court was untroubled by any costs that might be incurred in developing a system to limit the communities served or to provide less explicit conversation to more conservative communities. In conclusion, regarding this issue, the Court said:

> There is no constitutional barrier under *Miller* to prohibiting communications that are obscene in some communities under local standards even though they are not obscene in others. If Sable's audience is comprised of different communities with different local standards, Sable ultimately bears the burden of complying with the prohibition on obscene messages.[16]

Thus, the law in the United States in the era leading up to the Internet relied on community in determining the standards defining obscenity. The Court's concern that more conservative communities should not have to tolerate the material acceptable in more liberal communities meant that a national standard was inappropriate. The concerns of those who would mail obscene materials or provide obscene telephone conversation that their materials would be judged by the standards of the most conservative community, thereby limiting the access of those in more liberal communities, were not seen as valid. Providers of obscene materials in both media could determine what communities they were addressing. While they may not have had the knowledge of local community standards that a resident might, they were capable of making some determination of standards in these more remote communities and could tailor the material to the community served.

2. Europe

The European Court of Human Rights has also, in a real sense, used the concept of community in its obscenity jurisprudence. At least in the pre-Internet era, the Court was willing to let each of the member states provide its own definition of what would be considered obscene. "Community" may not have been the local community, as in a city, but the Court's recognition of differing standards from country to country indicates the same sort of approach.

This reliance on country-based standards was set out in *Handyside v. United Kingdom*.[17] *Handyside* was, in terms of the material at issue, a rather odd obscenity case, at least compared to the standard in the United States. The work at issue was a book titled *The Little Red Schoolbook*, a publication aimed at school children 12 and older, with a sale price of 30 pence that would make it accessible to them. What makes it odd by United States standards is that it did not contain explicit sexual depictions, even with the sort of lower level of explicitness required in the United States for material to be obscene when distributed to minors.[18]

The concern over the work in question was in the ideas it presented.[19] The book did contain a 26 page section covering a number of topics regarding sex, but again, the concern seems not to have been with a prurient appeal but with the possibility that minors would be corrupted by the ideas conveyed. There was, for example, an objection to a passage titled "Be yourself." The passage said:

> Maybe you smoke pot or go to bed with your boyfriend or girlfriend— and don't tell your parents or teachers, either because you don't dare to or just because you want to keep it secret. Don't feel ashamed or guilty about doing things you really want to do and think are right just because your parents or teachers might disapprove. A lot of these things will be more important to you later in life than the things that are "approved of."[20]

There was no mention that it was illegal to smoke pot and that sexual intercourse of minors below a particular age was also illegal.

There was also a passage, under the heading "Pornography," suggesting that, while someone who takes pornography as an indication of real life may well be disappointed, "it's quite possible that you may get some good ideas from it and you may find something which looks interesting and you haven't tried before."[21] Concerns that children might "feel it incumbent upon them to look for and practise such things"[22] made the passage objectionable.

Prosecution had been brought under the Obscene Publications Act of 1959, as amended by the Obscene Publications Act of 1964. The definition of obscenity under the amended Act is broad:

> [A]n article shall be deemed to be obscene if its effect or (when the article comprises two or more distinct items) the effect of any one of its items is, if taken as a whole, such as to tend to deprave and corrupt persons who are likely, having regard to all relevant circumstances, to read, see or hear the matter contained or embodied in it.[23]

There appears to be no requirement of explicit sexual content, so the book could be seen to be in violation of the act.

Again, the book would not be seen as obscene under United States law. And, the fact that it had been circulated in other parts of Europe and, indeed, even in other parts of the United Kingdom, indicates that England had adopted a potentially very broad definition of obscenity. The question before the European Court of Human Rights was whether this broad view was consistent with the rights guaranteed Europeans under Article 10(1) of the European Convention on Human Rights, which provides: "Everyone has the right to freedom of expression. This right shall include freedom to hold opinions and to receive and impart information and ideas without interference by public authority and regardless of frontiers...."[24] While establishing freedom of expression, the Convention, as with most free expression clauses other than that found in the First Amendment, provides for exceptions. Article 10(2) goes on to say,

> The exercise of these freedoms, since it carries with it duties and responsibilities, may be subject to such formalities, conditions, restrictions or penalties as are prescribed by law and are necessary in a democratic society, in the interests of national security, territorial integrity or public safety, for the prevention of disorder or crime, for the protection of health or morals, for the protection of the reputation or rights of others, for preventing the disclosure of information

received in confidence, or for maintaining the authority and impartiality of the judiciary.[25]

The English courts seems to have relied on the exception for the protection of health or morals, so the Court went on to examine whether that exception necessitated the prosecution of the book's distributor. In that regard, the Court said

> it is not possible to find in the domestic law of the various Contracting States a uniform European conception of morals. The view taken by their respective laws of the requirements of morals varies from time to time and from place to place, especially in our era which is characterised by a rapid and far-reaching evolution of opinions on the subject. By reason of their direct and continuous contact with the vital forces of their countries, State authorities are in principle in a better position than the international judge to give an opinion on the exact content of these requirements as well as on the "necessity" of a "restriction" or "penalty" intended to meet them.[26]

Rather than use the phrase "community standards," the European Court said that Contracting States have a "margin of appreciation" given both to the legislature and to the national courts interpreting statutes.[27] That did not mean that there could be no review by the European Court, but it does appear that there is great deference given to the standards of the member states.[28]

Müller v. Switzerland[29] is a more recent case, but still before the major development of the Internet. The subject matter there, three paintings, was more explicitly sexual than that in *Handyside*, since the paintings depicted sexual activities, including one involving bestiality. Swiss authorities seized the paintings and fined those involved in the exhibition. Eight years after the seizure, the paintings were returned to the artist. The defendants brought an action before European authorities, who in the first instance held that the seizure was in violation of Article 10, although the conviction was not. The Court of Human Rights, however, refused to find fault with either the confiscation or conviction.

The Swiss court had explained its view of obscenity.

> [A]lthough Mr. Müller's three works are not sexually arousing to a person of ordinary sensitivity, they are undoubtedly repugnant at the very least. The overall impression is of persons giving free rein to licentiousness and even perversion. The subjects—sodomy, fellatio, bestiality, the erect penis—are obvious morally offensive to the vast majority of the population. Although allowance has to be made for

changes in the moral climate, even for the worse, what we have here would revolutionise it. Comment on the confiscated works is superfluous; their vulgarity is plain to see and needs no elaborating upon.... Nor can a person of ordinary sensitivity be expected to go behind what is actually depicted and make a second assessment of the picture independently of what he can actually *see*. To do that he would have to be accompanied to exhibitions by a procession of sexologists, psychologists, art theorists or ethnologists in order to have explained to him that what he saw was in reality what he wrongly thought he saw.[30]

That court recognized that Müller was a serious artist but still felt that the painting should be withheld from the general public.[31]

At the European Court of Human Rights, the main issue was whether, under Article 10(2), the Swiss action could be considered "necessary in a democratic society." In that regard, the court discussed necessity and the "margin of appreciation."

The Court has consistently held that in Article 10(2) the adjective "necessary" implies the existence of a "pressing social need." The Contracting States have a certain margin of appreciation in assessing whether such a need exists, but this goes hand in hand with a European supervision, embracing both the legislation and the decisions applying it, even those given by an independent court. The Court is therefore empowered to give the final ruling on whether a "restriction" or "penalty" is reconcilable with freedom of expression as protected by Article 10.[32]

The Court saw its task to be determining whether or not the interference was proportionate to the legitimate aim and whether the Swiss court's reasoning had been "relevant and sufficient."[33] The court repeated its "margin of appreciation" discussion from *Handyside* and went on to say:

[H]aving inspected the original paintings, the Court does not find unreasonable the view taken by the Swiss courts that those paintings, with their emphasis on sexuality in some of its crudest forms, were "liable grossly to offend the sense of sexual propriety of persons of ordinary sensitivity." In the circumstances, having regard to the margin of appreciation left to them under Article 10(2), the Swiss courts were entitled to consider it "necessary" for the protection of morals to impose a fine on the applicants for publishing obscene material.[34]

US v J European approach

So, as in the United States, community plays a role in the obscenity jurisprudence of the European Union. It is found in the "margin of appreciation" and allows variations from country to country in terms of what will be considered obscene. This is not quite the same as the United States, in which "community" might refer to states but might also be based on more local attitudes. Nonetheless, the "margin of appreciation" is still a recognition of the role of community.

II. The Internet Age

With the advent of the Internet, or at least since its growth into a major medium, concerns about community took a completely different tack. While the concern in the United States had been that the people of Maine or Mississippi should not have to tolerate what was acceptable in New York or Las Vegas, now the concern became whether the people of Maine or Mississippi should be able to limit what those in New York or Las Vegas might see. In the pre-Internet age, a supplier of pornographic materials could limit the communities into which those materials were sent. If materials were not suitable for Maine and Mississippi, they could still be sent to New York and Las Vegas. The Internet, however, does not allow that limited distribution.

Once materials are placed on the Internet, they are available to anyone, anywhere, with Internet access. The receipt of pornographic materials cannot be limited only to more liberal communities. They may also be viewed in the most conservative communities. If obscenity charges could be filed in those conservative communities, and if community standards were based on the communities in which the charges were filed, the impact would carry over to other communities. Effectively, the Internet would be limited to materials that were acceptable in even the most puritanical communities. That impact, and the applicability of community standards for the Internet, had to be addressed.

1. The Response in the United States

There is an opinion from the Supreme Court of the United States taking on the issue in a slightly different context. The case, *Ashcroft v. American Civil Liberties Union*,[35] examined the Child Online Protection Act, which attempted to shield children from sexual material deemed to be "harmful to minors" on the Internet. While material might be "harmful to minors" without being obscene for adults, the definition of "harmful to minors" mirrored the *Miller* definition for obscenity, with reference to minors added to the prurient interest and offensiveness requirements and in limiting the serious value that might save a work from being obscene or harmful to minors to serious value for minors. Thus, concerns over the community standards issue in the obscenity context carried over to the analysis of this statute.

The Supreme Court concluded that the lack of a geographic community for the Internet did not provide adequate cause to declare the statute unconstitutional.[36] There was, however, no agreement as to why the statute's reference to "contemporary community standards" did not present a problem. The conclusion is arrived at only by adding up the votes of justices in the plurality and of those joining in two opinions concurring in the judgment.

The three justices' plurality opinion with respect to this issue was written by Justice Thomas. He relied on *Hamling* and *Sable* for the proposition that, where a statute is otherwise properly drawn, "requiring a speaker disseminating material to a national audience to observe varying community standards does not violate the First Amendment."[37] Furthermore, he said that the speaker's ability to target the material to particular communities was not integral to the analysis in either case.[38] Instead, he concluded that the companies involved in the earlier cases were required to adhere to the standards in the communities served simply because they sent their materials into those communities, and he saw no reason why the Internet required a different approach.[39]

> If a publisher chooses to send its material into a particular community, this Court's jurisprudence teaches that it is the publisher's responsibility to abide by that community's standards. The publisher's burden does not change simply because it decides to distribute its material to every community in the Nation. Nor does it change because the publisher may wish to speak only to those in a "community where avant-garde culture is the norm," but nonetheless utilizes a medium that transmits its speech from coast-to-coast. If a publisher wishes for its material to be judged only by the standards of particular communities, then it need only take the simple step of utilizing a medium that enables it to target the release of its material into those communities.[40]

While the step might be simple, its effect on the Internet would certainly be strong. The only way for a publisher to avoid prosecution in conservative communities would be to avoid placing material on the Internet. That would make the material inaccessible, at least through that medium, even in communities in which the material would be considered acceptable.

The other justices, who did not see the use of community standards as making the statute unconstitutional, adopted an approach that would have less impact on the Internet. Justice O'Connor suggested that the Court should adopt a "national standard for obscenity for regulation of the Internet."[41] She took the position that, since the Internet content provider can't control the geographic location of its audience, the adoption of this national standard was necessary, and she saw the Court's precedents as not forbidding such an adoption. The other justice taking this more protective approach to the Internet was Justice Breyer. He did not argue that a national standard was constitutionally required but said he believed that Congress intended that the term "community" refer to "the Nation's adult community taken as a whole...."[42]

In addition to the two opinions already discussed, there was a three justice concurrence written by Justice Kennedy, agreeing with Justices O'Connor and Breyer that "national variation in community standards constitutes a particular burden on Internet speech."[43] Justice Kennedy, however, was unsure that the adoption of a test based on a national community would eliminate the problem, because any actual standard applied to a particular case would vary from community to community.

Overall, there was a majority that concluded that the lack of geographic community did not mean that the Internet could not be regulated. While the specific context was with regard to materials harmful to minors, given the similarity of the definition involved to the definition of obscenity, the analysis seems likely to carry over to obscenity statutes. But, what more specific conclusions should be drawn remained unclear. Should purely local standards control in any prosecution, or should there be a national standard? That issue remained for consideration by lower courts.

The lower courts have, in fact, begun to grapple with the issue. The first few Internet obscenity cases to be considered after *Ashcroft*,[44] in what would seem to be a proper approach under their facts, relied on community standards in the place where the material was accessed. In *United States v. Moore*,[45] the material was judged by community standards in Texas, despite the defendant's arguments that a national standard for the Internet community should apply. The use of Texas standards is easily justified by the fact that the case did not involve material that was generally available on the Internet. Instead the charges were based on the use of instant messaging software to provide obscene material to a person under 16, where the defendant had reason to believe that the recipient was located in Texas. A similar result obtained in *United States v. Jenkins*.[46] There, the defendant believed the recipient to be a 13-year-old Canadian girl, and the court concluded that the standards of the community in which the materials were received applied.

Two other cases involve materials posted on the Internet, but the community issue in each case was fairly easily resolved. In *United States v. Rudzavice*,[47] the defendant had been charged with the interstate transfer of obscene materials to minors. The defendant argued that under *Ashcroft* the community standards of the place where the materials were received should apply. The Court did not really have to resolve the issue left over from *Ashcroft*, because what the defendant was objecting to was the use of the community standards of the location from which the materials were sent, and the court easily concluded that the defendant was required to abide by the community standards there. The second case, *United States v. Extreme Associates, Inc.*,[48] involved the use of the Internet to provide access to obscene materials. But, since access required membership, and the membership application required the address of the recipient, the defendant knew the community where the materials would be received and could be convicted using the community standards of the recipient's location.

Setting aside these easier cases, there are cases that directly raise the issue left by *Ashcroft*, and there is a circuit split in the results. In *United States v. Kilbride*,[49] the defendants had been charged with, among other things, interstate transportation of obscene material via the Internet. The material was spam advertising adult websites, where the spam itself was the basis for the charge. The case was tried in Arizona, where the defendants initially had their servers, before shifting their business operations to Mauritius and their server to the Netherlands. After conviction, the defendants argued on appeal that the trial court had committed error in instructing the jury to apply standards of communities other than the defendant's own community or of a global community.

The appellate court examined the various opinions from *Ashcroft*. Trying to draw a result from that mix of opinions, the court noted that only the three justice plurality supported the use of local community standards. Justice O'Connor saw a national standard as necessary, while Justice Breyer saw such a standard as contained in the statute. Justice Kennedy's three justice concurrence in the result was seen as agreeing with Justices O'Connor and Breyer, and Justice Stevens' dissent certainly could not be seen as being in agreement with the Justice Thomas plurality.

> Accordingly, five Justices concurring in the judgment, as well as the dissenting Justice, viewed the application of local community standards in defining obscenity on the Internet as generating serious constitutional concerns. At the same time, five justices concurring in the judgment viewed the application of a national community standard as not or likely not posing the same concerns by itself.[50]

Thus, local community standards were unacceptable, and the Court concluded that a national community standard must be applied.

The circuit split with *Kilbride* is found in *United States v. Little*.[51] The defendants in that case sold sexually explicit videos. The videos were advertised on websites, and it was the advertising trailers for those videos that were the basis for several of the counts charged.[52] Those trailers clearly raise the *Ashcroft* issue, since they were generally available on the Internet. The trial court had applied local Florida community standards, and the appellate court saw no constitutional violation. The court recognized the Ninth Circuit's opinion in *Kilbride* but declined to follow the result reached by that court. In the court's view, "[t]he portions of the *Ashcroft* opinion and concurrences that advocated a national community standard were dicta, not the ruling of the Court."[53] Thus, in the view of the 11th circuit, *Miller* still controlled, and the trial court had not erred in instructing the jury that the materials were to be judged based on the community standards of the Florida district in which the trial was conducted.

2. The Response in Europe

The European Court of Human Rights seems not to have dealt with the issue of a conviction of a non-resident non-citizen for violating the obscenity laws of a member state. There is a case involving Internet receipt of materials held to be obscene in the United Kingdom. In *Perrin v. United Kingdom*,[54] the defendant was a French national but a resident of the United Kingdom. He operated a website through a company based in the United States. The webpage that was initially accessed contained pornographic images, and he provided a link labeled "subscription to our best filthy sites." A police officer, to access those sites, provided a name, address and credit card details. The charges were based on the preview page and two other pages accessed by subscription.

Interestingly, the defendant was convicted with regard to the preview page but acquitted with regard to the other two. This, presumably, makes sense in terms of access by the unwitting web surfer, in the instance of the preview page, as opposed to the intentional access of someone seeing the subscription pages. But, from the point of view of community standards, the preview page raises a more difficult issue than the subscription pages. It was accessible everywhere, and might be subject to charges anywhere, while the site operator could have limited access to the subscription pages based on the address provided.

On his appeal to the European Court, the defendant raised the issue of the inability to limit access based on geography. He argued that, since the major steps towards publication had taken place in the United States and because of the worldwide nature of the Internet, he could not be reasonably expected to know the legal requirements and definitions in all countries in which the material might be accessed. The Court did not find that argument relevant.

> In the present case, the Court notes that the applicant was a resident
> of the United Kingdom. As a result, he cannot argue that the laws of
> the United Kingdom were not reasonably accessible to him. More-
> over, he was carrying on a professional activity with his Internet site
> and could therefore be reasonably expected to have proceeded with a
> high degree of caution when pursuing his occupation and to take legal
> advice.[55]

The defendant also raised the issue that is central here, arguing that "there
should not be a wide margin of appreciation in this area because that would
amount to imposing moral standards on publishers of a web page that are not
regarded as necessary in the society where the major steps concerned with publication took place."[56] The Court was unmoved by the argument.

> [T]he fact that dissemination of the images in question may have been
> legal in other States, including non-Parties to the Convention such as
> the United States, does not mean that in prescribing such dissemina-
> tion within its own territory and in prosecuting and convicting the
> applicant, the respondent State exceeded the margin of appreciation
> afforded to it.[57]

Thus, the language makes it appear that the European Court is willing to allow
community standards, through its "margin of appreciation," to apply to material on the Internet. But, this case may not be a good test of that principle.
The defendant was a resident of the United Kingdom and was charged in the
United Kingdom. The dispositive case would have to be one in which the defendant was neither a citizen nor a resident of the country in which the material was accessed and charges were brought.

The resolution of this issue may be even more important for Europe than
for the United States, because the "margin of appreciation" applies in Europe
in contexts in which community standards would not be relevant in the United
States. In the case of *Wingrove v. United Kingdom*,[58] the British Board of Film
Classification refused any classification for a film representation of St. Teresa.
The representation involved some nudity and, at one point, St. Teresa engaged
in a sexual act with the crucified Christ. While the situation might seem to implicate obscenity law, the refusal to classify was based on the United Kingdom's
criminal blasphemy law. The director of the film challenged the refusal before
the European Court of Human Rights. The Court applied the same sort of
reasoning as that present in the obscenity cases, saying "The Court recognises
that the offence of blasphemy cannot by its very nature lend itself to precise legal
definition. National authorities must therefore be afforded a degree of flexi-

bility in assessing whether the facts of a particular case fall within the accepted definition of the offence."[59] Furthermore:[60]

> a wider margin of appreciation is generally available to the Contracting States when regulating freedom of expression in relation to matters liable to offend intimate personal convictions within the sphere of morals or, especially, religion. Moreover, as in the field of morals, and perhaps to an even greater degree, there is no uniform European conception of the requirements of "the protection of the rights of others" in relation to attacks on their religious convictions. What is likely to cause substantial offence to persons of a particular religious persuasion will vary significantly from time to time and from place to place, especially in an era characterised by an ever growing array of faiths and denominations. By reason of their direct and continuous contact with the vital forces of their countries, State authorities are in principle in a better position than the international judge to give an opinion on the exact content of these requirements with regard to the rights of others as well as on the "necessity" of a "restriction" intended to protect from such material those whose deepest feelings and convictions would be seriously offended.

Neither case involved the Internet, so the issue of material posted in one country being the basis for blasphemy charge in another country unrelated to the posting but due solely to access does not arise. But if there were an attempt to bring such a charge the perhaps even wider "margin of appreciation" in blasphemy cases would raise even more concern than its application in obscenity cases.

Conclusion

The reliance on community presents a real challenge in regulating material posted on the Internet. The concern that content on the Internet will be limited to material that is acceptable in the least tolerant communities is a very real concern. If obscenity charges can be brought in the states of Maine in Mississippi for material posted to the Internet from New York or Las Vegas, where the material might be seen as acceptable, then the standards of Maine to Mississippi will control what is generally available in the medium. The same could be true in Europe, where the standards of the most restrictive country, assuming the limits set out are within the "margin of appreciation," would provide a general limit for Internet content in Europe.

The solution in the United States would appear to be the adoption of a standard based on a national community with regard to what is suitable for the Internet. This may not provide the people of Maine or Mississippi with the shielding they might want. But, that is a reasonable compromise between a conclusion that obscenity law simply cannot apply to the Internet, and the absolutely wide open Internet that would lead to, and the approach that would let the most restrictive communities set the limits for the entire country.

In Europe, there is even more need to address the issue. The "margin of appreciation" appears to allow countries to limit a far wider range of material than would be allowed in the United States. In the United States, review by the federal courts seems more substantive. While the European Court of Human Rights has indicated that there are limits to the margin allowed, given the case law, those limits seem far broader than would be acceptable in the United States. Thus, differences from country to country would seem potentially, and actually, far greater than the differences from community to community in the United States. The impact of the "margin of appreciation" is then greater, and the most restrictive countries would be able to limit more material than would the most restrictive communities in the United States.

This difference in range of application is explained by the natures of the provisions being applied. In the United States, the First Amendment speaks in rather absolute terms, but there is an exception for obscene materials. The protection of expression under the European Convention of Human Rights contains an exception not aimed solely at obscene material; the exception allows for the protection of morality. A definition of "morality" is, of necessity, far broader than definition of "obscenity." The task of the United States courts has, therefore, been easier. In delineating the obscene the Court focused on differentiating between acceptable and unacceptable depictions of sexual conduct. In determining what is necessary for the protection of morality, the European Court would seem to have to take a broader view. Even though the difference in approach is reasonable, this lack of specificity involving morality and the "margin of appreciation" does allow for greater differences in Europe, and more conservative countries may have more impact on the Internet than the more conservative states in the United States.

Given the importance of the "margin of appreciation" to European law the solution is not likely to involve its elimination. Nor is it likely that the European Court would take on the role of limiting the definition of the morality that would justify a limitation on expression. The better approach would likely be enforcement of jurisdictional rules. If Internet based charges can only be brought by countries against their own citizens or residents or against individuals who are conducting their business in that country, it makes sense to allow a "margin of appreciation" in such cases. The most restrictive country will not control the Internet, but only that portion of the Internet originating, in some sense, within its borders.

That will, of course, mean that content on the Internet will include material unacceptable in the most restrictive country. That might not be satisfactory to those countries wishing to limit their residents' access to objectionable material. But, the only alternative would seem to be to provide greater power to authorities in the Council of Europe to set communitywide standards as to what expression that is to be protected, at least on the Internet. However, that call for greater power flies in the face of the current attitudes of most Contracting States.[61]

Notes

1. Can Newspapers Survive in an Internet Era?

1. *See* Russell L. Weaver, From Gutenberg to the Internet: Free Speech, Advancing Technology and the Implications for Democracy (Carolina Academic Press, forthcoming).

2. *Id.*

3. *See* Sharon LaFraniere, *Activists Crack China's Wall of Denial About Air Pollution*, The New York Times, at A4 (Jan. 28, 2012).

4. *See* Michael Schwartz, *In Russia, Viral Videos Make Electoral Politics a Bit Cleaner*, The New York Times, at 1 (Nov. 25, 2011).

5. *See* Eleanor Beardsley, *Social Media Gets Credit for Tunisian Overthrow*, National Public Radio, Weekend Edition Sunday (Jan. 16, 2011), http://www.npr.org/2011/01/16/132975274/Social-Media-Gets-Credit-For-Tunisian-Overthrow.

6. *See* Deborah Amos, *Blogging and Tweeting, Egyptians Push for Change*, National Public Radio (Aug. 26, 2010), http://www.npr.org/templates/story/story.php?storyId=129425721.

7. For conflicting views, see Rachel K. Gibson and Stephen J. Ward (eds.), Reinvigorating Democracy: British Politics and the Internet (2000); Joe Trippi, The Revolution Will Not Be Televised : Democracy, the Internet, and the Overthrow of Everything (2004); Peter M Shane (ed.), Democracy Online : The Prospects for Political Renewal Through the Internet (2004); Andrew Chadwick, Internet Politics: States, Citizens, and New Communication Technologies (2006); Cass R Sunstein, Republic.com 2.0 (2007); Michael Margolis and Gerson Moreno-Riano, The Prospect of Internet Democracy (2009); Matthew Hindman, The Myth of Digital Democracy (2009); Stephen Coleman and Peter M. Shane (eds.), Connecting Democracy (2012).

8. *See* Neal Conan, *Should Objectivity Still Be the Standard in News?*, National Public Radio, Talk of the Nation (Nov. 16, 2010), http://www.npr.org/2010/11/16/131361367/should-objectivity-still-be-the-standard-in-news.

9. *See Room for Debate: Do We Need Network TV?*, The New York Times (Feb. 27, 2009) (blog), http://roomfordebate.blogs.nytimes.com/2009/02/27/how-network-tv-brought-america-together/.

10. *See* John Nichols, *The Nation: Walter Cronkite America's Anchorman*, National Public Radio (July 20, 2009), http://www.npr.org/templates/story/story.php?storyId=106796633.

11. Copy of Royal Charter for the continuance of the British Broadcasting Corporation (Cm 6925, London, 2006) para.4; An Agreement Between Her Majesty's Secretary of State for Cul-

ture, Media and Sport and the British Broadcasting Corporation (Cm 6872, London, 2006) para.5. See Colin McCabe, Olivia Stewart, eds., The BBC and public service broadcasting (1986); Asa Briggs, The history of broadcasting in the United Kingdom (1995).

12. Communications Act 2003, ss.363–368.

13. See Hugh Cudlipp, The prerogative of the harlot: press barons & power (1980); Jeremy Tunstall, Newspaper power: the new national press in Britain (1996).

14. See Associated Press, *Comcast Drives Growth with Pricier Bundles*, National Public Radio (Oct. 27, 2010), http://www.npr.org/templates/story/story.php?storyId=130854321.

15. See R. Greenslade, *Note Book BBC gloom over bright Sky*, *The Daily Telegraph*, at 6 (Nov. 22, 2005).

16. See Michael J. De la Merced, *Tribune Files for Bankruptcy*, *The New York Times*, Deal Book Blog (Dec. 8, 2008), http://dealbook.nytimes.com/2008/12/08/tribune-files-for-bankruptcy/; *see also* David Folkenflik, *Imagining a City Without its Daily Newspaper*, National Public Radio's *Morning Edition* (Feb. 5, 2009), http://www.npr.org/templates/story/story.php?storyId=100256908; Alex Jones, Losing the News: The Future of the News That Feeds Democracy (2009); Wilson Lowrey & Peter J. Gade, Changing the News: The Forces Shaping Journalism in Uncertain Times (2011).

17. See Staff and Wire Dispatches, *Newspaper Circulation Tumbling: ABC Audit Shows Decline Accelerating*, *The Courier-Journal*, at B6 (Oct. 27, 2009).

18. See Howard Kurtz, *Industry Shudders as Famed Newspaper Closes*, *The Courier-Journal*, Forum Section, at A7 (March 3, 2009); *Why Newspapers Can't Be Saved, But the News Can*, *The New York Times*, The Opinion Pages, Opinionater (blog) (Mar. 16, 2009), http://opinionator.blogs.nytimes.com/2009/03/16/why-newspapers-cant-be-saved-but-the-news-can/?scp=24&sq=media%20newspapers%20guardians%20democracy&st=cse.

19. See Richard Perez-Pena, *Newspaper Circulation Falls by More Than 10%*, *The New York Times*, at B3 (Oct. 27, 2009).

20. *Id.*

21. See Richard Perez-Pena, *Newspaper Ad Revenue Could Fall as Much as 30%*, *The New York Times*, at B3 (Apr. 15, 2009).

22. See Tim Arango, *Fall in Newspaper Sales Accelerates to Pass 7%*, *The New York Times*, at B3 (Apr. 28, 2009).

23. *See Newspaper Circulation Falls*, note 19, at B3.

24. *Id.*

25. See Jeremy W. Peters, *USA Today to Remake Itself to Stress Digital Operations*, *The New York Times*, at B1 (Aug. 28, 2010).

26. OECD Working Party on the Information Economy, The Evolution Of News And The Internet (DSTI/ICCP/IE(2009)14/FINAL).

27. See Richard Pérez-Pena, *Gannett Plans to Furlough Workers*, *The New York Times*, at B12 (Jan. 15, 2009).

28. *See Id.*

29. See Richard Perez-Pena, *McClatchy Plans to Cut 15% of Staff*, *The New York Times*, at B5 (Mar. 10, 2009).

30. *See Id.*

31. See Richard Perez-Pena, *Detroit Newspapers May Sharply Cut Home Delivery*, *The New York Times*, at B3 (Dec. 13, 2008).

32. See Richard Perez-Pena, *Tribune, Major News Chain, Seeks Bankruptcy Protection*, *The New York Times* A1 (Dec. 9, 2008).

33. *See McClatchy Plans to Cut 15%, supra* note 29.

34. *See* Stephanie Clifford, *Conde Nast Reports Sharp Drop in Ad Pages, The New York Times,* at B3 (Nov. 12, 2009).

35. *See* Ashley Parker, *Washington Times Faces Uncertainty, The New York Times,* at B1 (Dec. 1, 2010).

36. *See* Kurtz, *supra* note 18, at A7.

37. *See* Kirk Johnson, *The Rocky Says Goodbye, Taking a Part of its City's Past with It, The New York Times,* at A11 (Feb. 28, 2009).

38. *See Tribune, Major News Chain, Seeks Bankruptcy Protection, supra* note 32, at A1.

39. Joel Rose, *Philadelphia Newspaper Inc. Files for Chapter 11,* National Public Radio's Morning Edition (Feb. 23, 2009), http://www.npr.org/templates/story/story.php?storyId=101024311.

40. *See* Richard Pérez-Pena, *As Cities Go From Two Papers to One, Talk of Zero, The New York Times,* at A1 (Mar. 11, 2009).

41. *See Id.*

42. *See* Joseph Plambeck, *Creditors Win Auction for Philadelphia Newspapers, The New York Times,* at B3 (Apr. 29, 2010).

43. *See* Brooke Gladstone, *Are Newspapers Dead Yet?,* National Public Radio, On the Media (Jan. 28, 2011) (citing The *Tuscon Citizen, The Rocky Mountain News, The Baltimore Examiner, Kentucky Post, Cincinnati Post, King County Journal,* and *Union City Register Tribune*). http://www.onthemedia.org/2010/jul/16/are-newspapers-dead-yet/transcript/

44. *Id.*

45. 0 *See* Brian Stelter, *News Corp.'s Net Income More Than Doubles, Leds by Its Cable Networks, The New York Times,* at B4 (Feb. 3, 2011); Tanzina Vega, *Time Warner Raises Dividend as Earnings Beat Forecast, The New York Times,* at B4 (Feb. 3, 2011).

46. News of the World to close amid hacking scandal (http://www.bbc.co.uk/news/uk-14070733).

47. Declining newspaper sales threaten toilet roll (Declining newspaper sales threaten toilet roll (http://www.telegraph.co.uk/finance/newsbysector/mediatechnologyandtelecoms/media/7637589/Declining-newspaper-sales-threaten-toilet-roll.html).

48. *Sharp Decline in Profit at Washington Post Co., The New York Times,* at B2 (Feb. 26, 2009).

49. *See* Richard Perez-Pena & Mary Chapman, *In a Grand Experiment, 2 Daily Newspapers Now Not So Daily, The New York Times,* at A14 (Mar. 31, 2009).

50. *Id.*

51. *See* Andrew Ross Sarkin, *DealBook: Rocky Mountain News is Shutting Down, The New York Times* (Feb. 26, 2009).

52. Richard Perez-Pena, *Hearst Threatens to End San Francisco Newspaper, The New York Times,* at B9 (Feb. 25, 2009); *San Francisco: A No Newspaper Town?,* CNN (Feb. 25, 2009).

53. *See* Kurtz, *supra* note 18, at A7.

54. *See* William Yardley & Richard Perez-Pena, *In Seattle, A Newspaper Loses Its Paper Routes, The New York Times,* A1 (March 17, 2009).

55. *See* Richard Perez-Pena, *Seattle Paper is Resurgent as a Solo Act, The New York Times,* at B1 (Aug. 10, 2009).

56. *See* Kurtz, *supra* note 18, at A7.

57. *See McClatchy Plans to Cut 15%, supra* note 29.

58. *See Hearst Threatens to End, supra* note 52.

59. *See Id.*

60. *See* Shira Ovide, *At Tribune Co., Leaving Behind Bankruptcy and Old Ways, The Wall Street Journal,* at B1 (July 26, 2010).

61. *See* Richard Perez-Pena, *Times Co. Announces Temporary Salary Cuts, The New York Times,* at B6 (Mar. 27, 2009).

62. *See At Tribune Co., supra* note 60, at B1.

63. *See* Richard Perez-Pena, *4 Michigan Markets Will Lose Daily Newspapers, as Ailing Industry Tries to Cope, The New York Times,* at B8 (Mar. 24, 2009).

64. *Id.*

65. *See Detroit Newspapers May Sharply Cut Home Delivery, supra* note 31.

66. *Id.* (referring to *The Detroit Free Press, The Detroit News,* and other smaller newspapers).

67. *See As Cities Go From Two Papers to One, supra* note 40.

68. *See Id.*

69. *See* Kurtz, *supra* note 18, at A7.

70. *Id.* ("*The New York Times* has borrowed $250 million from a Mexican financier at 14 percent interest....").

71. *Id.*

72. *See* Richard Perez-Pena, *Times Moves to Trim 100 in Newsroom, The New York Times,* at B1 (Oct. 20, 2009).

73. *See* Holly Ramer, *New Hampshire Aids Paper, The Courier-Journal,* at A13 (Nov. 15, 2009).

74. *See* Kurtz, *supra* note 18, at A7 (*quoting San Francisco Chronicle* Editor-at-Large Phil Bronstein).

75. *See As Cities Go From Two Papers to One, supra* note 40.

76. *See* Verena Dobnik, *Insiders: Boston Threat a Warning to Newspapers, The Courier-Journal,* at A2 (Apr. 5, 2009).

77. *See* Richard Perez-Pena, *Boston Globe Workers Reverse Course and Agree to Cuts, The New York Times,* at B5 (July 21, 2009).

78. *See Times Co. Announces Temporary Salary Cuts, supra* note 61.

79. *See As Cities Go From Two Papers to One, supra* note 40.

80. *Id.*

81. Marc Fisher, *Bloggers Can't Fill the Gap Left by Shrinking Press Corps, The Courier-Journal,* Forum Section, at A7.

82. *Id.*

83. *Id.*

84. *See* Kurtz, *supra* note 18, at A7.

85. *See Newspaper Leighoffs,* National Public Radio, On the Media (July 24, 2009), http://www.onthemedia.org/2009/jul/24/neswpaper-leighoffs/transcript/.

86. BBC's Thompson warns of news quality decline, Press Gazette 11 July 2007 (http://www.pressgazette.co.uk/story.asp?storycode=38206).

87. BBC budget cut by 16% in spending review, George Osborne confirms (http://www.guardian.co.uk/media/2010/oct/20/bbc-cuts-spending-review).

88. Everette E Dennis and Melvin L DeFleur, Understanding media in the digital age (2009) chaps. 4, 8; James Curran and Jean Seaton, Power without responsibility: the press, broadcasting, and new media in Britain (7th ed., 2009).

89. *See A Newspaper Loses Its Paper Routes, supra* note 54 ("Other newspapers have closed and many more are threatened. But the transition to an all-digital product for The P-I will be especially closely watched in an industry that is fast losing revenue and is casting around for a new economic model.").

90. *See As Cities Go From Two Papers to One, supra* note 40.

91. *See* Richard Perez-Pena & Tim Arango, *Adding Fees and Fences on Media Sites, The New York Times,* at B1 (Dec. 28, 2009).

92. *See McClatchy Plans to Cut 15%, supra* note 29, at B5.

93. *See* Russell Adams, *Rocky Mountain News Shuts Down: Scripps Fails to Find Buyer for Denver Newspaper; Dailies at Risk in Other Metropolitan Markets, The New York Times,* at B1 (Feb. 27, 2009).

94. *See* Richard Pérez-Pena, *Papers Facing Worst Year for Ad Revenue, The New York Times,* at C3 (Jun. 23, 2008).

95. *See* Brian Stelter, *Cable Networks Trying to Build on Their Gains in Ratings, The New York Times,* at C5 (May 26, 2008). During the 2012 political campaign, cable news networks gained market share vis-a-vis television news. *See* Brian Stelter, *For Campaign News, Most Turn to Cable, The New York Times,* at B3 (Feb. 8, 2012).

96. *See* Bob Garfield, *The Point of Twitter,* National Public Radio, On the Media (Nov. 26, 2010), http://www.onthemedia.org/2010/nov/26/the-point-of-twitter/transcript/.

97. *See As Cities Go From Two Papers to One, supra* note 40; David A. L. Levy and Rasmus Kleis Nielsen, The Changing Business of Journalism and its implication for Democracy (2010).

98. *See* http://www.monster.com/.

99. *See* http://hotjobs.yahoo.com/.

100. http://www.jobsite.co.uk/.

101. http://www.fish4.co.uk/.

102. *See* Felicity Barringer, *HELP WANTED: Newspapers Seek Cyber Partners to Fight On-Line Ads, The New York Times* (Aug. 30, 1999).

103. http://www.ebay.com/.

104. http://www.craigslist.org/about/sites

105. *See Craigslist Meets the Capitalists, The New York Times* (Dec. 8, 2006) (blog), http://dealbook.nytimes.com/2006/12/08/craigslist-meets-the-capitalists/.

106. *See Imagining a City Without Its Daily Newspaper, supra* note 16.

107. *See As Cities Go From Two Papers to One, supra* note 40.

108. *See* Claire Cain Miller, *Ad Shift Throws Blogs a Business Line: Small Web-Based Media Networks Attract Big-Ticket Marketers, The New York Times,* at B1 (Sept. 14, 2009).

109. *Id.*

110. *See* Julie Bosman, *Online Newspaper Ads Gaining Ground on Print, The New York Times,* at C3 (Jun. 6, 2006); John Plunkett, Mail Online revenue growth hits new high as print ads decline 8 February 2012 (http://www.guardian.co.uk/media/2012/feb/08/mail-online-revenue-growth).

111. *See As Cities Go From Two Papers to One, supra* note 40 ("But no one yet has unlocked the puzzle of supporting a large newsroom purely on digital revenue....").

112. *See* Eric Pfanner, *German Publisher Lays Out Plan to Save Newspapers from the Internet; A German Plan to Save Newspapers from Death by Internet: Springer Offers Strategy for Publishers and Net Firms to Work Together, International Herald Tribune,* at 21 (Dec. 7, 2009).

113. *See* Bob Garfield, *Government Intervention to Save Journalism*, National Public Radio, On the Media (Jan. 28, 2011), http://www.onthemedia.org/2011/jan/28/government-intervention-to-save-journalism/transcript/.

114. *See* Bob Garfield, *Getting Desperate*, National Public Radio, On the Media (Feb. 20, 2009), http://www.onthemedia.org/2009/feb/20/getting-desperate/transcript/.

115. See House of Commons Culture Media and Sports Committee, Future for local and regional media (2009-10 HC 43) para.41.

116. *See* David Carr, *Papers Push to Get Out of a Box*, *The New York Times*, The Media Equation, at B1 (Apr. 13, 2009) (discussing the Associated Press' effort to be paid for reuse of its content by other organizations such as Google); Michael Moran, *No Such Thing as Free News*, National Public Radio, (Apr. 21, 2009), http://www.npr.org/templates/story/story.php?storyId=103316249.

117. *See* Perez-Pena & Arango, *supra* note 91.

118. *See* Eric Pfanner, *European Newspapers Find Creative Ways to Thrive in the Internet Age*, *The New York Times*, at B4 (Mar. 30, 2009).

119. *See* David Folkenflik, *Jeff Jarvis: Rewriting Media's Business Model (Again)*, National Public Radio, All Things Considered (Oct. 6, 2009), http://www.npr.org/templates/story/story.php?storyId=113512103.

120. *See* Eric Pfanner, *The Paper That Doesn't Want to be Free*, *The Courier-Journal*, at B1 (Aug. 17, 2009).

121. *Id.*

122. *See* Perez-Pena & Arango, *supra* note 91.

123. *See The Paper That Doesn't Want to be Free*, *supra* note 120, at B7.

124. *Id.*

125. *Id.*

126. *Id.*

127. Josh Holliday, Times loses almost 90% of online readership 20 July 2010 (http://www.guardian.co.uk/media/2010/jul/20/times-paywall-readership).

128. John Plunkett, Times and Sunday Times digital subscriptions to double in price 23 February 2012 (http://www.guardian.co.uk/media/2012/feb/23/times-digital-subscriptions-double-price).

129. *See* Bob Garfield, *Should Newspapers Charge for Content Online?*, National Public Radio, On the Media (Jan. 28, 2011), http://www.onthemedia.org/2011/jan/28/should-newspapers-charge-for-content-online.

130. *Id.*

131. *Id.* (Quoting Alan Murray).

132. *Id.*

133. *Id.*

134. *See The Paper That Doesn't Want to be Free*, *supra* note 120.

135. *See Id.*

136. *See Should Newspapers Charge for Content Online?*, *supra* note 129.

137. *Id.*

138. *Id.* (quoting Mr. Alan Murray of *The Wall Street Journal*).

139. *See The Paper That Doesn't Want to be Free*, *supra* note 120, at B7.

140. *Id.*

141. *See Should Newspapers Charge for Online Content?*, *supra* note 129.

142. *Id.*

143. *Id.*

144. *Id.*

145. http://www.gmgplc.co.uk/wp-content/uploads/2011/09/GNM_AR_1011.pdf.

146. *See, e.g.,* http://pqasb.pqarchiver.com/courier_journal/access/2221997001.html?FMT=ABS&date=Dec+26%2C+2010.

147. *See* David Folkenflik, *"New York Times" Considers Risk and New Revenue,* National Public Radio (July 19, 2009), http://www.npr.org/templates/story/story.php?storyId=106774623.

148. *See* Melissa Block, *The New York Times to Reinstitute Pay Wall,* National Public Radio, All Things Considered (Jan. 20, 2010), http://www.npr.org/templates/story/story.php?storyId=122777083.

149. *See* Eric Pfanner, *French Publishers Plan Digital Newstand: Online and Mobile Users Would Reach Content Via a Single Paid-Access Site, International Herald Tribune,* at 16 (Dec. 6, 2010).

150. *See* David Folkenflik, *"New York Times* Unveils Metered Online Pay Wall," National Public Radio, All Things Considered (Mar. 17, 2011),http://www.npr.org/2011/03/17/134621239/new-york-times-unveils-metered-online-paywall.

151. *See* Wesley Wilson, *C-J Offers New Options, Rates for Readers, Louisville Courier-Journal* (May 10, 2012).

152. *See* David Carr, *The Media Equation: For Murdoch, It's Try, Try Again, The New York Times,* at B1 (Aug. 10, 2009).

153. *Id.*

154. *See "New York Times" Considers Risk and New Revenue, supra* note 147.

155. Josh, Holliday, Mail Online becomes world's second most popular newspaper site 19 April 2011 (http://www.guardian.co.uk/media/2011/apr/19/mail-online-website-popular).

156. http://www.bbc.co.uk/news/magazine-16746785.

157. *See Newspaper Circulation Falls, supra* note 19, at B3.

158. *Id.*

159. *See* Eric Pfanner, *Internet Companies and Ad Agencies Go From Old Enemies to New Friends, The New York Times,* at B7 (July 4, 2009). http://www.nytimes.com/2009/07/04/business/media/04digital.html?scp=1&sq=internet%20companies%20ad%20agencies&st=cse.

160. *See* Martin Peers, *Mixed Ad Message From Newspaper, The Wall Street Journal,* Heard on the Street, at B12 (July 29, 2010).

161. *Id.*

162. *Id.*

163. *See* Jeff Kaye and Stephen Quinn, Funding journalism in the digital age: business models, strategies, issues and trends (2010).

164. *See* Block, *supra* note 148 (interviewing Professor Jay Rosen of New York University).

165. *See* House of Commons Culture Media and Sports Committee, Future for local and regional media (2009-10 HC 43) para 238.

166. Advertising has been accepted for sites directed at foreign users only: http://www.bbc.co.uk/bbc.com/faq/.

167. BBC Annual Report and Accounts 2010/11 (2011) 2–11.

168. James Murdoch hits out at BBC and regulators at Edinburgh TV festival 28 August 2009 (http://www.guardian.co.uk/media/2009/aug/28/james-murdoch-bbc-mactaggart-edinburgh-tv-festival).

169. *See Why Newspapers Can't Be Saved, But the News Can, supra* note 18.

170. *Id.*

171. *Id.*

172. James Murdoch hits out at BBC and regulators at Edinburgh TV festival 28 August 2009 (http://www.guardian.co.uk/media/2009/aug/28/james-murdoch-bbc-mactaggart-edinburgh-tv-festival).

173. *See* Irving Fang, A History of Mass Communication: Six Information Revolutions 56 (1997).

174. *See* Alicia C. Shepard, *Deep Throat's Legacy to Journalism*, National Public Radio (Dec. 19, 2008). http://www.npr.org/templates/story/story.php?storyId=98532461.

175. *See Imagining a City Without Its Daily Newspaper, supra* note 16.

176. App. no. 17488/90, 1996-II, para.39.

177. *See No Such Thing as Free News, supra* note 116.

178. http://www.bbc.co.uk/news/magazine-16746785.

179. *See* Kurtz, *supra* note 18, at A7; *As Cities Go From Two Papers to One, supra* note 40.

180. *Id.* (*quoting* former *Miami Herald* Executive Editor Tom Fiedler).

181. *See* Kurtz, *supra* note 18, at A7 (quoting Dean Nicholas Lemann, Columbia University, School of Journalism).

182. *See* Brooke Gladstone, *Stopping the Presses*, National Public Radio, On the Media (Feb. 20, 2009), http://www.onthemedia.org/2009/feb/20/stopping-the-press/transcript/.

183. *Id.*

184. *See No Such Thing as Free News, supra* note 116.

185. Dan Zak, Woodward and Bernstein: Could the Web generation uncover a Watergate-type scandal? 4 April 2012 (http://www.washingtonpost.com/lifestyle/style/woodward-and-bernstein-could-the-web-generation-uncover-a-watergate-type-scandal/2012/04/03/gIQAwErvtS_story.html?tid=sm_twitter_washingtonpost).

186. *Id.*

187. *See As Cities Go From Two Papers to One, supra* note 40.

188. *Id.*

189. *See Id.* (quoting Jeff Jarvis, City University of New York's graduate school of journalism).

190. *See* Kurtz, *supra* note 18, at A7 (quoting John Marshall of *Talking Points Memo* website).

191. *Id.*

192. *See* Bob Garfield, *Paper Trail*, National Public Radio, On the Media (Apr. 3, 2009) (quoting Professor Sam Schulhofer-Wohl, Princeton University), http://www.onthemedia.org/2009/apr/03/paper-trail/transcript/.

193. *See Stopping the Presses, supra* note 158.

194. *See* http://www.drudgereport.com/.

195. http://order-order.com/.

196. *See* A History of Mass Communication, *supra* note 173, at 234.

197. *Id.*

198. *See* Eric Alterman, What liberal media?: the truth about bias and the news (2004); Neil T Gavin, Press and television in British politics: media, money and mediated democracy (2007); John Street, Mass media, politics and democracy (2011).

199. *See Id.*

200. *Id.*

201. *Id.*

202. *See No Such Thing as Free News, supra* note 116.

203. *See* House of Commons Culture Media and Sports Committee, Future for local and regional media (2009-10 HC 43) para.261; Bob Garfield, *Is Hyperlocal the Future of News?*, National Public Radio, On the Media (Jan. 28, 2011), http://www.onthemedia.org/2010/jul/16/is-hyperlocal-the-future-of-news/transcript/ (quoting Mary Ann Giordano, Deputy Metro Editor, *The New York Times*).

204. *Id.*

205. *See* Claire Cain Miller & Brad Stone, *News Without Newspapers: "Hyperlocal" Updates From Blogs, Police, And Even Reporters, The New York Times*, at B1 (Apr. 13, 2009).

206. *Id.*

207. *Id.*

208. *Id.*

209. *Id.*

210. *Id.*

211. *See No Such Thing as Free News, supra* note 116.

212. *Id.*

213. *Id.*

214. http://mirror.wikileaks.info/.

215. *See Id.*

216. http://mirror.wikileaks.info/; *see also* Raphale G. Satter & Michael Weissenstein, *WikiLeaks' War Records Reveal Grim Accounts: Iraqis Accused of Torture Slayings, The Courier-Journal*, at A5 (Oct. 23, 2010).

217. *Id.*

218. *Id.*

219. *See* Scott Shane, *WikiLeaks Prompts New Round of Diplomatic Uproar: Envoys Fear for Sources' Safety as Reporters Sift Newly Released Cables for Revelations, The New York Times*, at A11 (Sept. 1, 2011).

220. *See* Eric Schmitt & Helene Cooper, *Document Leak Adds to Pressure on White House: Policy Faces Scrutiny, The New York Times*, at A1 (July 27, 2010).

221. *See* Bill Keller, *The Boy Who Kicked the Hornet's Nest, The New York Times Magazine*, at 34 (Jan. 30, 2011).

222. *See* Dina Temple Raston, *WikiLeaks Release Reveals Messier Side of Diplomacy*, National Public Radio (Nov. 28, 2010), http://www.npr.org/2010/11/28/131648175/wikileaks-releases-huge-cache-of-u-s-diplomatic-cables.

223. *See* Scott Shane & Andrew W. Lehren, *Leaked Cables Offer Raw Look at U.S. Diplomacy, The New York Times*, at A1 (Nov. 2, 2010).

224. *See* Ray Somaiya & Alan Cowell, *WikiLeaks Founder Said to Fear "Illegal Rendition" to U.S., The New York Times*, A6 (Jan. 12, 2001).

225. *See* David Folkenflik, *WikiLeaks: An Editor-in-Chief or Prolific Source?*, National Public Radio, Weekend Edition Saturday (July 31, 2010), http://www.npr.org/templates/

story/story.php?storyId=128870288 (discussing the release of some 90,000 classified documents relating to the Afghanistan war).

226. *See Leaked Cables Offer Raw Look, supra* note 223.

227. *See* Dina Temple Raston, *supra* note 222.

228. *See WikiLeaks Prompts New Round of Diplomatic Uproar, supra* note 219.

229. *See* Helene Cooper & Carlotta Gall, *Cables Depict a Roller-Coaster Trajectory for Karzai, From Exalted to Baffling, The New York Times*, A10 (Dec. 3, 2010).

230. *See* Scott Shane, Mark Mazetti & Dexter Filkins, *State's Secrets Day 5; Pervasive Afghan Graft, Starting at Top, The New York Times*, at A1 (Dec. 3, 2010).

231. *See* Rachel Donadio & Celestine Bohlen, *Caustic U.S. Views of Berlusconi Churn Italy's Politics, The New York Times*, A11 (Dec. 3, 2010).

232. *See* Bill Chappell, *WikiLeaks Begins Exposing 400,000 U.S. Documents About the Iraq War*, National Public Radio, The Two-Way (Oct. 22, 2010), http://www.npr.org/blogs/thetwo-way/2010/10/22/130760662/wikileaks-begins-exposing-400-000-u-s-documents-about-the-iraq-war.

233. *See* Ethan Bronner, *Leaked Documents Open a Door on Mideast Peace Talks, The New York Times*, A4 (Jan. 25, 2011).

234. *See* Reuters, *Former Swiss Banker is Arrested in WikiLeaks Case, After a Conviction, The New York Times*, at B3 (Jan. 20, 2011).

235. *See* James Glanz & John Markoff, *Vast Hacking by a China Fearful of the Web: Cables Depict Google Shock, Censorship and Cyberattacks, The New York Times*, at A1 (Dec. 5, 2010).

236. *See* Mary Beth Sherdan, *US-Mexico Relations Hit Bottom Over WikiLeaks, The Sydney Morning Herald*, at. 25 (Mar. 5–6, 2011).

237. *See* David Kirkpatrick, *Beyond Tunisia Unrest, Rage Over Wealth of Ruling Family, The New York Times*, at A10 (Jan. 14, 2011).

238. *Id.*

239. *See* Scott Shane, *Cables From American Diplomats Portray U.S. Ambivalence on Tunisia, The New York Times*, at 11 (Jan. 16, 2011).

240. *Id.*

241. *See* Dina Temple Raston, *supra* note 222.

242. *See WikiLeaks Founder Said to Fear "Illegal Rendition" to U.S., supra* note 224, at A6.

243. *See* Kim Severson & Robbie Brown, *WikiLeaks Cables Make Appearance in a Tale of Sunken Treasure and Nazi Theft, The New York Times*, at A10 (Jan. 7, 2011).

244. Adam Clark Estes, WikiLeaks Is Running Out of Media Friends 27 February 2012 (http://www.theatlanticwire.com/business/2012/02/wikileaks-running-out-media-friends/49184/).

245. *See* Brian Stelter & Noam Cohen, *In WikiLeaks' Growth, Some Control is Lost: Mad Scramble to be First to Reveal Secrets, The New York Times*, at A11 (Apr. 27, 2011).

246. *Id.*

247. *See* Keller, *supra* note 221, at 33.

248. http://cryptome.org/.

249. http://www.liveleak.com/.

250. *See* Ravi Somaiya, *Former WikiLeaks Colleagues Forming New Web Site, OpenLeaks, The New York Times*, at A10 (Feb. 7, 2011).

251. *See* Ravi Somaiya, *WikiLeaks Angry About Former Staff Member's Book, The New York Times*, A9 (Feb. 11, 2011) (the former associate is Mr. Daniel Domscheit-Berg who is described as a German computer scientist).

252. *See Former WikiLeaks Colleagues Forming New Web Site, supra* note 250.

253. *See* David Gura, *Online News Organizations Compete for Pulitzers*, National Public Radio, Morning Edition (Apr. 20, 2009), http://www.npr.org/templates/story/story.php?storyId=103222044.

254. *See* Richard Perez-Pena, *In Chicago, Ex-Editor Fights Back, The New York Times*, at B1 (Nov. 23, 2009).

255. *Id.*

256. *See* Michel Martin, *Pulitzer Awards First Prize to New Media Outlet*, National Public Radio, Tell Me More (Apr. 13, 2010), http://www.npr.org/templates/story/story.php?storyId=125902373.

257. *See* Noam Cohen, *Blogger, Sans Pajamas, Rakes Muck and a Prize, The New York Times*, at C1 (Feb. 25, 2008).

258. *See* Alex Cohen, *Nonprofit News Site Wins Coveted Media Award*, National Public Radio, All Things Considered (Apr. 7, 2009), http://www.npr.org/templates/story/story.php?storyId=102851849.

259. *See* Bob Garfield, *Post-Newspaper Journalism*, National Public Radio, On the Media (Aug. 21, 2009) (quoting Professor Jeff Jarvis, City University of New York), http://www.onthemedia.org/2009/aug/21/post-newspaper-journalism/transcript/.

260. http://order-order.com/2004/01/09/about-guidos-blog/.

261. See Pablo Boczkowski, Digitizing the News: Innovation in Online Newspapers (2004).

262. *See* Richard Perez-Pena, *Politico and Reuters Forge a News Distribution Alliance, The New York Times*, at B4 (Dec. 15, 2008).

263. *See* Jeremy W. Peters, *Political Blogs Are Ready to Flood the Campaign Trail, The New York Times*, at A1 (Jan. 30, 2011).

264. *Id.*

265. *Id.*

266. *Id.* (quoting Mr. VandeHei, *Politico's* Executive Editor and co-founder).

267. http://www.politico.com/.

268. *See* Jonathan Martin, Maggie Haberman, Anna Palmer & Kenneth P. Vogel, *Herman Cain Accused by Two Women of Inappropriate Behavior, Politico* (Oct. 31, 2011). http://www.politico.com/news/stories/1011/67194.html.

269. *See* Frank James, *News Corps. Contributions Raise Eyebrows*, National Public Radio, Its All Politics (Oct. 1, 2010), http://www.npr.org/blogs/itsallpolitics/2010/10/01/130261968/news-corp-s-gop-contributions-raise-eyebrows.

270. *See* Scott Horsley, *Before Politics, Huntsman Aspired to Rock Star Fame*, National Public Radio, All Things Considered (Oct. 12, 2011), http://www.npr.org/2011/10/12/141276651/before-politics-huntsman-aspired-to-rock-star-fame.

271. *See* Melissa Block, *Paper: Muslim Women Sidelined at Obama Rally*, National Public Radio, All Things Considered (June 18, 2008), http://www.npr.org/templates/story/story.php?storyId=91658107.

272. *See Political Blogs are Ready to Flood the Campaign Trail, supra* note 263.

273. *See* Kurtz, *supra* note 18, at A7.

274. *See Political Blogs are Ready to Flood the Campaign Trail, supra* note 263.

275. *See Id.*

276. *See* Liane Hansen, *New Website Texas Tribune Thrives, But How?*, National Public

Radio, Weekend Edition Sunday (Aug. 15, 2010), http://www.npr.org/templates/story/story.php?storyId=129210695.

277. *See Political Blogs are Ready to Flood the Campaign Trail, supra* note 263.

278. *Id.* (quoting Mr. John McIntyre, Chief Executive and co-founder).

279. *Id.*

280. *Id.*

281. *See Political Blogs are Ready to Flood the Campaign Trail, supra* note 263.

282. *Id.*

283. *Id.*

284. *See* NPR Staff, *Is Writing Online Without Pay Worth It?*, National Public Radio, Morning Edition (Feb. 15, 2011), http://www.npr.org/2011/02/15/133759724/is-writing-online-without-pay-worth-it.

285. *Id.*

286. *Id.*

287. http://www.huffingtonpost.ca/; http://www.huffingtonpost.co.uk/; http://www.huffingtonpost.fr/.

288. *See* David Carr, *News Erupts, and So Does a Web Debut, The New York Times*, at B1 (Nov. 9. 2009).

289. *Id.*

290. *See New Website Texas Tribune Thrives, But How?, supra* note 276.

291. *Id.*

292. *See News Erupts and So Does a Web Debut, supra* note 288, at B1 & B8.

293. *Id.*, at B8.

294. *See New Website Texas Tribune Thrives, But How?, supra* note 276.

295. *Id.*

296. *See* David Carr, *After a Year of Ruin, Some Hope, The New York Times*, at B1 (Dec. 21, 2009).

297. *Id.*

298. *See* Richard Perez-Pena, *Hearst's Seattle Paper May Move to Web, The New York Times*, at B5 (Mar. 6, 2009).

299. *Id.*

300. *Id.*, at B1.

301. http://www.indenvertimes.com/.

302. *See* David Folkenflik, *Newspapers Wade Into an Online-Only Future*, National Public Radio, All Things Considered (Mar. 20, 2009), http://www.npr.org/templates/story/story.php?storyId=102162128.

303. *Id.*

304. *See* Jennifer Preston, *When Unrest Stirs, Bloggers Are Already in Place, The New York Times*, at B3 (Mar. 14, 2011).

305. *Id.*

306. *Id.*

307. *Id.*

308. *Id.*

309. *See* Brian Stelter, *A Grass Roots Newscast Gives a Voice to Struggles, The New York Times*, at B3 (Oct. 24, 2011).

310. www.democracynow.org.

311. *See A Grass Roots Newscast, supra* note 309.

312. *Id.*

313. *Id.*

314. *Id.*

315. *Id.*

316. *Id.*

317. *See* David Carr, *Journalist, Provocateur, Maybe Both, The New York Times*, The Media Equation, at B2 (July 26, 2010).

318. *See* Jennifer Mascia, *A Web Site That's Not Afraid to Pick a Fight, The New York Times*, at B1 (July 12, 2010).

319. *Id.*

320. *Id.*

321. *See* Bob Garfield, *New and Old Media in Post-Katrina New Orleans*, National Public Radio, On the Media (Sept. 10, 2010), http://www.onthemedia.org/2010/sep/10/new-and-old-media-in-post-katrina-new-orleans/transcript/.

322. *Id.*

323. *See* Bob Garfield, *The Road to Non-Profit*, National Public Radio, On the Media (Aug. 21, 2009), http://www.onthemedia.org/2009/aug/21/the-road-to-non-profit/transcript/.

324. *Id.*

325. *See Nonprofit News Site Wins Coveted Media Award, supra* note 258.

326. *Id.*

327. *See A Web Site That's Not Afraid to Pick a Fight, supra* note 318.

328. *Id.*

329. *See* David Carr, *A Protest's Ink-Stained Fingers, The New York Times*, The Media Equation, at B1 (Oct. 10, 2011).

330. *See Id.*

331. *See Id.*, at B3.

332. *Id.*, at B3.

333. *See A Protest's Ink-Stained Fingers, supra* note 329, at B3.

334. *Id.*, at B3.

335. *Id.*

336. *Id.*

337. http://www.guardian.co.uk/commentisfree/uk-edition.

338. *See* A HISTORY OF MASS COMMUNICATION, *supra* note 173, at 51–53.

339. *As Cities Go From Two Papers to One, supra* note 40 (quoting Jeff Jarvis, City University of New York's graduate school of journalism).

340. *See* Jeremy W. Peters & Brian Stelter, *News Corp. Heralds Debut of The Daily, an iPad-Only Newspaper, The New York Times*, at B1 (Feb. 3, 2011).

341. *Id.*

342. *Id.*

343. *Id.*, at B4.

344. *Id.*

345. *Id.*

346. *See A Newspaper Loses Its Paper Routes, supra* note 89.

347. *See Newspapers Wade Into an Online-Only Future, supra* note 302.

348. *See A Newspaper Loses Its Paper Routes, supra* note 89.

349. The publication can be found at Seattlepi.com.

350. *See Newspapers Wade Into an Online-Only Future, supra* note 302.

351. *Id.*

352. *Id.* (the article goes on to note that the MinnPost in the Minneapolis-Twin Cities area, does the same thing).

353. *Id.*

354. *Id.*

355. *Id.*

356. *Id.*

357. www.KYPost.com.

358. *See Newspapers Wade Into an Online Only Future, supra* note 302.

359. *Id.*

360. *Id.*

361. *See Newspapers Wade Into an Online Only Future, supra* note 302.

362. *Id.*

363. *See* Richard Perez-Pena, *Seattle Paper is Resurgent as a Solo Act, The New York Times,* at B1 (Aug. 10, 2009).

364. See for example HC Deb, 25 March 2009, vol.490 col.304, Andrew Gwynne.

365. Roy Greenslade, 32nd regional weekly closure of the year (24 December 2011) (http://www.guardian.co.uk/media/greenslade/2011/dec/24/newspaper-closures-downturn).

366. *See* Bercovici, J., *Warren Buffett and Newspapers: Infatuation or Cold Calculation?, Forbes'* (2012) http://www.forbes.com/sites/jeffbercovici/2012/05/24/warren-buffett-and-newspapers-infatuation-or-cold-calculation/.

367. *See* House of Commons Culture Media and Sports Committee, Future for local and regional media (2009-10 HC 43) para 57.

368. House of Commons Culture Media and Sports Committee, Future for local and regional media (2009-10 HC 43) para.263.

369. http://www.levesoninquiry.org.uk/.

370. http://www.levesoninquiry.org.uk/wp-content/uploads/2012/02/Submission-by-Paul-Staines.pdf.

371. *See* Dramatico Entertainment Ltd v. British Sky Broadcasting Ltd [2012] EWHC 1152 (Ch).

372. *See Why Newspapers Can't Be Saved, But the News Can, supra* note 18.

373. *Id.*

374. *Id.*

375. *See When Unrest Stirs, supra* note 304.

376. *See* Peter Wayner, *Stretching the Truth Just Became Easier (and Cheaper): Free Software Allows Anyone to Tweak a Picture, Whether by Expanding a Background or Deleting a Blemish, The New York Times,* at B7 (Jan. 31, 2008).

377. *See Journalist, Provocateur, supra* note 317, at B2.

378. *See* Jennifer Preston & Brian Stelter, *Cellphone Cameras Become World's Eyes and Ears on Protests Across the Middle East, The New York Times,* at A11 (Feb. 19, 2011).

379. *See* Bob Garfield, *The Rush to Report,* National Public Radio, On the Media (Jan. 21, 2011), http://www.onthemedia.org/2011/jan/21/the-rush-to-report/transcript/.

380. *Id.*

381. *See* Michael Martin, *"Shop Talk": The Sherrod Shuffle*, National Public Radio, Tell Me More (July 23, 2010), http://www.npr.org/templates/story/story.php?storyId=128720704.

382. *See* Brian Stelter, *When Race is the Issue, Misleading Coverage Sets Off an Uproar: Accusations Can Take Root Online, Then Move to TV or Radio*, The New York Times, at B1 (July 26, 2010).

383. *See* David Carr, *New Rules for the Way We Watch*, The New York Times, The Media Equation, at B1 (Dec. 26, 2011).

384. *Id.*

385. *Id.*

2. The New Media in the New World: Are They Behaving Badly or Doing Their Job?

1. *See*, Zemel v. Rusk, 381 U.S. 1, 17 (1965) ("The right to speak and publish does not necessarily provide for the unrestrained right to gather information.").

2. *Id.*; *see also*, Wolfson v. Lewis, 924 F. Supp. 1413, 1417 (E.D. Pa. 1996) (holding that "the First Amendment does not, therefore, shield the press from crimes or torts committed in pursuit of a story").

3. Timothy Dyk, *Newsgathering, Press Access, and the First Amendment*, 44 Stan. L. Rev. 927 (1992).

4. At least two states, Virginia and New York, do not recognize any tort of intrusion at all. For Virginia *see*, WJLA-TV v. Levin, 264 Va. 140, 160 n.5 (Va. 2002); for New York *see*, Howell v. New York Post Co., Inc., 81 N.Y. 2d 115, 123–24 (N.Y. 1993).

5. Although there is an undoubted right to gather news from any source by means within the law, this does not mean that the First Amendment compels others—private persons or governments—to supply information. *See*, Branzburg v. Hayes, 408 U.S. 665 (1972).

6. *See, e.g.* Campus Commc'n v. Earnhardt, 821 So. 2d 388 (Fla. 5th Dist. Ct. App. 2002); State v. Rolling, 22 Med. L. Rep. 2264 (Fla. Cir. Ct. 1994).

7. *See*, Pearson v. Dodd, 410 F.2d 701, 705 (D.C. Cir. 1969) ("[I]n analyzing a claimed breach of privacy, injuries from intrusion and injuries from publication should be kept clearly separate.").

8. Pell v. Procunier, 417 U.S. 817, 833 (1974) (quoting Branzburg v. Hayes, 408 U.S. 665 (1972)).

9. The First Amendment does not confer a license on the press to violate valid criminal laws. *Branzburg*, 408 U.S. at 691. *See*, Dietemann v. Time, Inc., 449 F.2d 245 (9th Cir. 1971) (holding employees of magazine liable for gaining entrance to plaintiff's personal office using hidden cameras and recording devices without plaintiff's permission).

10. Courts have recognized a general right to inspect and copy public records and documents. The right is justified by the interest of citizens in keeping a watchful eye on the workings of public agencies. Nixon v. Warner Commc'ns, Inc., 435 U.S. 589 (1978).

11. The right that individuals have against unreasonable searches and seizures in their homes is rooted and explicitly stated in the Fourth Amendment. U.S. Const. amend. IV.

12. The illegality of the acquisition of the information can impose liability on the newsgatherer as well as the publisher, depending upon the publisher's knowledge at the time of

publication. *See*, Boehner v. McDermott, 484 F.3d 573 (D.C. Cir. 2007); Peavy v. WFAA-TV, Inc., 221 F.3d 158, 172 (5th Cir. 2000); Quigley v. Rosenthal, 427 F.3d 1232 (10th Cir. 2005); Pearson v. Dodd, 410 F.2d 701, 705 (D.C. Cir. 1969).

13. *Boehner*, 484 F.3d 573; *Quigley*, 427 F.3d 1232.

14. Bartnicki v. Vopper, 532 U.S. 514 (2001) (finding that a stranger's illegal conduct does not remove the First Amendment shield from speech which contains matters of public concern); Pearson v. Dodd, 410 F.2d 701 (D.C. Cir.1969).

15. Peavy v. WFAA-TV, Inc., 221 F.3d 158, 172 (5th Cir. 2000).

16. Anderson v. Strong Mem'l Hosp., 151 A.D.2d 1033 (N.Y. App. Div. 1989).

17. Miller v. Nat'l Broad. Co., 187 Cal. App. 3d 1463 (Cal. Ct. App. 1986).

18. *Id.*

19. Nader v. General Motors Corp., 25 N.Y.2d 560 (N.Y. 1970). *See, e.g.*, Galella v. Onassis, 487 F.2d 986 (2d Cir. 1973).

20. *E.g.*, Although the family of Nicole Catsouras successfully lobbied to remove from Internet sites photographs of her gruesome automobile accident death, a recent Google search for the images revealed nearly 75,000 hits. Search of "Nikki Catsouras accident photos" on Google.com returns 74,900 results as of Nov. 22, 2010.

21. Requires: (1) extreme and outrageous conduct by discloser with the intention of causing or reckless disregard of the probability of causing, emotional distress; (2) the third party to suffer severe or extreme emotional distress; and (3) the discloser's conduct to be the actual or proximate cause of the third party's suffering. Catsouras v. Dep't of California Highway Patrol, 181 Cal. App. 4th 856 (Cal. Ct. App. 2010).

22. This cause of action protects the commercial value of the picture or representation of an individual or performer. Gritzke v. M.R.A. Holding, LLC, 2002 WL 32107540 (N.D. Fla. 2002).

23. If the right to one's image or likeness was licensed to a third party, then that party may have an interest in the use of the decedent's image or likeness past their death. Tyne v. Time Warner Entm't Co., 901 So. 2d 802 (Fla. 2005).

24. *See, e.g.*, State v. Rolling, 22 Med. L. Rep. 2264 (Fla. Cir. Ct. 1994); New York Times v. NASA, 782 F. Supp. 628, 631 (D.D.C. 1991); Campus Commc'n v. Earnhardt, 821 So. 2d 388 (Fla. 5th Dist. Ct. App. 2002).

25. Hustler Magazine, Inc. v. Falwell, 485 U.S. 46 (1988).

26. *Id.*

27. An individual cannot simply state "I think" to receive constitutional protection. Milkovich v. Lorain Journal Co., 497 U.S. 1, 20 (1990). If the statement is of public concern, then it must contain a provably false connotation in order to not be considered an "opinion." Philadelphia Newspapers, Inc. v. Hepps, 475 U.S. 767 (1986).

28. Partington v. Bugliosi, 56 F.3d 1147 (9th Cir. 1995); Celle v. Filipino Reporter Enters., Inc., 209 F.3d 163 (2d Cir.2000); Krinsky v. Doe, 159 Cal. App. 4th 1154 (Cal. Ct. App. 2008).

29. For example, if a true statement is incomplete or misleading a person can still be harmed despite the validity of the information. *See*, Rapp v. Jews for Jesus, Inc. 944 So. 2d 460, 465 (Fla. 4th Dist. Ct. App. 2006).

30. Not all jurisdictions recognize the tort of false light, but generally to prove false light, one must show that (1) defendant publicized information that presented plaintiff to public in a false light, (2) the false light was highly offensive to a reasonable person, and (3) the defendant knew or should have known of this falsity. Mitchell v. Griffin Television, LLC,

60 P.3d 1058, 1061 (Okla. Civ. App. 2002). *But see*, Gannett Co., Inc. v. Anderson, 947 So. 2d 1 (Fla. 1st Dist. Ct. App. 2006) (finding that there is no difference between a false light invasion of privacy claim and defamation claim, as the occurrence of defamation can be from an implied inference based off a true statement), *aff'd*, 994 So. 2d 1048 (Fla. 2008).

31. Diaz v. Oakland Tribune, Inc., 139 Cal. App. 3d 118 (Cal. Ct. App. 1983); Cason v. Baskin, 155 Fla. 198 (Fla. 1944).

32. Masson v. New Yorker Magazine, Inc., 501 U.S. 496 (1991).

33. Generally, the elements of a defamation claim are: "(a) a false and defamatory statement concerning another; (b) an unprivileged publication to a third party; (c) fault amount at least to negligence on the part of the publisher; and (d) either actionaability of the statement irrespective of special harm or the existence of special harm caused by the publication." Restatement (Second) of Torts § 558 (2011).

34. Steinbuch v. Cutler, 518 F.3d 580 (8th Cir. 2008).

35. *Diaz*, 139 Cal. App.3d at 126 ("matter which was once of public record may be protected as private facts where disclosure of that information would not be newsworthy"); *Cason*, 155 Fla. 198.

36. For instance, the European Union's Charter of Fundamental Rights recognizes human dignity as an inviolable right that must be respected and protected. Charter of Fundamental Rights of the European Union, ch. 1, art. 1, 2000 O.J. (C 364) 1 (EC).

37. New York Times Co. v. Sullivan, 376 U.S. 254, 279–80 (1964).

38. Gertz v. Robert Welch, Inc., 418 U.S. 323 (1974).

39. Photographs were taken of Princess Caroline of Monaco engaging in private activities. A German federal constitutional court, interpreting German law, enjoined the publication of those photographs that included images of her children because of the private nature of the activity. The court did not, however, protect the images of the Princess shopping and relaxing on the beach. Von Hannover v. Germany, 2004-III Eur. Ct. H.R. 294, §25.

40. Smith v. Daily Mail Publ'g Co., 443 U.S. 97, 102 (1979); *see also*, Florida Star v. BJF, 491 U.S. 524 (1989) (holding that punishment for publication of truthful information may—if at all—be lawful only when it is narrowly tailored to serve state interest of the highest order).

41. Bartnicki v. Vopper, 532 U.S. 514 (2001) (finding that a stranger's illegal conduct in obtaining information does not suffice to remove First Amendment protection about a matter of public concern when that information is then disclosed); Pearson v. Dodd, 410 F.2d 701, (D.C. Cir. 1969) (holding that publication of illegally obtained information of public interest does not impose liability even if publisher had knowledge of the illegal acquisition).

42. *See, e.g.*, Sipple v. Chronicle Publ'g Co., 154 Cal. App. 3d 1040 (Cal. Ct. App. 1984).

43. James Whitman, *The Two Western Cultures of Privacy: Dignity Versus Liberty*, 113 Yale L.J. 1151 (2004).

44. *Id.*

45. *Sipple*, 154 Cal. App. 3d 1040.

46. *Id.*

47. *See* Mark Stephens, *New Celebrities of the Libel Courts*, Times (U.K.), July 18, 2006, *available at* http://business.timesonline.co.uk/tol/business/law/article687881.ece.

48. New York Times v. United States, 407 U.S. 713 (1971).

49. The report "History of the U.S. Decision-Making Process on Viet Nam Policy" was copied and given to both the New York Times and Washington Post.

50. *Rupert Murdoch's phone-hacking scandal: A timeline*, The Week, August 11, 2011, http://theweek.com/article/index/217378/rupert-murdochs-phone-hacking-scandal-a-timeline.

51. *Id.*

52. John F. Burns and Ravi Somaiya, *WikiLeaks Found on the Run, Trailed by Notoriety*, NEW YORK TIMES, October 23, 2010, http://www.nytimes.com/2010/10/24/world/24assange.html.

53. Tim Lister and Emily Smith, *Flood of WikiLeaks calbes includes identities of dozens of informants*, CNN, August 31, 2011, http://www.cnn.com/2011/US/08/31/wikileaks.sources/index.html?hpt=hp_t2.

54. Jeanne Whalen, *WikiLeaks Blames Paper for Breach*, WALL STREET JOURNAL, September 2, 2011, http://online.wsj.com/article/SB1000142405311190471660457654415395648390.html?mod=e2tw.

55. Galella v. Onassis, 487 F.2d 986 (2d Cir. 1973). Interestingly, the Reporters Committee for Freedom of the Press has compiled a reference guide for photographers to assist them in not violating state privacy laws when taking pictures. *See* Photographer's Guide to Privacy, *available at* http://www.rcfp.org/pullouts/photographers/index.php (last visited Apr. 30, 2009).

56. *Galella*, 487 F.2d at 992. Although arrested after harassing John, Galella's harassment also extended to Onassis and her daughter Caroline as well. Some examples brought out at trial include invading the children's private school, driving a powerboat "uncomfortably close" to Onassis while she swam and disrupting Caroline when she played tennis.

57. Pamela McClintock, *Governator Snaps Back at Paparazzi*, VARIETY, Oct. 2, 2005, http://www.variety.com/article/VR1117930079.html?cs=1&s=h&p=0.

58. Bartnicki v. Vopper, 532 U.S. 514 (2001).

59. Earnhardt v. Volusia County, Office of the Med. Exam'r, No. 2001-30373-CICI (Fla. Cir. Ct. July 10, 2001).

60. There are websites advising photographers of the limits of privacy in the US and in other countries. *See* Photographers' Guide to Privacy, *supra* note 55.

61. State v. Rolling, 22 Med. L. Rep. 2264 (Fla. Cir. Ct. 1994).

62. Although mainstream media would not have published such gruesome photos, there was concern that the tabloid press would.

63. Campus Commc'n. v. Earnhardt, 821 So. 2d 388 (5th Dist. Ct. App. 2002).

64. *Id.*

65. The law controlling such records allows them to be kept confidential during the course of an investigation but must be released upon request after its completion.

66. Anderson v. Strong Mem'l Hosp., 573 N.Y.S.2d 828 (N.Y. Sup. Ct. 1991).

67. *See* Torsten Kleinz, CCC Publishes Fingerprints of Wolfgang Schäuble, the German Home Secretary, Heise Online, March 31, 2008, http://www.heise.de/english/newsticker/news/105728.

68. *Mosley v. News of the World* [2008] EWHC 1777 (QB). But Mosley lost his case in the European Court of Human Rights in which he asserted that the law should always require the media to give notice of stories intrusive into privacy: *Mosley v. United Kingdom*, App. no. 48009/08, 10 May 2011.

69. *See,* Sandler v. Calcagni, 565 F. Supp. 2d 184 (D. Me. 2008).

70. *Id.* at 198 (quoting RESTATEMENT (SECOND) OF TORTS §652D cmt. c (1977)).

71. *See* Martin Beckford, *United Nations Orders Labour to Stop Reality TV Shows Exploiting Children*, THE TELEGRAPH, Oct. 3, 2008, *available at* http://www.telegraph.co.uk/

news/newstopics/politics/labour/3129928/United-Nations-orders-Labour-to-stop-reality-TV-shows-exploiting-children.html.

72. Shulman v. Group W. Prods., Inc., 955 P.2d 469 (Cal. 1998).

73. Lucas v. Fox News Network, LLC, 2001 WL 100181 (11th Cir. 2001).

74. Hornberger v. ABC, Inc., 351 N.J. Super. 577 (N.J. Super. Ct. 2002).

75. Sheryl Gay Stolberg, *With Apology, Fired Official is Offered a New Job*, N.Y. TIMES, July 21, 2010, *available at* http://www.nytimes.com/2010/07/22/us/politics/22sherrod.html.

76. *See*, BBC NEWS, *Palin E-mail Hack Details Emerge*, Sept. 19, 2008, *available at* http://news.bbc.co.uk/2/hi/technology/7624809.stm and ASSOCIATED PRESS, *AP Refuses Secret Service Request for Palin's "Hacked" Emails*, Sept. 18, 2008, *available at* http://www.editorandpublisher.com/eandp/news/article_display.jsp?vnu_content_id=1003851598.

77. Steve Doughty, *We will not be gagged, m'lud: As Ryan Giggs is named in Parliament as cheating star after weeks of legal farce, mps launch a defiant message*, The Daily Mail, May 24, 2011, http://www.dailymail.co.uk/news/article-1389841/Ryan-Giggs-named-Parliament-cheating-super-injunction-star.html; *Giggs (previously known as CTB) v. News Group Newspapers Ltd* [2012] EWHC 431 (QB).

78. James Robinson, *How super-injunctions are used to gag investigative reporting*, THE GUARDIAN, Oct. 13, 2009, *available at* http://www.guardian.co.uk/uk/2009/oct/13/super-injunctions-guardian-carter-ruck.

79. This case emphasizes the jurisdictional issues that can arise with respect to the media and intrusion. *See*, Stephen Bell Wellington, *Names Found Online Despite Judge's Ruling*, COMPUTERWORLD, Sept. 2, 2008, *available at* http://computerworld.co.nz/news.nsf/scrt/1788882685C346E5CC2574B70035FCF6.

80. In fact, the New Jersey Supreme Court recently held that the New Jersey Shield Law did not apply to online message boards based on the nature of the messages boards and how they were not "similar to traditional news sources" which did qualify under the law. Too Much Medica, LLC v. Hale, 206 N.J. 209, 216 (N.J. 2011).

81. Krinsky v. Doe, 159 Cal. App. 4th 1154 (Cal. Ct. App. 2008).

82. *Id.*

83. Cohen v. Google, Inc. 887 N.Y.S. 2d 424 (N.Y. Sup. Ct. 2009) (holding the despite blogger's contention that the blog was a less serious form of dissemination where hyperbole and was expected, the statements made contain assertions of objective fact, that if proven false would provide the predicate for a defamation claim).

84. *See*, Amos Maki, *Police Back Off Blogger Pursuit—Subpoena for Critic's ID Pulled; Logo Use Still Issue*, RED ORBIT, Sept. 5, 2008, http://www.redorbit.com/news/technology/1545469/police_back_off_blogger_pursuit_subpoena_for_critics_id. Interestingly, the U.S. Supreme Court has already ruled that the First Amendment protects anonymous speech, especially when that speech is political in nature. McIntyre v. Ohio Elections Commission, 514 U.S. 334 (1995).

3. The Institutional Press, the Internet, and the Paradox of the Press Clause

1. U.S. Const. amend. I.

2. *Id.* ("Congress shall make no law ... abridging the freedom of speech, or of the press").

3. 408 U.S. 665, 704 (1972).

4. *See generally, e.g.*, Cohen v. Cowles Media, 501 U.S. 663 (1991) (considering whether the First Amendment prohibits promissory estoppel claims against a newspaper by a confidential source); Zurcher v. Stanford Daily, 436 U.S. 547 (1978) (considering press claim for exemption from search warrant); *Branzburg*, 408 U.S. 665 (considering press claim for exemption from subpoena).

5. *See generally, e.g.*, Houchins v. KQED, Inc., 438 U.S. 1 (1978) (considering press claim for special access to prisons); Pell v. Procunier, 417 U.S. 817 (1974) (same); Saxbe v. Wash. Post Co., 417 U.S. 843 (1974) (same); The United States Senate Rules Governing Radio and Television Correspondents' Galleries, http://www.senate.gov/galleries/radiotv/criteria.htm (last visited May 27, 2011) (granting access to the congressional press corps to a defined set of media institutions).

6. *See, e.g.*, Freedom of Information Act, 5 U.S.C. §552(a)(4)(A)(ii) (2012) (imposing the cost of "document search, duplication, and review" on FOIA requests by members of the public, but exempting "a representative of the news media" from the costs of document search and review).

7. *See generally, e.g.*, Press-Enterprise v. Sup. Ct., 478 U.S. 1 (1986) (access to judicial proceedings); Waller v. Georgia, 467 U.S. 39 (1984) (same); Press-Enterprise v. Sup. Ct., 464 U.S. 501 (1984) (same); Globe Newspapers v. Super. Ct. Cal., 457 U.S. 596 (1982) (same); Richmond Newspapers v. Virginia, 448 U.S. 555 (1980) (same); Times-Picayune Pub. Corp. v. Schulingkamp, 419 U.S. 1301 (1974) (same).

8. *See, e.g.*, David A. Anderson, *Freedom of the Press*, 80 Tex. L. Rev. 429, 518–20 (2002) (hereinafter "Anderson, *Freedom*") (suggesting that the values of the Press Clause may in fact motivate legislative grants of privileges to the press).

9. The Supreme Court's concern with discrimination among members of the press has been most prevalent in the context of taxation. *See* Leathers v. Medlock, 499 U.S. 439 (1991); Texas Monthly v. Bullock, 489 U.S 1, 25 (1989) (White, J., concurring in the judgment); Arkansas Writers' Project v. Ragland, 481 U.S. 221 (1987); Minneapolis Star v. Minn. Comm'r of Revenue, 460 U.S. 575 (1983).

10. *Branzburg*, 408 U.S. at 704.

11. *See, e.g.*, Eugene Volokh, *Freedom for the Press as an Industry, or for the Press as a Technology? From the Framing to Today*, 160 U. Penn. L. Rev. 459 (2012) (arguing that the original meaning of the Press Clause understood "the press" as a technology, rather than an industry); *see also, e.g.*, First Nat'l Bank v. Bellotti, 435 U.S. 765, 799–800 (1978) (Burger, J., concurring) (arguing that the Speech Clause protects expression, while the Press Clause protects the freedom to disseminate that expression).

12. *See, e.g.*, Linda L. Berger, *Shielding the Unmedia: Using the Process of Journalism to Protect the Journalist's Privilege in an Infinite Universe of Publication*, 39 Hous. L. Rev. 1371, 1378 (2003) ("When everyone can be a member [of the Press], the club can no longer promise special treatment."); Sonja R. West, *Awakening the Press Clause*, 58 U.C.L.A. L. Rev.

1025, 1056 (2011) ("We need to resist the urge to overprotect press freedoms through an overly broad definition of the press for one primary reason—it results in a disappearance of press protections.").

13. Jos. Burstyn, Inc. v. Wilson, 343 U.S. 495, 502 (1952).

14. *See, e.g., id.* at 448 n. 97 (citing cases up to 1966); Cohen v. Cowles Media, 501 U.S. 663 (1991); Press-Enterprise v. Sup. Ct., 478 U.S. 1 (1986); Waller v. Georgia, 467 U.S. 39 (1984); Press-Enterprise v. Sup. Ct., 464 U.S. 501 (1984); Globe Newspapers v. Super. Ct. Cal., 457 U.S. 596 (1982); Richmond Newspapers v. Virginia, 448 U.S. 555 (1980); Zurcher v. Stanford Daily, 436 U.S. 547 (1978); Houchins v. KQED, Inc., 438 U.S. 1 (1978); Pell v. Procunier, 417 U.S. 817 (1974); Saxbe v. Wash. Post Co., 417 U.S. 843 (1974); Times-Picayune Pub. Corp. v. Schulingkamp, 419 U.S. 1301 (1974); Branzburg v. Hayes, 408 U.S. 665 (1972). *But see* Anderson, *Freedom, supra* note 8, at 448 n.97 (citing two cases dealing with non-members of the institutional press).

15. *See* Anderson, *Freedom, supra* note 8, at 448–49 (noting that in the mid-twentieth century, the identity of the press was "self-evident").

16. *See, e.g.,* Anderson, *Freedom, supra* note 8, at 448–49 ("The middle decades of the twentieth century—the 1930s, 1940s, 1950s, and 1960s—were the heyday of the Press Clause in the Supreme Court.")

17. *See, e.g.,* Suzanne Kirchoff, "The U.S. Newspaper Industry in Transition," Congressional Research Service, July 8, 2009, *available at* http://www.fas.org/sgp/crs/misc/R40700.pdf, at 4 (Even as late as the 1980s "many newspapers continued to enjoy extremely profitable, quasi-monopoly status in their communities."); *see also id.* at 3 (In 1930 only 21% of American cities had competing daily papers, a number that had fallen to 2% by 1971.); Eric Alterman, *Out of Print: the Death and Life of the American Newspaper*, New Yorker, Mar. 31, 2008, at 48. ("Until recently, own[ing] the dominant, or only, newspaper in a mid-sized American city was … a kind of license to print money.") (quoted in Ryan Benjamin Witte, *It's My News Too! Online Journalism and Discriminatory Access to the Congressional Periodical Press Gallery*, 12 Yale J. L. & Tech. 208, 214 (2009–2010).)

18. *Cf.* Adam Cohen, *The Media That Needs Citizens: The First Amendment and the Fifth Estate*, 85 So. Cal. L. Rev. 1, 75–83 (2011) (arguing that new media journalists should adopt an "architecture of accountability" that would aim at the same goals as the professional norms of traditional journalists).

19. Indeed, one can discern the beginning of the fracturing of the category "professional press" itself, as journalists come under more pressure to blog and otherwise act in ways not consistent with our traditional understanding of press norms. *See infra* note 58 (noting that traditional journalists at the New Orleans *Times-Picayune* will now be required to blog also); *see also* Paul Bradshaw, "When Journalists Blog: How It Changes What They Do," http://www.nieman.harvard.edu/reportsitem.aspx?id=100696 (discussing the results of a survey of journalists who have begun blogging).

20. One can overstate the novelty of this challenge. *See, e.g.,* Jos. Burstyn, Inc. v. Wilson, 343 U.S. 495, 501 (1952). (rejecting the argument that motion pictures do not transmit ideas, and quoting with approval an earlier Supreme Court opinion that said " 'The line between the informing and the entertaining is too elusive for the protection of that basic right (a free press).' " (quoting Winters v. New York, 333 U.S. 507, 510 (1948)). Nevertheless, at the very least the rise of Internet sites that explicitly seek to transmit information and opinion on matters of public affairs raises this challenge to new levels of difficulty.

21. Volokh, *supra* note 11.

22. Patrick Charles & Kevin O'Neill, "Saving the Press Clause From Ruin: The Customary Origins of a 'Free Press' As Interface to the Present and Future," ___ Utah. L. Rev. ___ (2012).

23. This understanding of the press echoes views identified by prominent European scholars on press freedom. *See, e.g.,* Eric Barendt, Freedom of Speech (2nd ed., 2005) 421–422 (identifying as "attractive" a view of freedom of the press that that sees it as instrumental, extending only as far as necessary in order to promote broader free speech values, in particular, self-government) (citing J. Lichtenberg, "Foundations and Limits of the Freedom of the Press," in J. Lichtenberg, ed., *Democracy and the Mass Media* 104 (Cambridge U.P. 1990)).

24. Randall Bezanson, *Whither the Press*, 97 Iowa L. Rev. 1259, 1271 (2012) ("Bezanson, *Whither*") (defining the function of the press as "first, the provision of information and opinion to the polity by a truth-seeking process of public-oriented judgment about relevance and need; and second, independence from government in the gathering, sifting and distribution of that information"); *see also* Randall Bezanson, *Means and Ends and Food Lion: The Tension Between Exemptions and Independence in Newsgathering By the Press*, 47 Emory L.J. 895, 896–897 (1998) (Bezanson, *Means and Ends*) (reflecting this basic understanding of press freedom).

25. West, *supra* note 12.

26. *See* Anderson, *Freedom, supra* note 8, at 510–11.

27. *See, e.g.,* Anderson, *Freedom, supra* note 8, at 510 (expressing concern that such challenges might lead government decision-makers to minimize the benefits provided to the press, for fear of provoking litigation alleging unconstitutional discrimination against other self-described press organs).

28. Cohen, *supra* note 18.

29. *See id.* at 3 ("As the Fourth Estate ebbs, an Internet-based Fifth Estate is emerging, including solo blogs, group-discussion websites, Twitter news bulletins, crowd-sourced news research, and WikiLeaks disclosures, among others. This new sector is a mixture of different kinds of actors: some are clearly journalists, some are communicators who would never be confused with journalists, and some lie in between.").

30. 783 F.2d 1532 (11th Cir. 1986).

31. *See id.* at 1533; *cf.* Witte, *supra* note 17, at 212 ("The online journalist might be a former reporter for a major publication who decides to research, report, and publish his own news online. She might be a journalism school graduate.").

32. *Jersawitz*, 783 F.2d at 1533.

33. *Id.* at 1534. This holding forced Jersawitz to assert a more general equal protection claim, which the court easily rejected. *See id.* at 1534–35.

34. *See, e.g.,* Pell v. Procunier, 417 U.S. 817 (1974).

35. *Cf.* Anderson, *Freedom, supra* note 8, at 510 (noting that, if Press Clause were construed to give special privileges to the press, anyone denied those privileges would have a potential constitutional claim).

36. *Compare* Leathers v. Medlock, 499 U.S. 439, 447 (1991) (upholding differential tax rates for different media when there was no realistic prospect that the scheme discriminated on the basis of content) *with* Arkansas Writers' Project v. Ragland, 481 U.S. 221 (1987) (striking down differential tax rates that were explicitly content-based).

37. *Compare, e.g.,* Ariz. Rev. Stat. Ann. §12-2214(A) (2011) (limiting applicability of subpoenas directed at "a person engaged in gathering, reporting, writing, editing, pub-

lishing or broadcasting news to the public, and which relates to matters within these news activities") *with* ALA. CODE § 12-21-142 (2011) (extending privileges to newspapers, construed by a court to exclude magazines) *and* ARK. CODE ANN. § 43-917 (2011) (extending a privilege to "any editor, reporter, or other writer for any newspaper or periodical, or radio station, or publisher of any newspaper or periodical or manager or owner of any radio station"). *But see* Dept. of Rev. v. Magazine Pub. of America, 604 So. 2d 459 (Fl. 1992) (striking down, as content-based and thus violative of the First Amendment, a state tax exemption for newspapers, when part of the definition of what constitutes a newspaper includes "whether it contains 'reports of current events and matters of general interest which appeal to a wide spectrum of the general public.'") (internal citation omitted).

38. *See* Matthew Nisbet, *Is America a Joke? Researcher Examines* The Daily Show's *Impact on Political Culture*, BIGTHINK (Sept. 15, 2010 11:29 PM), http://bigthink.com/ideas/24044 (noting a scholar's statement that *The Daily Show* was "able to challenge elite frames and offer alternative framing of issues"); see also Anderson, *Freedom, supra* note 8, at 507 ("[T]he familiar boundaries that [in the past] enabled us to identify the press ... could be replaced by more functional definitions, but that would require some consensus about what functions deserve special protection. The consensus reflected in conventional thought about freedom of the press was more elitist, more paternalistic, and more collectivist than is acceptable to present tastes."). *Cf.* Rancho Publications v. Sup. Ct., 68 Cal. App 4th 1538, 1544 (1999) (construing California's press shield law to require that the person invoking the shield prove that he was "engaged in legitimate journalistic purposes, or have exercised judgmental discretion in such activities").

39. *See infra.* note 72 (noting sociological and professional factors that influence how the professional press identifies and covers news); Anderson, *Freedom, supra* note 8, at 507 ; Cohen, *supra* note 18, at 34–37 (arguing that the traditional press's concern for objectivity "has diminished the American press's traditional role in promoting interest group formation"); Michael Schudson, *Why Democracies Need an Unlovable Press*, *in* FREEING THE PRESS: THE FIRST AMENDMENT IN ACTION (Timothy Cook, ed., 2005) 73–86.

40. *See, e.g.*, Cohen, *supra* note 18, at 27–28 (noting examples where the traditional media collectively made certain choices about what content to report and what to suppress, or at least ignore).

41. Anderson, *Freedom, supra* note 8, at 528–29.

42. *See* Bezanson, *Whither, supra.* note 24 (challenging Professor Volokh's "press-as-technology" conclusion); Charles & O'Neill, *supra.* note 22 (concluding that the founding generation's understanding of "the press" was influenced at least in part by the role newspapers had played in promoting democratic self-government).

43. *Cf. id.* at 441– 45 (suggesting the difficulty of defining the press, for purposes of the Press Clause, as all media).

44. Today, by contrast, a large number of major press entities comprise but a part of a corporate conglomerate's holdings. Disney owns ABC, until recently General Electric owned NBC and, arguably, the Washington Post Corporation is primarily focused on its Kaplan educational assets rather than the *Post* itself. *See, e.g.*, *id.* at 455–57 (noting several of these, and other, examples).

45. 408 U.S. at 704.

46. Part of that ideal conception may have also derived from the personalities of many of the owners and managers of press institutions of that era—personalities that valued the

professional qualities of excellence, objectivity and independence from advertisers. *See, e.g., id.* at 452–53 (noting examples from newspapers and broadcast entities).

47. On the other hand, at least one scholar has argued that an embryonic institutional press had come into existence during the Revolutionary period, and showed at least some of the governmental "watchdog" character that Justice Stewart identified as the primary role of what he considered "the Press." Charles Clark, *The Press the Founders Knew, in* FREEING THE PRESS, *supra* note 37, at 46–48.

48. *See* Anderson, *Freedom, supra* note 8, at 506 (noting the Court's gradual turn to using the more general, and perhaps pejorative, term "media" in place of "press").

49. *See, e.g.,* Anderson, *Freedom, supra.* note 8 at 470–471.

50. *See* Bezanson, *supra* note 24, at 1271 ("[F]irst, the provision of information and opinion to the polity by a truth-seeking process of public-oriented judgment about relevance and need; and second, independence from government in the gathering, sifting and distribution of that information.... [T]he brilliance of the idea of the press ... was its premise of disinterestedness and devotion to the ... ideal of truth.")

51. *See, e.g.,* Chris Edelson, "Lies, Damned Lies, and Journalism: Why Journalists Are Failing to Vindicate First Amendment Values and How a New Definition of 'The Press' Can Help," http://ssrn.com/abstract=2106096.

52. *See* Cohen, *supra* note 18, at 75–83.

53. *See supra.* note 12.

54. Berger, *supra* note 12, at 1411–16.

55. Russell Weaver, Clive Walker & Geoffrey Bennett, *Can Newspapers Survive in an Internet Era?* (noting both online news organizations of national scope, such as the *Huffington Post,* and hyper-local news blogs (citing Bob Garfield, Is Hyperlocal the Future of News?, National Public Radio, On the Media (Jan. 28, 2011), http://www.onthemedia.org/2010/jul/16/is-hyperlocal-the-future-of-news/transcript/); *but see* text accompanying *infra* notes 58–60 (noting how some media outlets are melding traditional and non-traditional journalistic functions).

56. *Cf.* O'Grady, 139 Cal. App. 4th at 1457 ("declin[ing] the implicit invitation to embroil [itself] in questions of what constitutes 'legitimate journalis[m]' despite precedent identifying that inquiry as relevant to when the state's reporter shield law applies").

57. *See generally* Berger, *supra* note 12; *see also* Kaufman v. Islamic Soc. Of Arlington, 291 S.W.3d 130 (Tex. App. Ct. 2009) (determining that the question of who is entitled to journalistic privileges turns, at least in part, on consideration of the editorial process).

58. *See, e.g.,* Dylan Stableford, *New Orleans to Lose its Daily Newspaper,* THE CUTLINE (May 24, 2012), http://news.yahoo.com/blogs/cutline/orleans-soon-no-longer-daily-newspaper-153740196.html (noting that one newspaper's traditional reporters are now expected to blog throughout the day).

59. *See, e.g.,* Frédéric Filloux, *Aggregators: The Good Ones vs. The Looters,* MONDAY NOTE (Sept. 19, 2010, 6:58 PM), http://www.mondaynote.com/2010/09/19/aggregators-the-good-ones-vs-the-looters/.

60. *See* Michael Calderone, *Huffington Post Awarded Pulitzer Prize,* Huffington Post (April 17, 2012, 7:47 AM) http://www.huffingtonpost.com/2012/04/16/huffington-post-pulitzer-prize-2012_n_1429169.html. *See also* Kirchoff, *supra.* note 17 at 11 (noting the general trend of some news sites combining aggregation and original reporting).

61. *See, e.g.,* Cohen, *supra* note 18, at 26 (noting examples).

62. *See also, e.g.,* O'Grady v. Sup. Ct., 139 Cal. App. 4th 1423, 1457 (206) (suggesting that the decline of space scarcity with the rise of online communication alters the way courts should review the question whether an online communicator exercised editorial judgment when simply reprinting a document rather than editing it for presentation to the public). This issue arose again when observers noted that the traditional journalism sources that disseminated information posted by Wikileaks exercised traditional editorial judgment when declining to post or publicize, unredacted, all the information possessed by Wikileaks. *See* "Anger as Wikileaks Releases All U.S. Cables Unredacted," http://www.bbc.co.uk/news/world-us-canada-14765837, Sept. 2, 2011.

63. *See* Bradshaw, *supra.* note 19 (discussing journalists' views of how blogging impacts their professional conduct).

64. *See* Marshall McLuhan & Quentin Fiore, The Medium is the Message (Jerome Agel as Coordinator, 1967).

65. *See, e.g.,* Nisbet, *supra.* note 38 (noting a scholar's statement that *The Daily Show* was "able to challenge elite frames and offer alternative framing of issues"); *see also* Anderson, *Freedom, supra* note 8, at 507 ("[T]he familiar boundaries that [in the past] enabled us to identify the press ... could be replaced by more functional definitions, but that would require some consensus about what functions deserve special protection. The consensus reflected in conventional thought about freedom of the press was more elitist, more paternalistic, and more collectivist than is acceptable to present tastes.").

66. *See* text accompanying *supra* notes 30−35.

67. Jersawitz v. Hanberry, 783 F.2d 1532, 1534 (11th Cir. 1986).

68. *See* Anderson, *supra* note 15.

69. *See, e.g.,* Randall Bezanson, *The Developing Law of Editorial Judgment,* 78 Neb. L. Rev. 754, 760 (1999) (suggesting that a reporter's privilege to withhold sources should be available when the publication is "useful and important for the maintenance of freedom in a self-governing society").

70. *See, e.g.,* RonNell Anderson Jones, *Rethinking Reporters' Privilege,* ___ Mich. L. Rev. (2012) (MS at 17 & n. 157) (suggesting that providing protection to the gathering of information useful for democratic self-government necessarily requires distinguishing speech based on its content).

71. *Cf.* Anderson, *Freedom, supra* note 8, at 507 ("[T]echnological and business changes ... are obliterating the familiar boundaries that enabled us to identify the press.... The confluence of technological, business, and ideological forces now at work, together with constitutional and political objections to the discrimination that press preferences requires, may cause 'the press' as a legally preferred institution to simply disappear in an ocean of information.").

72. *See* Schudson, *supra* note 38, at 73−86 (discussing the sociological and professional factors that influence how the institutional press defines and covers news); Cohen, *supra* note 18, at 27–29, 31–37 (noting instances where new media do a superior job in vindicating the values of a free press).

73. *Cf.* Barendt, *supra* note 23 (identifying contribution to democratic debate as a possible way to identify persons or conduct protected by freedom of the press guarantees).

74. *See* Volokh, *supra* note 11.

75. *See, e.g.,* Consumers' Union v. Periodical Correspondents' Assn, 515 F.2d 1341 (5th Cir. 1975) (finding non-justiciable a challenge to Congress's limitations regarding the press entities that enjoy the right to enter the press section of the congressional gallery).

76. *See, e.g.,* Bezanson, *Whither, supra* note 24; Bezanson, *Means and Ends, supra* note 24.

77. *Cf.* Anderson, *Freedom, supra* note 8 at 473 (suggesting that Bezanson's criterion of concern for the public interest may be too narrow, to the extent it ignores the role of the press in creating a community by deciding which information is important for the community to receive).

78. *See, e.g.,* Archibald Cox, *The Role of Congress in Constitutional Determinations,* 40 CINCINNATI L. REV. 199, 230 (1971) (some government-drawn lines are arbitrary "in the sense that [they] make[] a sharp cut off at some point in a range shading from one extreme to the other by infinitely small differences of degree"); William D. Araiza, *The Section 5 Power and the Rational Basis Standard of Equal Protection,* 79 Tulane L. Rev. 519, 546 (2005) (arguing that legislatures are better at drawing lines that are arbitrary in this sense).

79. *See, e.g.,* Lee v. Dept. of Justice, 401 F.Supp.2d 123,140 (D.D.C. 2005) ("The proliferation of communications media in the modern world makes it impossible to construct a reasonable or useful definition of reporter.").

80. *Cf.* Charles & O'Neill, *supra.* note 22 (reviewing the pre-1787 intellectual history of the concept of "freedom of the press" as evidence of the framers' understanding of the term).

81. *Cf.* Anderson, *Freedom, supra* note 8, at 515 ("[A]nswers [to the questions arising out of preferential treatment for the press] do not flow from constitutional principle, but from judgments about matters of degree and prudence"). *Compare O'Grady,* 139 Cal. App. 4th at 1457 (refusing to "embroil" itself in the question what constitutes legitimate journalism) *with* Time, Inc. v. Price v. Time, Inc. 416 F.3d 1327 (11th Cir. 2005) (applying the literal wording of an Alabama shield statute that protected newspapers but not magazines, to exclude a sports magazine from its protection).

82. *See* Geoffrey Stone, *Why We Need a Federal Reporter's Privilege,* 34 HOFSTRA L. REV. 39, 47 (2005) ("Courts necessarily proceed on the basis of precedent, and they are quite sensitive to the dangers of 'slippery slopes.' Legislation, however, properly considers problems 'one step at a time' and legislators need not reconcile each law with every other law in order to meet their responsibilities. For the Court to recognize a journalist-source privilege but not, for example, a privilege of journalists to commit burglary or wiretapping, would pose a serious challenge to the judicial process. But for Congress to address the privilege issue without fretting over journalistic burglary or wiretapping is simply not a problem. This is a fundamental difference between the judicial and legislative processes.") (paragraph break omitted); *see also* Cox, *supra* note 78 at 231 (arguing that the drawing of such distinctions reflect "questions of fact in the first instance, characterization or degree after the raw data is assembled, and ultimately of balance and relative importance" and that the drawing of such distinctions is characteristically allocated to legislatures).

83. Anderson, *Freedom, supra* note 8, at 518.

84. *See, e.g.,* Robert Post & Reva Siegel, *Equal Protection By Law: Federal Antidiscrimination Legislation After* Morrison *and* Kimel, 110 YALE L.J. 441 (2000) (calling for judicial deference to federal legislation implementing the Equal Protection Clause).

85. *Compare, e.g.,* First National Bank v. Bellotti, 435 U.S. 765, 795 (Burger, C.J., concurring) (noting the difficulty of distinguishing between press corporations and other corporation, and thus expressing caution about allowing restrictions on corporate political speech) *with* City of Cleburne v. Cleburne Living Center, 473 U.S. 432 (1985) (refusing to grant heightened equal protection scrutiny to the mentally retarded, given the difficulties courts would face in reviewing classifications involving the mentally retarded, and in deciding

claims for heightened protection by groups similar to the mentally retarded). This argument in favor of legislative action echoes Lawrence Sager's classic argument about judicial under-enforcement of constitutional norms. *See* Lawrence Sager, *Fair Measure: The Legal Status of Underenforced Constitutional Norms*, 91 HARV. L. REV. 1212 (1978).

86. Thanks to Professor Joseph Tomain for suggesting this.

87. *Cf.* Anderson, "Freedom," *supra*. note 8 at 518 ("Constitutional adjudication is necessarily general; it is difficult to argue that the First Amendment guarantees access to government records except those relating to bank examinations or geological reports. A constitutional right of access would be broad, at least until the litigation process produced specific exceptions. Maybe the press argument that there should be fewer exceptions to the rights of access is correct, but that should be decided on the merits, not imposed by the unavoidable generality of constitutional decision-making.").

88. *See, e.g.*, Time, Inc. v. Price v. Time, Inc. 416 F.3d 1327 (11th Cir. 2005) (applying the literal wording of an Alabama shield statute that protected newspapers but not magazines, to exclude a sports magazine from its protection).

89. *See, e.g.*, Jones, *supra*. note 70 at MS 17 ("[W]hile perhaps expected and even appropriate when designing the contours of a reporter's privilege as a statutory matter, [the definitional line-drawing implicit in defining the press] is at best knotty as a basis for constitutional doctrine") (internal citation omitted).

90. *See, e.g.*, Citizens United v. Federal Election Comm'n, 130 S.Ct. 876 (2010) (noting the presumptive unconstitutionality of both these types of speech restrictions).

91. *See, e.g.*, Minneapolis Star v. Minn. Comm'r of Revenue, 460 U.S. 575 (1983) (expressing concern whenever government singles out the press, or distinguishes among its members); *Magazine Publishers, supra*. note 37 (finding a state tax exemption for newspapers content-based and therefore unconstitutional when the identification criteria entail government review of the publication's content).

92. Anderson, *Freedom, supra* note 8, at 512.

93. *See* text accompanying *supra* notes 84–85.

94. *Cf.* Katzenbach v. Morgan, 384 U.S. 641, 656–658 (1966) (considering the argument that congressional legislation designed to enforce the Equal Protection Clause itself violates that clause); *see also* Northwest Austin Mun. Util. Dist. No. 1 v. Holder, 129 S. Ct. 2504, 2512 (2009) (expressing concern that the race-conscious government action mandated under parts of the Voting Rights Act might itself violate the Fourteenth Amendment).

95. *Cf.* Leathers v. Medlock, 469 U.S. 439 (1991) (allowing government to discriminate among different members of the press as long as the discrimination does not narrowly single out the burdened members and is content-neutral); *see also* Stone, *supra* note 82 at 48 (arguing that the definitional problem "poses a much more manageable issue in the context of legislation," and arguing that legislative distinctions ought to be upheld as long as they are viewpoint neutral and reasonable).

96. 384 U.S. 641 (1966).

97. *See, e.g.*, City of Boerne v. Flores, 521 U.S. 507 (1997) (holding that Congress exceeded its power to enforce the Free (religious) Exercise Clause when it enacted a statute that reinstated a religious freedom test the Court itself had rejected several years earlier); Board of Trustees v. Garrett, 531 U.S. 356 (2001) (holding that Congress exceeded its power to enforce the Equal Protection Clause when it enacted a statute protecting a group the Court itself had already decided did not merit heightened equal protection scrutiny); Dickerson v.

United States, 530 U.S. 428 (2000) (striking down a federal statute governing the admissibility of prisoners' confessions when that law adopted a standard for judging the confession's voluntariness that conflicted with a judicially-announced standard the Court had earlier suggested was simply a safe-harbor, prophylactic rule that was not itself constitutionally mandated).

98. *See, e.g.*, Bezanson, *Means and Ends, supra* note 24 (arguing that the press's independence from government would be compromised if it came to depend on government's provision of special benefits).

99. *See* Anderson, *Freedom, supra* note 8, at 514.

4. Does the Internet Require Rethinking First Amendment Theory?

1. *See* Freedman v. Maryland, 380 U.S. 51 (1965), Times Film v. Chicago, 365 U.S. 43 (1961).

2. *See* City of Erie v. PAP's A.M., 529 U.S. 277 (2000).

3. *See* Metromedia, Inc. v. City of San Diego, 453 U.S. 490 (1981).

4. *See* Kovacs v. Cooper, 366 U.S. 77 (1949).

5. *See* Schneider v. State, 308 U.S. 147 (1939).

6. *See* e.g. Frisby v. Schultz, 487 U.S. 474 (1988).

7. Movies may have been an exception at one time to this principle (*see* Times Films v. Chicago, 365 U.S. 43 (1961)), but that no longer seems to be the law. (*See* Freedman v. Maryland, 380 U.S. 51 (1965).)

8. *See* City of Erie v. PAP's A.M., 529 U.S. 277 (2000).

9. *See* Ward v. Rock Against Racism, 491 U.S. 781 (1989).

10. Though that's not enough to preclude them. *See* Schneider v. State, 308 U.S. 147 (1939).

11. *Cf* Frisby v. Schultz, 487 U.S. 474 (1988), upholding a prohibition of focused picketing of a residence.

12. See http://www.snopes.com/.

13. In my view, ill. *See* e.g. Arnold H. Loewy, Obscenity, Pornography, and First Amendment Theory, 2. W&M Bill of Rights J. 471 (1993).

14. *See* Ginzburg v. United States, 383 U.S. 463 (1966) (dissenting opinion); Jacobellis v. Ohio, 378 U.S. 184, 197 (concurring opinion).

15. *See* e.g. United States v. Williams, 553 U.S. 285 (2008) (Internet), New York v. Ferber, 458 U.S. 747 (1982) (Elsewhere).

16. Specifically, New York Times v. Sullivan 376 U.S. 254 (1964), and its progeny.

17. *See* RUSSELL WEAVER, FROM GUTENBERG TO THE INTERNET: FREE SPEECH, ADVANCING TECHNOLOGY AND THE IMPLICATIONS FOR DEMOCRACY (2013).

18. 376 U.S. 254 (1964).

19. 132 S. Ct. 2537 (2012).

20. 18 U.S.C. §704.

21. 617 F. 3d 1198 (2010). Rehearing *en banc* denied, 638 F. 3d 666 (2011).

22. 638 F. 3d at 674–675.

23. *See* Arnold H. Loewy, A Dialogue on Hate Speech, 36 F.S.U. L. Rev. 67 (2008).

24. *See* Russell L. Weaver, Nicholas Delpierre, and Laurence Boissier, Holocaust Denial and Governmentally Declared "Truth": French and American Perspectives, 41 T.T. L. Rev 495 (2009).

25. For example, in Beauharnais v. Illinois, 343 U.S. 250 (1952), the Supreme Court dealt with a white supremacist who had many demeaning things to say about African-Americans, including their "rapes and robberies." Could we imagine holding a trial whereby a trier of fact determined truth. Would any rapes and robberies suffice? Would it have to be more than the number committed by Caucasians? Would any number have the be discounted by the quality of the neighborhood in order to be "true"? etc.

26. *See* Butler v. Michigan, 352 U.S. 380 (1957) at p.383. See also Reno v. American Civil Liberties Union, 521 U.S. 844 (1997).

27. *See* Thomas v. Collins, 323 U.S. 516, 545 (1945) (concurring opinion).

5. The Promise and Peril of Protesting in the Internet Era

1. Sarah Joseph, *Social Media, Political Change and Human Rights*, 35 B.C. Int'l & Comp. L. Rev.145, 157–63 (2012).

2. Leonid Bershidsky, *Post a Link, Go To Jail: Russia Tries to Silence Protest*, Bloomberg.com, July 18, 2012, available at http://www.bloomberg.com/news/2012-07-18/post-a-link-go-to-jail-russia-tries-to-silence-protest.html.

3. Adam Gabbatt, *Canada Student Protests Erupt into Political Crisis with Mass Arrests*, The Guardian (London), May 24, 2012, available at http://www.guardian.co.uk/world/2012/may/24/canada-student-fee-protest-arrests.

4. Ronald Krotoszynski & Clint Carpenter, *The Return of Seditious Libel*, 55 UCLA L. Rev. 1239 (2008); Timothy Zick, *Speech and Spatial Tactics*, 84 Tex. L. Rev. 581 (2006).

5. Zick, *supra* note 4.

6. Christina E. Wells, *Privacy and Funeral Protests*, 87 N. C. L. Rev. 151 (2008).

7. Kevin Francis O'Neill, *Disentangling the Law of Public Protest*, 45 Loy. L. Rev. 411, 463–74 (1999).

8. *See generally* Alicia D'Addario, *Policing Protest: Protecting Dissent and Preventing Violence Through First And Fourth Amendment Law*, 31 NYU Rev. L. & Soc. Change 97 (2006); Jerome H. Skolnick, *Democratic Policing Confronts Terror and Protest*, 33 Syr. J. Int'l L. & Com. 191 (2005). On policing of the Occupy movement, *see* Mary Slosson, *Oakland Police May Face Sanctions Over Handling of Occupy Protests*, Reuters.com, May 2, 2012, available at http://www.reuters.com/article/2012/05/02/us-usa-occupy-may1-oakland-idUSBRE8 4104T20120502.

9. Zick, *supra* note 4, at 585 (quoting Martin v. City of Struthers 319 U.S. 141, 143 (1943)); *see also* Owen M. Fiss, *Silence on the Street Corner*, 26 Suffolk U. L. Rev. 1 (1992).

10. Perry Educ. Ass'n v. Perry Local Educators' Ass'n 460 U.S. 37, 45 (1983). *See infra* nn. 19–22 and accompanying text.

11. *See, e.g.* Timothy Zick, *Space, Place, and Speech: The Expressive Topography,* 74 Geo. Wash. L. Rev. 439, 457 (2006).

12. Robert C. Post, *Recuperating First Amendment Doctrine*, 47 Stan. L. Rev. 1264 (1997); *see also* C. Edwin Baker, *Unreasoned Reasonableness: Mandatory Parade Permits and Time,*

Place and Manner Regulations, 78 Nw. U. L. Rev. 937, 937; Krotoszynski & Carpenter, *supra* note 4, at 1260–61; Zick, *supra* note 11, at 440.

13. *See* http://sopastrike.com/ (discussing online strike).

14. *See, e.g.,* http://occupywallst.org/ (Occupy Movement's webpage); Seth F. Kreimer, *Technologies of Protest: Insurgent Social Movements and the First Amendment in the Era of the Internet*, 150 U. Pa. L. Rev. 119, 131–42 (2001) (discussing social organizing on the Internet).

15. Samuel J. Rascoff, *Domesticating Intelligence*, 83 S. Cal. L. Rev. 575 (2010).

16. Karson K. Thompson, *Not Like An Egyptian: Cybersecurity and the Internet Kill Switch Debate*, 90 Tex. L. Rev. 465, 465 (2011).

17. Seth F. Kreimer, *Censorship By Proxy: The First Amendment, Internet Intermediaries, and the Problem of the Weakest Link*, 155 U. Pa. L. Rev. 11 (2006).

18. Hudgens v. NLRB, 424 U.S. 507, 520 (1976); Lloyd Corp. v. Tanner, 407 U.S. 551, 568 (1972).

19. Ashutosh Bhagwat, *Associational Speech*, 120 Yale L.J. 978, 1016 (2011) ("[W]here if not in the public forum can public assembly occur?").

20. Hague v. CIO, 307 U.S. 496, 515 (1939).

21. Perry Education Ass'n v. Perry Local Educators Ass'n, 460 U.S. 37, 45 (1983).

22. *Hague*, 307 U.S. at 516.

23. *Perry*, 460 U.S. at 46; *see also* R.A.V. v. City of St. Paul, 505 U.S. 377, 382 (1992).

24. *See, e.g.,* Hill v. Colorado, 530 U.S. 703 (2000) (Colorado law restricting certain protests near health clinics); Grayned v. City of Rockford, 408 U.S. 104 (1972) (statute regulating disruptions around school as applied to protestors). There are strong arguments that some statutes regulating protestors in certain spaces are not content neutral, *see infra* pp. 42–46 and accompanying text, but to the extent that they are considered to be so, the Court applies intermediate scrutiny.

25. Clark v. Community for Creative Non-Violence, 468 U.S. 288, 293 (1984).

26. *See Clark*, 468 U.S. at 293 (upholding National Park Service regulation banning protestors from sleeping overnight in a national park); Frisby v. Shultz, 487 U.S. 474 (1988) (upholding ordinance banning targeted picketing near residential homes); Ward v. Rock Against Racism, 491 U.S. 781 (1989) (upholding a municipal regulation requiring concert performers to use city amplification equipment); Kovacs v. Cooper, 336 U.S. 77, 81 (1949) (upholding law banning use of amplified sound trucks on city streets). For discussion of outcomes after applying this test, *see* Ashutosh Bhagwat, *The Test That Ate Everything: Intermediate Scrutiny in First Amendment Jurisprudence*, 2007 Ill. L. Rev. 783.

27. *See* Lovell v. City of Griffin, 303 U.S. 444, 451–53 (1938); City of Lakewood v. Plain Dealer Publishing Co., 486 U.S. 750, 759–60 (1988).

28. Cox v. New Hampshire, 312 U.S. 569, 574 (1941).

29. *Id.* at 575–76.

30. *Perry*, 460 U.S. at 45; Cornelius v. NAACP Legal Defense & Educ. Fund, Inc., 473 U.S. 788, 802 (1985).

31. Ark. Educ. Tele. Comm'n v. Forbes, 523 U.S. 666, 677 (1998); *Cornelius*, 473 U.S. at 802.

32. *Perry*, 460 U.S. at 45.

33. *Id.* at 46.

34. *Id.* The Court has also discussed a "limited public forum," which is a designated forum that the government can limit by speaker or subject matter. *Perry*, 460 U.S. at 46

n.7. As others have noted, however, the distinction between the limited public forum and the non-public forum is theoretically incoherent. Zick, *supra* note 11, at 439 n.2. Furthermore, the Court applies essentially the same rules in the limited public forum as in the non-public forum. *See* Pleasant Grove City v. Summum, 555 U.S. 460 (2009).

35. Zick, *supra* note 4, at 615.

36. Robert C. Post, *Between Governance and Management: The History and Theory of the Public Forum*, 34 UCLA L. Rev. 1713, 1759–60 (1987).

37. *See generally* Zick, *supra* note 11. For example, a quiet sit-in in a public library to protest racial discrimination at that library may be far more effective and important to protestors than a protest held on a public street. *See* Brown v. Louisiana, 383 U.S. 131 (1966).

38. Krotoszynski & Carpenter, *supra* note 4, at 1260–61; Post, *supra* note 12, at 1261–65; Christina E. Wells, *Fear and Loathing in Constitutional Decision-making*, 2005 Wiscon. L. Rev. 115, 211; Zick, *supra* note 11, at 440.

39. Krotoszynski & Carpenter, *supra* note 4, at 1258–59; William E. Lee, *Lonely Pamphleteers, Little People, and the Supreme Court: the Doctrine of Time, Place and Manner Regulations of Expression*, 54 Geo. Wash. L. Rev. 757, 782 (1986); Wells *supra* note 38, at 214; Zick, *supra* note 4, at 598.

40. *Ward*, 491 U.S. at 800; Turner Broad. Sys., Inc. v. FCC, 520 U.S. 180, 195–96 (1997); *see also* Krotoszynski & Carpenter, *supra* note 4, at 1260–61.

41. *See supra* notes 4–8.

42. Krotoszynski & Carpenter, *supra* note 4, at 1265–75; Zick, *supra* note 4, at 634–35.

43. Wells, *supra* note 38, at 163–68, 175–78; Zick, *supra* note 4, at 633.

44. Zick, *supra* note 4, at 635.

45. Baker, *supra* note 12, at 971–72.

46. Zick, *supra* note 4, at 634.

47. Baker, *supra* note 12, at 946, 1014. Some courts strike down permitting requirements for small groups in order to protect spontaneity. Grossman v. City of Portland, 33 F.3d 1200 (9th Cir. 1994). But they generally uphold requirements for large groups assuming they meet the Supreme Court's criteria described *supra* nn. 27–29.

48. Baker, *supra* note 12, at 942; William E. Lee, *Modernizing the Law of Open Air Speech: The Hughes Court and the Birth of Content Neutral Balancing*, 13 Wm. & M.B. Rt. J. 119, 1261–63 (2005).

49. In keeping with the Court's original vision for such schemes, *see supra* nn. 27–29, most ordinances contain a provision allowing officials to deny a permit if a protest "would present an unreasonable danger to health or safety." *See* Thomas v. Chicago Park Dist., 534 U.S. 316, 318 n.1 (2002).

50. Baker, *supra* note 12, at 942 ("[N]egative consequences of dissent often appear more likely than they are in fact, and those consequences that actually will occur often appear more objectionable, worse, than they actually would be."); *see also* Wells, *supra* note 38, at 158–72, 211–14 (discussing psychological phenomena leading to overassessment of risk both generally and in context of protests).

51. D'Addario, *supra* note 8, at 97 n.6.

52. *Id.* at 114–23 (discussing Fourth and First Amendment scrutiny for protestor arrests).

53. Baker, *supra* note 12, at 981.

54. For a discussion of various technologies, *see* Joseph, *supra* note 1, at 146–50.

55. Kreimer, *supra* note 14, at 124–25, 131–33.

56. David Kirkpatrick & Mona El-Naggar, *Protest's Old Guard Falls in Behind the Young*, N.Y. Times, Jan. 31, 2011, at A1; *see also* Russell L. Weaver, From Gutenberg to the Internet: Free Speech, Advancing Technology, and the Implications for Democracy 75–85 (in press) (manuscript on file with the author).

57. *See* http://en.wikipedia.org/wiki/Occupy_Wall_Street. *See also* Weaver, *supra* note 56, at 105.

58. Joseph, *supra* note 1, at 157–61; Weaver, *supra* note 56, at 75–80.

59. For the video depicting the pepper spray incident *see*, *NYPD Police Pepper Spray Occupy Wall Street Protestors (Anthony Bologna)*, http://www.youtube.com/watch?v=TZ05rWx1pig. On the lack of media coverage, *see* Nate Silver, *Police Clashes Spur Coverage of Wall Street Protests*, FiveThirtyEight, Oct. 7, 2011, http://fivethirtyeight.blogs.nytimes.com/2011/10/07/police-clashes-spur-coverage-of-wall-street-protests/.

60. *See* Silver, *supra* note 59; Weaver, *supra* note 56, at 106.

61. Kreimer, *supra* note 14, at 127.

62. Heather "Digby" Parton, *Militarizing the Police: How the Drug War and 9/11 Led to Battle Dressed Cops Cracking Down on Peaceful Protests*, AlterNet, Nov. 14, 2011, http://www.alternet.org/occupywallst/153062/militarizing_the_police:_how_the_drug_war_and_9_11_led_to_battle-dressed_cops_cracking_down_on_peaceful_protests?page=entire.

63. Erika Niewdowski, *Occupy Wall Street Protestors Sue Over Free Speech, Use of Force*, Huff. Post, Dec. 22, 2011, http://www.huffingtonpost.com/2011/12/22/occupy-wall-street-protesters-sue-free-speech_n_1166372.html; Matt Taibbi, *UC Pepper Spray Incident Reveals Weakness Up Top*, Rolling Stone, Nov. 22, 2011, available at http://www.rollingstone.com/politics/blogs/taibblog/uc-davis-pepper-spray-incident-reveals-weakness-up-top-20111122 (linking to video).

64. *Id.*; Timothy Zick, Speech Out of Doors: Preserving First Amendment Liberties in Public Places 254–55 (2009). Police use different models when policing protests, ranging from "negotiated management," which requires police to negotiate with protestors before a protest occurs, to "escalated force," where police use force to shut down protests when protestors resist police direction. One or any combination of these methods can be used at any protest. *See* Jennifer Earl, *A Lawyer's Guide to Repression Literature*, 67 Nat'l Law. Guild Rev. 3, 15–17 (2010).

65. http://www.change.org/about.

66. U.S. Const., amend. 1. Individuals have started petitions seeking change by businesses as well as government officials. *See* http://www.change.org/petitions/tell-bank-of-america-no-5-debit-card-fees (discussing successful petition to stop bank debit card fee).

67. *See* Jack C. Schechter, Trademark Law Community Blog, Jan. 20, 2012, available at 2012 WLNR 208008. These criticisms stem from provisions in SOPA that allow government officials to obtain court orders (1) requiring Internet Service Providers to prevent subscribers from accessing "foreign infringing sites"; (2) barring search engines, such as Google, from providing the domain name of infringing sites if asked; (3) barring Payment Network Providers, such as PayPal, from completing payment transactions related to such sites; and (4) barring Internet Advertising Services from providing ads for such sites or from receiving compensation from those sites. *Id.*

68. Jenna Wortham, *Public Outcry over Anti-Piracy Bills Began as Grassroots Grumbling*, N.Y. Times, Jan. 19, 2012, available at http://www.nytimes.com/2012/01/20/technology/public-outcry-over-antipiracy-bills-began-as-grass-roots-grumbling.html?_r=1&pagewanted=all.

69. *Id.*

70. *Id.*

71. *See* http://en.wikipedia.org/wiki/Protests_against_SOPA_and_PIPA#cite_note-54. Visitors to the page could also look up their congressional representatives. A screen shot of the Wikipedia page as well as several other pages is available at the above-referenced citation.

72. Wortham, *supra* note 68.

73. *See* Kreimer, *supra* note 14, for discussions of other forms of online activism.

74. Mark Fenster, *Disclosure's Effects: WikiLeaks and Transparency*, 97 Iowa L. Rev. 753, 759 (2012).

75. *Id.* at 762–64; Yochai Benkler, *A Free Irresponsible Press: Wikileaks and the Battle Over the Soul of the Networked Fourth Estate*, 46 Harv. C.R.-C.L. L. Rev. 311, 315–30 (2011). Professor Benkler notes that WikiLeaks "goes out of its way" to assure that the overwhelming bulk of the material it posts is accurate, thus distinguishing itself from other aggregation sites such as Liveleak. *Id.* at 320.

76. *See* Michael D. Horvath, U.S. Army Counterintelligence Ctr., *Wikileaks.org—An Online Reference to Foreign Intelligence Services, Insurgents, or Terrorist Groups?* (Mar. 18, 2008), available at http://www.wired.com/images_blogs/threatlevel/2010/03/wikithreat.pdf.

77. 18 U.S.C. 793(e) prohibits anyone who has "unauthorized possession of … information relating to the national defense which information the possessor has reason to believe could be used to the injury of the United States or the advantage of any foreign nation" from "willfully communicat[ing], deliver[ing], [or] transmit[ing] … the same to anyone not entitled to receive it." This is the law most mentioned in connection with prosecutions of Assange.

78. *See, e.g.,* Ewan MacAskill, *Julian Assange Like a High-Tech Terrorist, says Joe Biden,* The Guardian (London), Dec. 19, 2010, available at http://www.guardian.co.uk/media/2010/dec/19/assange-high-tech-terrorist-biden; Fox News' *Bob Beckel Calls For 'Illegally' Killing Assange: 'A Dead Man Can't Leak Stuff'* (VIDEO), The Huffington Post (Dec. 7, 2010, 5:50 PM), http://www.huffingtonpost.com/2010/12/07/fox-news-bob-beckel-calls_n_793467.html.

79. *See, e.g.,* Jonathan Peters, *WikiLeaks, the First Amendment, and the Press*, Harv. L. & Pol'y Rev., Apr. 18, 2011, available at http://hlpronline.com/2011/04/wikileaks-the-first-amendment-and-the-press/.

80. *See* Christina E. Wells, *Contextualizing Disclosure's Effects, WikiLeaks, Balancing, and the First Amendment*, forthcoming Iowa L. Rev. Bull. (2012) (discussing law and likely application to Assange if prosecuted in the U.S.).

81. *See* Fenster, *supra* note 74, at 774–81 (discussing Assange's theory of radical resistance through disclosure).

82. *See* Oxford English Dictionary, available at http://www.oed.com/view/Entry/153191?rskey=ZiLE8C&result=1&isAdvanced=false#eid (defining protest as "[t]he expression of social, political, or cultural dissent from a policy or course of action …").

83. Whether the point of protecting free expression is to force government officials to listen to one's petition for redress of grievance, *see* Krotoszynski & Carpenter, *supra* note 4, or to allow people to assemble for purposes of self-governance, *see* Bhagwat, *supra* note 19, or so that public opinion serves as a check on government action, *see* Vincent Blasi, *The Checking Value in First Amendment Theory*, 1977 Am. B. Found. Research J. 521, most free speech theories have some form of government accountability as a primary goal.

84. United States v. Rosen, 445 F. Supp. 2d 602 (E.D. Va. 2006).

85. *See* Wells, *supra* note 80 for further discussion.

86. New York Times v. Sullivan, 376 U.S. 264 (1964).

87. Joseph, *supra* note 1, at 167–68; Rascoff, *supra* note 15, at 580 n.16; Matthew C. Waxman, *National Security Federalism in the Age of Terror*, 64 Stan. L. Rev. 289, 313 (2012).

88. *See* Laird v. Tatum, 408 U.S. 1 (1972).

89. Laura Batchelor, *Occupy Wall Street Lands on Private Property*, CNN.Com, Oct. 6, 2011, available at http://money.cnn.com/2011/10/06/news/companies/occupy_wall_street_park/index.htm. Officials during the Middle East uprisings aggressively engaged in online surveillance of protestors in an effort to block protests and to track down protestors for retaliation. Joseph, *supra* note 1, at 167–68. Officials of some repressive regimes seek technology to track dissidents online. Jamie Doward, *UK Exporting Surveillance Technology to Repressive Nations*, The Guardian (London), Apr. 7, 2012, available at http://www.guardian.co.uk/world/2012/apr/07/surveillance-technology-repress.ive-regimes.

90. Joseph Goldstein, *Police Warrant Squads Were Used to Monitor Wall Street Protestors, Suspects Say*, N.Y. Times, May 2, 2012, http://www.nytimes.com/2012/05/03/nyregion/warrant-squads-spied-on-wall-st-protesters-suspects-say.html?_r=1&ref=occupywallstreet.

91. *See, e.g.*, Danielle Keats Citron & Frank Pasquale, *Network Accountability for the Domestic Intelligence Apparatus*, 62 Hastings L.J. 1441 (2011).

92. Kreimer, *supra* note 14, at 121.

93. ACLU v. Reno, 521 U.S. 824, 868–70 (1997).

94. *See, e.g.*, Bl(a)ck Tea Soc'y v. City of Boston, 378 F.3d 8, 14 (1st Cir. 2004). *See also* Krotoszynski & Carpenter, *supra* note 4, at 1265–75; Zick, *supra* note 4, at 589–97.

95. Zick, *supra* note 4, at 648 (original emphasis).

96. Joseph, *supra* note 1, at 161–62; Weaver, *supra* note 56, at 76–77.

97. Weaver, *supra* note 56, at 76–77.

98. Michael Cabanatuan, *BART Admits to Stopping Cell Phone Service to Stop Protests*, SFGate.com, Aug. 13, 2011, available at http://www.sfgate.com/cgi-bin/article.cgi?f=/c/a/2011/08/12/BAEU1KMS8U.DTL.

99. *Id.*

100. *Id.*

101. Thompson, *supra* note 16.

102. *Id.* at 478–88 (discussing existing law and proposed bills some of which arguably contain Internet "kill" switches); Larry Greenemeier, *What is the Best Way to Protect U.S. Critical Infrastructure From a Cyber Attack*, Sci. Am., Feb. 4, 2011, available at http://www.scientificamerican.com/article.cfm?id=critical-infrastructure-kill-switch.

103. Eric Lichtblau & James Risen, *Officials Say U.S. Wiretaps Exceeded Law*, N.Y. Times, Apr. 15, 2009, available at http://www.nytimes.com/2009/04/16/us/16nsa.html?_r=2&hp; John Solomon & Barton Gellman, *Frequent Errors in FBI's Secret Records Requests*, Wash. Post (March 9, 2007), http:// www.washingtonpost.com/wpdyn/content/article/2007/03/08/AR2007030802356.html.

104. Greenemeier, *supra* note 102 (discussing increasing view of Internet as part of critical infrastructure similar to electrical, transportation and financial services).

105. *Id.* (quoting free speech advocate as saying that promises that proposed legislation didn't contain a kill switch weren't "reassuring" and that "the details suggest that this is a dangerous bill that threatens our free speech rights").

106. Kreimer, *supra* note 17, at 17–27.

107. Benkler, *supra* note 75, at 313–14.

108. *Id.* at 314.

109. *See* Kreimer, *supra* note 17, at 27–65 (drawing parallels between Internet "proxy" censorship and the McCarthy era).

6. Advancing Technology & Aging Democracy

1. MARSHALL MCLUHAN, UNDERSTANDING MEDIA: THE EXTENSION OF MAN (1964).

2. *Id.* at 26.

3. *Id.* at 33.

4. *Id.* at 26.

5. "Instagram is essentially a social network built around photography, offering mobile apps that let people add quirky effects to their smartphone snapshots and share them with friends." Jenna Wortham, *Facebook to Buy Photo-Sharing Service Instagram for $1 Billion*, N.Y. TIMES (April 9, 2012), http://bits.blogs.nytimes.com/2012/04/09/facebook-acquires-photo-sharing-service-instagram/.

6. Evelyn M. Rusli, *Facebook Buys Instagram for $ 1 Billion*, N.Y. TIMES (April 9, 2012), http://dealbook.nytimes.com/2012/04/09/facebook-buys-instagram-for-1-billion/.

7. Nick Bilton, *Instagram Users Fail to Welcome Their New Overlord*, N.Y. TIMES (April 10, 2012), http://bits.blogs.nytimes.com/2012/04/10/on-instagram-backlash-about-facebook-acquistion/ (quoting tweets of Instagram users unhappy about Facebook's acquisition, including: "most of us on IG are on here because it's not FB not that there's anything wrong with FB it's just we like the community here …"; "FB just acquired Instagram for $1 billion … guess its [sic] time to quit Instagram before it becomes like FB/Myspace"; and "I think it would be great if every #Instagram user quit in the wake of the FB buy, leaving it worthless.").

8. *See, e.g.*, Kevin J. O'Brien, *Facebook Offers More Disclosure to Users*, N.Y. TIMES, (April 10, 2012) http://www.nytimes.com/2012/04/13/technology/facebook-offers-more-disclosure-to-users.html; David Streitfeld, *Data Harvesting at Google Not a Rogue Act, Report Finds*, N.Y. TIMES (April 28, 2012), http://www.nytimes.com/2012/04/29/technology/google-engineer-told-others-of-data-collection-fcc-report-reveals.html.

9. Eric Goldman, *Teaching Cyberlaw*, 52 ST. LOUIS U. L.J. 749, 751 (2008) (as of 2008, approximately one-half to two-thirds of U.S. law schools regularly offer at least one cyberlaw course). I imagine that percentage has increased since 2008.

10. Lawrence Lessig, *The Law of the Horse: What Cyberlaw Might Teach*, 113 HARV. L. REV. 501, 502 (1999).

11. ANGELE A. GILROY, CONG. RESEARCH SERV., RS22444, NET NEUTRALITY: BACKGROUND & ISSUES 1–2 (2008), http://www.fas.org/sgp/crs/misc/RS22444.pdf ("There is no single accepted definition of 'net neutrality.'"); Daren Read, *Net Neutrality & the Electronic Communications Regulatory Framework*, 20 INT'L J.L. & INFO. TECH. 48, 50 (2012) (same).

12. http://www.savetheinternet.com/net-neutrality.

13. Lawrence Lessig & Robert W. McChesney, *No Tolls on the Internet*, WASH. POST (June 8, 2006), http://www.washingtonpost.com/wp-dyn/content/article/2006/06/07/AR2006060702108_pf.html.

14. At least one commentator proposes a different, but closely-related concept, a generative internet theory. Jonathan L. Zittrain, *The Generative Internet*, 119 Harv. L. Rev. 1974, 1978. (2006) ("Those who make paramount 'network neutrality' derived from end-to-end theory confuse means and ends, focusing on 'network' without regard to a particular network's policy influence on the design of network endpoints such as PCs."). Zittrain theorizes that it is the generativity, not the open end-to-end principle, that must be preserved and that this generative construct enables the necessary dialogue about balancing cybersecurity and internet freedom. *Id.* at 1977–78.

15. Eduardo Porter, *Keeping the Internet Neutral*, N.Y. Times (May 8, 2012), http://www.nytimes.com/2012/05/09/business/economy/net-neutrality-and-economic-equality-are-intertwined.html.

16. *See* Turner Broadcasting System, Inc. v. Federal Communications Commission, 516 U.S. 622 (1994) (holding legislation requiring cable operators to carry local broadcast channels constitutionally permissible).

17. Comcast Network Management Practices Order, 23 FCC Rcd 13028 (2008). There are other examples of discrimination by an internet service provider that prevented its customers from accessing the content or application of their choice. An AT&T subsidiary prevented its internet customers from connecting to PayPal and other online payment systems because it sought to channel those customers to its partner, Direct Bill, one of PayPal's competitors. *Task Force on Competition Policy and Antitrust Law: Hearing on "Net Neutrality and Free Speech on the Internet," Before the H. Comm. on the Judiciary*, 110th Cong. (Mar. 11, 2008) (statement of Caroline Frederickson), http://judiciary.house.gov/hearings/pdf/Fredrickson080311.pdf. A rural telephone company that also provided broadband access via DSL blocked access to VoIP services because it competed with the company's telephone service. Madison River Communications, LLC and Affiliated Companies Order, 20 FCC Rcd 4295 (2005).

18. Comcast Corp. v. FCC, 600 F.3d 642 (D.C. Cir. 2010).

19. Preserving the Open Internet Broadband Indus. Practices, Report & Order, 25 FCC Rcd. 17,905 (Dec. 23, 2010).

20. The FCC's December 2010 report and order provides these rules:

  i. **Transparency.** Fixed and mobile broadband providers must disclose the network management practices, performance characteristics, and terms and conditions of their broadband services;

  ii. **No blocking.** Fixed broadband providers may not block lawful content, applications, services, or non-harmful devices; mobile broadband providers may not block lawful websites, or block applications that compete with their voice or video telephony services; and

  iii. **No unreasonable discrimination.** Fixed broadband providers may not unreasonably discriminate in transmitting lawful network traffic.

Id. at 17906 ¶ 1 (emphasis in original).

21. *See, e.g.*, Violet Blue, *Verizon Wireless Wants to "Edit" Your Internet Access*, CNET (July 11, 2012 3:09 PM), http://news.cnet.com/8301-13510_3-57470566-21/verizon-wireless-wants-to-edit-your-internet-access/.

22. http://www.freepress.net/ownership/chart#charts_cable-telecommunications.

23. *See* Ted Turner, *My Beef with Big Media: How Government Protects Big Media & Shuts Out Upstarts Like Me*, Wash. Monthly (July / August 2004), http://www.washingtonmonthly.com/features/2004/0407.turner.html.

24. Edward Wyatt, *F.C.C. Commissioner Leaving To Join Comcast*, N.Y. Times (May 11, 2011), http://mediadecoder.blogs.nytimes.com/2011/05/11/f-c-c-commissioner-to-join-comcast/.

25. *See, generally,* Tim Wu, The Master Switch: The Rise & Fall of Information Empires (2010).

26. Porter v. Bowen, 496 F.3d 1009 (9th Cir. 2007).

27. In June 2012, presidential candidate, Mitt Romney, embarked on a campaign trip and bus labeled, "Every Town Counts." Evoking McLuhan, a *New York Times* article on this and other presidential bus tours with slogans reads, "If medium is the message, bus tours are about running voters over with the theme." Sarah Wheaton, *Putting Their Trademarks on the Campaign Bus Tour,* N.Y. Times (June 19, 2012), http://query.nytimes.com/gst/fullpage.html?res=9C05E6DE1238F93AA25755C0A9649D8B63.

28. Romney's bus tour traveled to Iowa, Michigan, New Hampshire, Ohio, Pennsylvania and Wisconsin. Ari Shapiro, *Romney Rolls Into States Where 'Every Town Counts',* Nat'l Pub. Radio (June 16, 2012), http://www.npr.org/2012/06/16/155169598/romney-rolls-into-states-where-every-town-counts.

29. Jamin B. Raskin, *Neither the Red States nor Blue States But the United States: The National Popular Vote & American Political Democracy,* 7 Election L.J. 188, 190–91 (2008). Raskin notes that "12 of the 13 least populous states are also in the dejected 'safe' column." *Id.* at 190. The safe small red states are Alaska, Idaho, Montana, North Dakota, South Dakota and Wyoming. *Id.* at 191. The safe small blue states are Delaware, Hawaii, Maine, Vermont and Washington D.C. *Id.* at 190.

30. John R. Korza, et al., Every Vote Equal: A State-Based Plan for Electing the President by National Popular Vote 15 (2d ed. 2008) (citing Peitro S. Nivola, Thinking About Political Polarization, The Brookings Inst. Pol'y Brief 139 (Jan. 2005); Committee for the Study of the American Electorate, President Bush, Mobilization Drives Propel Turnout to Post-1968 High (2004)).

31. *See* http://www.nationalpopularvote.com/index.php.

32. Korza, et al., *supra* note 30, *generally*; *see also* http://www.fairvote.org/what-is-the-national-popular-vote-plan#.T6qUn9WpSZS.

33. Art. IV, National Popular Vote Interstate Compact, http://www.nationalpopularvote.com/resources/43-Compact-TAATS-V43.pdf.

34. The eight states are California, Hawaii, Illinois, Maryland, Massachusetts, New Jersey, Vermont and Washington. http://www.nationalpopularvote.com/.

35. *See* Bush v. Gore, 531 U.S. 98 (2000).

36. http://www.cnn.com/ELECTION/2008/results/president/.

37. Whether the current iteration of the national popular vote plan is desirable or would be effective is unsettled. *See, e.g.,* Sanford Levinson, John McGinnis, Daniel H. Lowenstein, *Should we Dispense with the Electoral College?,* 156 U. Pa. L. Rev. PENNumbra 10 (2007) (a proponent and two opponents of a national popular vote debate the issue). Another scholar doubts that a national popular vote is normatively more desirable than some form of a malapportioned process for electing the president and is certain that the current national popular vote interstate compact adopted by eight states and Washington D.C. is the wrong way to approach the issue because it will create more problems than it solves. Norman R. Williams, *Reforming the Electoral College: Federalism, Majoritarianism, & the Perils of Subconstitutional Change,* 100 Geo. L.J. 173 (2011). Williams concludes that a constitutional amendment is the appropriate way to effect this legal change, assuming it is a desirable change at all.

38. There are alternatives to the current national popular vote interstate compact. *E.g.* Alexander S. Benkley, *The Good, the Bad, & the Ugly: Three Proposals to Introduce the Nationwide Popular Vote in U.S. Presidential Elections*, 106 MICH. L. REV. FIRST IMPRESSIONS 110 (2008) (briefly outlines alternative proposals).

39. Paul Ohm, *The Fourth Amendment in a World Without Privacy*, 81 MISS. L.J. 1309, 1310 (2012) ("Every year, companies … spend millions of dollars developing new services that track, store, and share the words, movements, and even the thoughts of their customers.… Millions now own sophisticated tracking devices (smartphones) studded with sensors and always connected to the Internet.").

40. Samuel D. Warren & Louis D. Brandeis, *The Right to Privacy*, 4 HARV. L. REV. 193 (1890).

41. William L. Prosser, *Privacy*, 48 CALIF. L. REV. 383 (1960). Prosser's other three invasion of privacy torts are: (1) appropriation; (2) public disclosure of private facts; and (3) false light.

42. Adam Pabarcus, *Are "Private" Spaces on Social Networking Websites Truly Private? The Extension of Intrusion Upon Seclusion*, 38 WM. MITCHELL L. REV. 391 (2012) (intrusion upon seclusion should apply to private areas on social networking websites); Jane Yakowitz, *Space Invaders: Intrusion in the Digital Age*, 88 NOTRE DAME L. REV. (forthcoming 2012) (intrusion claims better serve online privacy interests and avoid conflict with the First Amendment than privacy theories focused on dissemination and re-use of information).

43. Margaret Jane Radin, Commentary, *Boilerplate Today: The Rise of Modularity & The Waning of Consent*, 104 MICH. L. REV. 1223, 1231 (2006).

44. *Id.*

45. Randy Barnett, *A Consent Theory of Contract*, 86 COLUM. L. REV. 269, 269 (1986).

46. *Id.*

47. Randy Barnett, *The Sounds of Silence: Default Rules & Contractual Consent*, 78 VA. L. REV. 821 (1992). Barnett tempers his vision of consent theory by stating that legal enforcement based on a theory of manifested consent is subject to limitations for reasons of justice and fairness. Randy Barnett, Afterword, *… And Contractual Consent*, 3 S. CAL. INTERDISC. L.J. 421, 435 (1993).

48. *See* Lawrence Kalevitch, *Gaps in Contracts: A Critique of Consent Theory*, 54 MONT. L. REV. 169, 181 (1993).

49. *Id.* at 184.

50. Todd D. Rakoff, *Contracts of Adhesion: An Essay in Reconstruction*, 96 HARV. L. REV. 1173 (1983). Rakoff proposes that boilerplate terms should be presumptively enforceable.

51. *See, generally*, Nancy J. King, *Direct Marketing, Mobile Phones, & Consumer Privacy: Ensuring Adequate Disclosure & Consent Mechanisms for Emerging Mobile Advertising Practices*, 60 FED. COMM. L.J. 229 (2008).

52. *See* Kalevitch, *supra* note 48, at 182.

53. *See* Rakoff, *supra* note 50.

54. PATRICIA L. BELLIA, ET AL., CYBERLAW: PROBLEMS OF POLICY & JURISPRUDENCE IN THE INFORMATION AGE 328 (3d ed. 2007).

55. James Risen & Eric Lichtblau, *Bush Lets U.S. Spy On Callers Without Courts*, N.Y. TIMES (December 16, 2005), http://www.nytimes.com/2005/12/16/politics/16program.html?pagewanted=all.

56. James Risen, *Obama Voters Protest His Switch on Telecom Immunity*, N.Y. TIMES (July 2, 2008), http://www.nytimes.com/2008/07/02/us/politics/02fisa.html.

57. Noam Cohen, *A Political Agitator Finds a Double-Edged Weapon*, N.Y. TIMES (July 6, 2008), http://www.nytimes.com/2008/07/06/us/politics/06website.html.

58. Eric Lichtblau, *More Demands on Cell Carriers*, N.Y. TIMES (July 8, 2012), http://www.ny-times.com/2012/07/09/us/cell-carriers-see-uptick-in-requests-to-aid-surveillance.html?page-wanted=all ("In the first public accounting of its kind, cellphone carriers reported that they responded to a startling 1.3 million demands for subscriber information last year from law enforcement agencies seeking text messages, caller locations and other information in the course of investigations.").

59. Erwin Chemerinsky, *Rethinking State Action Doctrine*, 80 Nw. U. L. Rev. 503, 507 (1985) ("The state action requirement is undesirable because it requires courts to refrain from applying constitutional values to private disputes even though there is no other form of effective redress.").

60. 326 U.S. 501 (1946).

61. Amalgamated Food Employees Union v. Logan Valley Plaza, Inc., 391 U.S. 308 (1968); Lloyd Corporation v. Tanner, 407 U.S. 551 (1972); Hudgens v. National Labor Relations Board, 424 U.S. 507 (1976). In *Logan Valley*, the Court held that a privately owned shopping violated the First Amendment by enjoining a protest against one of its tenant's that refused to unionize. The Court reasoned that the shopping center was functionally equivalent to the business district in *Marsh*. Logan Valley, 391 U.S. at 318. Four years later, the Court did not expressly overrule *Logan Valley*, but made a questionable distinction. In *Lloyd Corporation*, the Court held that a privately owned shopping mall did not violate the First Amendment when it prohibited individuals from distributing handbills protesting the draft and Viet Nam War. The Court distinguished *Logan Valley* by stating the material difference between the cases was the content of the messages. In *Logan Valley*, the protest related to one of the mall's tenants, whereas in *Lloyd Corporation* the handbills were unrelated to the mall's activities. Lloyd Corporation, 407 U.S. at 561–567. Thus, the former could not be banned, but the latter could. Four years later, the Court declared that *Lloyd Corporation* overruled *Logan Valley sub silentio* because the First Amendment does not permit control of speech in malls to depend on the content of the speech. Hudgens, 424 U.S. at 518. In a subsequent case, however, the Court upheld the constitutionality of a provision of the California Constitution that protected the free speech and petition rights of individuals in privately-owned shopping malls. Pruneyard Shopping Center v. Robins, 447 U.S. 74 (1980).

62. Turner Broadcasting, *supra* note 16, at 657 ("First Amendment's command that government not impede the freedom of speech does not disable the government from taking steps to ensure that private interests not restrict, through physical control of a critical pathway of communication, the free flow of information and ideas.").

63. To be sure, however, "constitutional jurisprudence, built firmly atop a foundation of state action, does not lend itself easily to the idea that private action can give rise to constitutional problems." Ohm, *supra* note 39, at 1388.

64. U.S. CONST. amend. IX. In recent years, several scholars have expounded upon the history, meaning and possibilities for Ninth Amendment jurisprudence going forward. *E.g.* KURT T. LASH, THE LOST HISTORY OF THE NINTH AMENDMENT (2009); DANIEL A. FARBER, RETAINED BY THE PEOPLE: THE "SILENT" NINTH AMENDMENT & THE CONSTITUTIONAL RIGHTS AMERICANS DON'T KNOW THEY HAVE (2007); CALVIN R. MASSEY, SILENT RIGHTS: THE NINTH AMENDMENT & THE CONSTITUTION'S UNENUMERATED RIGHTS (1995).

65. Kurt T. Lash, *Three Myths of the Ninth Amendment*, 56 Drake L. Rev. 875, 877 (2008) (explaining that the language of the Ninth Amendment is expansive and protects a variety of rights, including: "(1) alienable and unalienable rights; (2) positive rights; (3) individual rights; (4) collective revolutionary rights; (5) majoritarian democratic rights; and the retained rights of the sovereign states."). There are, however, other interpretations of the Ninth Amendment. *E.g.* Randy Barnett, *The Golden Mean Between Kurt & Dan: A Moderate Reading of the Ninth Amendment*, 56 Drake L. Rev. 897, 898–99 (Barnett believes that Lash's interpretation goes too far and that the Ninth Amendment, "recognizes all of the individual liberties of the people; however, it does not recognize a collective right that goes beyond that.").

66. John Lennon, "Imagine" (released 1971) ("You may say I'm dreamer, but I'm not the only one. I hope someday you'll join us."). I am far from the only one exploring new ways to protect liberty interests in the face of long-standing interpretations of constitutional law. In challenging the continuation of the state action doctrine, Chemerinsky states: "History shows that if doctrines and concepts are attacked long enough and hard enough they may begin to crumble." Chemerinsky, *supra* note 59, at 556. Ohm explains that privacy has been a proxy for Fourth Amendment protection, but it is no longer a useful proxy in the digital age. Ohm, *supra* note 39, at 1354. Instead, the "new Fourth Amendment" must protect against "power" if it is to continue serving as "an important bulwark of liberty in these changing times." *Id.* at 1355. Finally, JoEllen Lind explains how the Ninth Amendment provides an opportunity to reconceptualize the relationship between individual liberty and community as interdependent, as opposed to in conflict. JoEllen Lind, *Liberty, Community, & the Ninth Amendment*, 54 Ohio St. L.J. 1259 (1993).

67. *See* David Schizer, *Subsidizing the Press*, 3 J. Legal Analysis 1, 30–31 (2011) ("This issue [of political feasibility] should not be overemphasized, since it is worth knowing about strong proposals, even if they would encounter stiff political opposition.").

68. James Boyle, The Public Domain: Enclosing the Commons of the Mind 35 (2008) ("... we have been expanding intellectual property rights relentlessly ..."); *see also* Yochai Benkler, *Free as the Air to Common Use: First Amendment Constraints on Enclosure of the Public Domain*, 74 N.Y.U. L.Rev. 354, 354 ("We are in the midst of an enclosure movement.").

69. Boyle, *supra* note 68, at 51 ("Congress would, and still does, literally hand over the lawmaking process to the industries involved, telling them to draft their intra-industry contract in the form of a law, and then return to Congress to have it enacted.").

70. Jonathan Weisman, *In Fight Over Piracy Bills, New Economy Rises Against Old*, N.Y. Times (Jan. 18, 2012), http://www.nytimes.com/2012/01/19/technology/web-protests-piracy-bill-and-2-key-senators-change-course.html/?pagewanted=all ("Legislation that just weeks ago had overwhelming bipartisan support and had provoked little scrutiny generated a grass-roots coalition on the left and the right."); Timothy B. Lee, *Conservatives Lining Up in Opposition to SOPA*, Arstechnica (Dec. 27, 2011 9:35 AM), http://arstechnica.com/tech-policy/2011/12/sopa-faces-growing-opposition-among-conservatives/.

71. U.S. Const. art. I, §8 cl. 8 ("The Congress shall have power ... To promote the Progress of Science and useful Arts, by securing for limited Times to Authors and Inventors the exclusive Right to their respective Writings and Discoveries.").

72. Thomas Jefferson Letter to Isaac McPherson (Aug. 13, 1813), *in* The Writings of Thomas Jefferson (Andrew A. Lipscomb & Albert Ellery Bergh eds. 1905), http://press-

pubs.uchicago.edu/founders/documents/a1_8_8s12.html ("Considering the exclusive right to invention as given not of natural right, but for the benefit of society, I know well the difficulty of drawing a line between the things which are worth to the public the embarrassment of an exclusive patent, and those which are not.").

73. 17 U.S.C. § 302.

74. 1 Stat. 124 (1790).

75. Lawrence Lessig, "Laws that Choke Creativity," TED TALK (Mar. 2007), http://www.ted.com/talks/larry_lessig_says_the_law_is_strangling_creativity.html.

76. *See also* BOYLE, *supra* note 68, at 158 ("The copyright term could be shortened or we could require renewal every twenty-eight years.").

77. This concession, however, does not apply to the procedural flaws in SOPA and the Protect IP Act that violate standard First Amendment law. For analysis on why these bills violated the First Amendment, see Laurence Tribe, *The "Stop Online Piracy Act" Violates the First Amendment* (Dec. 2011), http://www.net-coalition.com/wp-content/uploads/2011/08/tribe-legis-memo-on-SOPA-12-6-11-1.pdf; Marvin Ammori, *Memorandum to Congress: PROTECT IP, SOPA, & Standard First Amendment Analysis* (Dec. 2011), http://ammori.files.wordpress.com/2011/12/ammori-first-amd-sopa-protectip.pdf.

78. Dissenting from the seminal hot news misappropriation decision, Justice Brandeis made the following enlightening and often quoted observation:

> But the fact that a product of the mind has cost its producer money and labor, and has a value for which others are willing to pay, is not sufficient to ensure to it this legal attribute of property. The general rule of law is, that the noblest of human productions—knowledge, truths ascertained, conceptions, and ideas—become, after voluntary communication to others, free as the air to common use.

International News Service v. Associated Press, 248 U.S. 215, 250 (Brandeis, J., dissenting).

79. *Hearing on "Net Neutrality and Free Speech on the Internet," supra* note 17 (statement of Michelle Combs), http://www.openinternetcoalition.org/files/CCA_Testimony.pdf.

80. Although these bills were defeated, efforts continue to increase protection of purported intellectual property rights. *E.g.* Cyrus Farivar, *SOPA Architect Now Pushing for IP Attaché Legislation,* ARSTECHNICA (July 11, 2012 7:00 PM), http://arstechnica.com/tech-policy/2012/07/sopa-architect-now-pushing-for-ip-attache-legislation/.

7. The Difference Between Online and Offline Communication as a Factor in the Balancing of Interests with Freedom of Speech

1. BVerfGE 65, 1.

2. Recht auf informationelle Selbstbestimmung, BVerfGE 65, 1, 43.

3. Cp. Art. 2 (b) of the Data Protection Directive 95/46/EG.

4. This principle is not strictly adhered by within the Data Protection Directive, as Art. 8 provides for a higher degree of protection for so-called "sensitive information", e.g. information on health, political or religious affiliation etc.

5. EuGH 16.12.2008-C-73/07.

6. See for a comparative and international approach to the problem of net neutrality and its potential solutions INDRA SPIECKER GEN. DOEHMANN AND JAN KRAEMER (EDS.), NET NEUTRALITY AND OPEN ACCESS (2011).

7. CETS 196.

8. Michael L Katz and Carl Shapiro, *Network externalities, competition, and compatibility*, 75 AMERICAN ECONOMIC REVIEW 424 (1985); Stan J. Liebowitz and Stephen E. Margolis, *Network Externality: An Uncommon Tragedy*, 8 JOURNAL OF ECONOMIC PERSPECTIVES 133 (1994); Manuela Mosca, *On the origins of the concept of natural monopoly*, 15 EUROPEAN JOURNAL ON HISTORY OF ECONOMIC THOUGHT 317 (2008).

9. See above at I.

10. See as a starting point for the information asymmetry literature George Akerlof, *The Market for Lemons: Quality Uncertainty and the Market Mechanism*, 84 QUARTERLY JOURNAL OF ECONOMICS 488 (1970).

11. Art. 4 of the Data Protection Directive.

12. Art. 3 of the Data Protection Regulation Proposal.

13. See above II 1.

14. For the purposes of this paper, the potential dangers of digital storage will not be further considered.

15. More on one particular means in the digital and online world below at II.7.

16. This again leads to the problem who may distribute information about a person: Can anyone in a public place as a street be photographed (according to general offline standards in the E.U. and the U.S: no) and then be checked for his identity and further information about him via Internet services (according to general practice: yes)?

17. The best solution against the indestructible Internet memory so far is a common name so no clear identification can be made. However, with face recognition software readily available, this might not be as effective as it is now.

18. See e.g. §6a and §28b German Federal Data Protection Law (BDSG).

19. As many online services have discovered the possibility of collecting information about their users, it has become a way of financing these services.

20. The German Constitutional Court has stressed this explicitly, that the amount of people potentially addressed by an infringement has severe consequences for the estimation of the level of intensity of the infringement, see e.g. BVerfGE 120, 378, 398 and 401 f.

8. Defamation and the Net: Anonymity, Meaning and ISPs

1. (2011–12 HL 203/ HC 930-I).

2. Ibid, para 92.

3. *Reno v. American Civil Liberties Union*, 929 F Supp 824, 883 (ED Pa 1996) per Dalzell District Judge.

4. The classic exposition of this case is by DR Johnson and D Post, "Law and Borders: The Rise of Law in Cyberspace" (1996) 48 *Stanford Law Rev* 1367.

5. 210 CLR 575, para 125.

6. Note 1, para 93.

7. This is still true of obituaries.

8. http://order-order.com/.

9. Under the UK Contempt of Court Act 1981, sect 10, a person may not be required to disclose "the source of information contained in a publication for which he is responsible," unless certain conditions are met to the satisfaction of the court, for example, that disclosure is necessary in the interests of justice or for national security.

10. *Totalise v. Motley Fool* [2001] EMLR 29.

11. See the evidence of Mark Gracey, Chair of Internet Service Providers Association Content Liability Subgroup to the Joint Committee, (n 1 above), Vol II, p 286 and note 124. Of course a court may rely on common sense assessment of evidence to determine who is responsible for sending defamatory messages on a social media site such as Facebook: *Applause Store Productions v. Raphael* [2008] EWHC 1781 (QB).

12. *Totalise Ltd v. The Motley Fool* (n 10 above) at para 27.

13. [2002] EMLR 20, at paras 25–26.

14. *Talley v. California* 362 US 60 (1960); *McIntyre v. Ohio Elections Commission* 514 US 334 (1995).

15. See the dissent of Scalia J in *McIntyre* (n 14 above).

16. *Dendrite International Inc v. Doe* 775 A 2d 756 (NJ Super AD 2001).

17. *Doe I and Doe II v. Individuals* (known as *AutdoAdmit*) 561 F Supp 2d 249 (D Comm 2008).

18. *Author of a Blog v. Times Newspapers* [2009] EMLR 22.

19. See E Barendt "Bad News for Bloggers" (2009) 1 *Journal of Media Law* 141; K Hughes, "No Reasonable Expectation of Anonymity?" 2 *Journal of Media Law* 169.

20. Committee on Defamation (Cmnd 5909, 1975) para 92.

21. Under the government's Defamation Bill, as under its earlier draft Bill, the defence replacing the common law fair comment defence is to be named "Honest Opinion," a change designed to reflect its character of protecting an honest expression of opinion.

22. *Lisa Krinsky v. Doe 6*, 72 Cal Reporter 3d 231 (Cal App 6 Dist 2008).

23. Ibid, at 238. For commentary, see LB Lidsky, "Anonymity in Cyberspace: What Can We Learn from John Doe?" 50 *Boston College Law Review* 1373, 1381–84 (2009).

24. *SPX Corp v. John Doe* 253 F Supp 2d 974 (ND Ohio 2003).

25. *Doe v. Cahill* 884 A2d 451, 465 (Del 2005), on which see SE Molloy, "Anonymous Bloggers and Defamation: Balancing Interests on the Internet" (2006) 84 *Washington Law Rev* 1187.

26. [2008] EWHC 1797 (QB), para 14.

27. *Sheffield Wednesday Football Club v. Hargreaves* [2007] EWHC 2375 (QB), para 16–18.

28. N 1 above, para 95.

29. GH Reynolds, "Libel in the Blogosphere: Some Preliminary Thoughts" (2006) 84 *Washington University Law Rev* 1157, 1166–67 recommends that the level of harm should be "fairly high" for claimants to recover libel damages in Internet cases.

30. *Elton John v. Guardian News and Media* [2008] EWHC 3066 (QB).

31. Reynolds (n 29 above) at 1165; M Nied, "Damage Awards in Internet Defamation Cases: Reassessing Assumptions about the Credibility of Online Speech," (2010) *Alberta Law Review* (Online Supplement, October)

32. WH Dutton and G Blank, *Next Generation Users: The Internet in Britain* (Oxford Internet Survey 20-11 Report), pp. 46–47. On the other hand, non-Internet users and former users placed most trust in radio and television.

33. See Molloy (n x above) at 1191, and DJ Solove, "A Tale of Two Bloogers: Free Speech and Privacy in the Blogosphere" (2006) 84 *Washington University Law Rev* 1195.

34. N 24 above.

35. N 30 above.

36. N 26 above.

37. N 24 above.

38. See the judgment of Tugendhat J in *Thornton v. Telegraph Media Group* [2010] EWHC 1414 (QB).

39. 129 F 3d 327 (1997).

40. *Bunt v. Tilley* [2006] EWHC 407 (QB), para 36. Also see para 23, where he said that for a person to be held responsible, there should be knowing involvement in the process of publication of the *relevant words* (his emphasis).

41. See the recent decision of Richard Parkes QC, sitting as Judge of the High Court, in *Davison v. Habeeb* [2011] EWHC 3031 (QB), esp at paras 38–48.

42. Electronic Commerce (EC Directive) Regulations 2002, SI 2002/2013.

43. Ibid, reg 17.

44. Notably PEN and Index on Censorship.

45. Evidence of ISPA to the Joint Committee, (n 1) Vol II (Ev 56 p 267.

46. See the evidence of Index on Censorship to the Joint Committee, (n 1) Vol II (Ev 48) p 83.

47. Ibid, Ev 64, p 274.

48. N 1 above, para 103.

49. *The Government's Response to the Report of the Joint Committee on the Draft Defamation Bill*, Cm 8295, 2012, paras 77–80.

50. Ibid, para 79.

51. Ibid, paras 85–88, and see Defamation Bill 2012, clause 5.

52. [1997] EMLR 139.

53. See the article by Y Karniel, "Defamation on the Internet—A New Approach to Libel in Cyberspace," 2 *Journal of International Media and Entertainment Law* 215 (2009).

54. Molloy (n x above) at 1191.

9. Free Speech in the Internet Era: Developments "Online" in Defamation and Privacy Law—Brief Observations

1. CTB v. News Group Newspapers Ltd [2011] EWHC 1232 (QB).

2. Edward Craven, *Case Law: CTB v. News Group Newspapers: privacy law and the judiciary* (http://inforrm.wordpress.com/2011/05/16/case-law-ctb-v-news-group-newspapers-privacy-law-and-the-judiciary-edward-craven/) (last visited 1 April 2013).

3. *Jameel v. Wall Street Journal Europe SPRL* [2007] 1 AC 359.

4. *CTB v. News Group Newspapers Ltd & Anor* [2011] EWHC 1326 (QB) (23 May 2011) at para. 14.

5. "Ryan Giggs named by MP as injunction footballer," 23 May 2011 BBC News (http://www.bbc.co.uk/news/uk-13503847) (last visited 1 April 2013).

6. *U.S. Asks Twitter for WikiLeaks Data*, Wall Street Journal (online), (http://online.wsj.com/article/SB10001424052748704482704576072081788251562.html) (last visited 1 April 2013).

7. See http://wikileaks.org/Banking-Blockade.html (last visited 1 April 2013).

8. "Julian Assange: WikiLeaks 'insurance' file could unleash secrets should website get taken down," New York Daily News (http://articles.nydailynews.com/2010-12-05/news/27083351_1_wikileaks-new-servers-fox-news) (last visited 1 April 2013).

9. See http://www.rawstory.com/rs/2010/12/05/gingrich-assange-enemy-combatant/ (on Fox News coverage) (last visited 1 April 2013).

10. The U.S's weak legal case against Wikileaks, Time Magazine (http://www.time.com/time/specials/packages/article/0,28804,2034088_2034097_2035994,00.html) (last visited 1 April 2013).

11. See http://sydneypeacefoundation.org.au/peace-projects/sydney-peace-foundation-gold-medal/ (last visited 1 April 2013).

12. See Joint Committee on the Draft Defamation Bill, Draft Defamation Bill (2010–12 HL 203/HC 930) and Government Response (Cm.8295, 2012).

13. Tamiz v. Google Inc Google UK Ltd [2012] EWHC 449 (QB) (02 March 2012).

14. Graham Smith, *What the Defamation Bill means for the internet* (http://inforrm.wordpress.com/2012/05/17/what-the-defamation-bill-means-for-the-internet-graham-smith/) (last visited 1 April 2013).

15. 2003/31/EC.

16. Graham Smith, *What the Defamation Bill means for the internet* (http://inforrm.wordpress.com/2012/05/17/what-the-defamation-bill-means-for-the-internet-graham-smith/) (last visited 1 April 2013).

17. See *Norwich Pharmacal Co. & Others v. Customs and Excise Commissioners* [1974] AC 133.

18. Graham Smith, *What the Defamation Bill means for the internet* (http://inforrm.wordpress.com/2012/05/17/what-the-defamation-bill-means-for-the-internet-graham-smith/) (last visited 1 April 2013).

19. *Ibid.* Graham Smith.

20. "James McClean closes Twitter account after death threats following Ireland selection for Euro 2012," *The Independent*, 28 May 2012 (http://www.independent.co.uk/sport/football/international/james-mcclean-closes-twitter-account-after-death-threats-following-ireland-selection-for-euro-2012-7723274.html) (last visited 1 April 2013).

21. Google reroutes China search, INBLive news, 23 March 2010, (http://ibnlive.in.com/news/google-reroutes-china-search-beijing-fumes/111891-11.html?from=tn?from=rssfeed).

22. "Google blames Chinese censors for outage," Los Angeles Times, 31 March 2010 (http://articles.latimes.com/2010/mar/31/business/la-fi-china-google31-2010mar31) (last visited 1 April 2013).

23. Google Says Bye Bye to User Privacy, David DiSalvo, Forbes Magazine, 24 January 2012, (http://www.forbes.com/sites/daviddisalvo/2012/01/24/google-says-bye-bye-to-user-privacy/) (last visited 1 April 2013).

24. See http://www.whitehouse.gov/the-press-office/2012/02/23/we-can-t-wait-obama-administration-unveils-blueprint-privacy-bill-rights (last visited 1 April 2013).

25. *Chambers v. DPP* [2012] EWHC 2157 (Admin).

26. News: "Twitter Joke" Case goes to the High Court—Gervase de Wilde, Inforrm's Blog, 8 February 2012, (http://inforrm.wordpress.com/2012/02/08/news-twitter-joke-case-goes-to-the-high-court-gervase-de-wilde/) (last visited 1 April 2013).

27. http://www.cps.gov.uk/consultations/social_media_consultation.html (last visited 1 April 2013).

10. Now Trending: Loving the Internet Terrorist?

1. The first reference to this can be found in the Old Testament, where it states: "Thou shalt not avenge, nor bear any grudge against the children of thy people, but thou shalt love thy neighbour as thyself." *Leviticus* 19:18.

2. According to the New Testament, one's neighbor is not confined to those who share one's beliefs. Thus, the question of who one's neighbor is, for these purposes, is illustrated by the story of the Good Samaritan, the Samaritans being a people who were despised by the Jews as heretics and depicted as being possessed by demons. *See Luke* 10:30–37, *John* 4:9, 8:48.

3. As Neil Duxbury notes, this rule, known as the golden rule, can be found in one form or another "in all cultures, and numerous studies show that it has been endorsed in all of the major and most minor religions," Neil Duxbury, *Golden Rule Reasoning, Moral Judgment and the Law*, 84 NOTRE DAME L. REV. 1529, 1531 (2009) (citing to LEONIDAS JOH. PHILIPPIDIS, DIE "GOLDENE REGEL" 11–15 (1933); H.T.D. ROST, THE GOLDEN RULE 15 (1986); JEFFREY WATTLES, THE GOLDEN RULE 15–67 (1996)).

4. This prayer, often referred to as the serenity prayer, is attributed to Dr. Rheinhold Niebuhr, but it may predate him. Fred R. Shapiro, *Who Wrote the Serenity Prayer?* July/August 2008 http://www.yalealumnimagazine.com/issues/2008_07/serenity.html.

5. One could add any number of others to the list, be it African Americans, immigrants, people in GLBT community (or communities), women, or that best friend, who, when there is no one else around, is always there to kick, the trusty dog.

6. MEATLOAF, TWO OUT OF THREE AIN'T BAD (Epic Records 1977).

7. According to Jennifer E. Manning, "Ninety-nine percent of the Members of the 112th Congress cite a specific religious affiliation." *Membership of the 122th Congress: A Profile, in* THE CONGRESSIONAL RESEARCH SERVICE REPORT R41647, 5–6 (March 1, 2011), *available at* http://www.senate.gov/reference/resources/pdf/R41647.pdf. Of those, 7% percent report being Jewish, 57% report being Protestant, 29% report being Catholic and the rest are reportedly "Greek Orthodox, Quaker, Unitarian Universalist, and The Church of Jesus Christ of Latter-Day Saints (Mormon)" with three Buddhists and two Muslims serving in the House of Representatives. *Id.* at 6. According to the Pew Forum on Religion and Public Life, Report on U.S. Religious Life Landscape (2008), 78.4% of those in the U.S. report being Christian, 5.8% are religious unaffiliated, 6.3% are secular unaffiliated, 2.4% are Agnostic, 1.7% are Jewish, 1.6% are Atheists, .7% are Buddhist, .7% are Unitarians or other liberal faiths, .6% are Muslim, .4% are Hindu, and .8% do not know or refused to answer. Religious Affiliation: Diverse and Dynamic, PEW FORUM ON RELIGION & PUBLIC LIFE (February 2008), http://religions.pewforum.org/pdf/report-religious-landscape-study-full.pdf. (last visited July 16, 2012).

8. The U.S. could benefit considerably from some of the wisdom of Frank Partnoy, George E. Barrett Professor of Law and Finance at San Diego University School of Law, in his latest book WAIT: THE ART AND SCIENCE OF DELAY (2012) (using behavior economics, neuroscience and case studies from across politics, economics, comedy, medicine and sports, to argue that: there are serious costs associated with rapid, short sighted decision making; we need to train ourselves to wait; and our society must learn to foster long term decision making).

9. *See* Sudha Setty, *No More Secrete Laws?: How Transparency of Executive Branch Legal Policy Doesn't Let the Terrorists Win*, 57 U. KAN. L. REV. 579, 621 (2009) (assessing our pol-

icy of keeping executive legal policy secret in times of armed conflict and arguing that other nations maintain more transparency and accessibility around the development of their legal policies under similar conditions, thus leading to greater integrity in their security programs).

10. Female terrorists are becoming more common, although they do not quite fit "our" picture of what a terrorist ought to be. In 2002, twenty women took part in the taking of 700 hostages in a Moscow theater. The same year, the first female suicide bombers appeared in Israel. Alexis B. Delaney & Peter R. Neumann, Another Failure of Imaginations?: The Spectacular Rise of the Female Terrorist, Int'l Herald Trib., Sept. 4, 2004, http://www.nytimes.com/ 2004/09/06/opinion/06iht-edneumann_ed3_.html?_r=1. "Women do act as terrorists— and as guerrillas, insurgents, revolutionaries, combatants, and militants." Susan N. Herman, *Women and Terrorism: Keynote Address*, 31 WOMEN'S RTS. L. REP. 258, 260 (2010) (discussing that the stereotype of woman as victims and not terrorists is a false misconception).

11. DAVID BARASH, PAYBACK: WHY WE RETALIATE, REDIRECT AGGRESSION AND SEEK REVENGE 100–01 (2011); *see also* VAMIK D. VOLKAN, THE NEED TO HAVE ENEMIES AND ALLIES (1988); DAVID BARASH, BELOVED ENEMIES: OUR NEED FOR OPPONENTS (1994).

12. NOAM CHOMSKY, TURNING THE TIDE (1985).

13. Shoon Kathleen Murray and Jason Meyers, *Do People Need Foreign Enemies? American Leaders' Beliefs after the Soviet Demise*, 43(5) JOURNAL OF CONFLICT RESOLUTION 555 (1999).

14. *Id.* at 566.

15. *Id.* at 566–567.

16. *Id.* at 567.

17. It is a win-win like the Cold War was a win-win, and like our relations with Cuba and Iran have been win-win situations. For discussion of the manipulation of threats by states, see FRANK FUREDI, INVITATION TO TERROR: THE EXPANDING EMPIRE OF THE UNKNOWN (2007).

18. After 9/11, Tim Russert asked then Vice President Cheney if the 9/11 attacks would result in lifting the restrictions placed on United States intelligence gathering. Vice President Cheney stated, yes; that one of the by-products of the attack was that the United States would see a thorough reassessment of how it operates and the kinds of people it deals with. Mr. Cheney answered that because these terrorists play by a whole set of different rules, it would force the U.S. to get "mean, dirty and nasty in order to take them on." He went on to say that: "We also have to work, though, sort of the dark side, if you will.... A lot of what needs to be done here will have to be done quietly, without any discussion, using sources and methods that are available to our intelligence agencies ... we need to make certain that we have not tied the hands, if you will, of our intelligence communities in terms of accomplishing their mission." Former Vice President Dick Cheney, *Meet the Press*, NBC's News (Sept. 16, 2001).

19. FRIEDRICH NIETZSCHE, BEYOND GOOD AND EVIL: PRELUDE TO A PHILOSOPHY OF THE FUTURE, *Aphorism* 146 (Walter Kaufmann trans., 1989). He also warned in the same aphorism that, "He who fights with monsters might take care lest he thereby become a monster." *Id.*

20. Azmat Khan, *New Study Asserts Drone Strikes in Pakistan Target Rescuers, Funerals,* PBS (February 6, 2012, 3:17 PM), http://www.pbs.org/wgbh/pages/frontline/afghanistan-pakistan/secret-war/new-study-asserts-drone-strikes-in-pakistan-target-rescuers-funerals/.

The study by Chris Woods and Christina Lamb of the Bureau of Investigative Journalism, based in City University London, is titled, "Obama terror drones: CIA tactics in Pakistan include targeting rescuers and funerals." As they note, "research by the Bureau has found that since Obama took office three years ago, between 282 and 535 civilians have been credibly reported as killed including more than 60 children. A three month investigation including eye witness reports has found evidence that at least 50 civilians were killed in follow-up strikes when they had gone to help victims. More than 20 civilians have also been attacked in deliberate strikes on funerals and mourners. The tactics have been condemned by leading legal experts." http://www.thebureauinvestigates.com/2012/02/04/obama-terror-drones-cia-tactics-in-pakistan-include-targeting-rescuers-and-funerals/ (last visited July 16, 2012).

21. This is not to say that killing innocent civilians is justified, even when horrible things happen to innocent civilians. There are many, however, that do. The use of "enhanced interrogation techniques" and other abuses of Guantanamo detainees have been used in al Qaeda's propaganda videos to recruit Islamic followers to join their cause. *See* James Gordon Meek, *Gitmo Fades as 'Recruiting Tool for al Qaeda'*, NY DAILY NEWS (January 25, 2010), http://www.nydailynews.com/blogs/dc/2010/01/gitmo-fades-as-recruiting-tool.html. It is reported that one of the top reasons that foreign fighters flocked to Iraq is because of the abuses carried out at Abu Ghraib and Guantanamo. *See* Matthew Alexander, *I'm Still Tortured by What I saw in Iraq*, WASHINGTON POST (November 30, 2008), http://www.washingtonpost.com/wp-dyn/content/article/2008/11/28/AR2008112802242.html.

22. Nathan C. Funk and Abdul Aziz Said, *Islam and the West, Narratives of Conflict and Conflict Transformation*, 9 INTERNATIONAL JOURNAL OF PEACE STUDIES 1, 2 (2004).

23. The point is not that all, or even most, terrorists come from Muslim countries. Rather, the U.S. approach to the "war on terror" has largely targeted Muslims, and our human rights abuses during this war have largely involved Muslims. *See* Parvez Ahmed, *Terror in the Name of Islam—Unholy War, Not Jihad*, 39 CASE W. RES. J. INT'L L. 759, 762–3 (2008).

24. *Id.* at 780. These polls indicate that we are not winning over hearts and minds.

25. *See* e.g. Charlie Savage, *Takeover: Return of the Imperial Presidency*, 48 WASHBURN L.J. 299 (2009).

26. James E. Campbell, *Why Bush Won the Presidential Election of 2004: Incumbency, Ideology, Terrorism, and Turnout*, 120 POLITICAL SCIENCE QUARTERLY 219, 225 (2005). Bush attempted to use the threat of terrorism to his political advantage. "Tom Ridge, the first secretary of homeland security, asserts in a new book that he was pressured by top advisers to President George W. Bush to raise the national threat level just before the 2004 election in what he suspected was an effort to influence the vote." Peter Baker, *Bush Official, in Book, Tells of Pressure on '04 Vote*, N.Y. TIMES, August 21, 2009, at A19.

27. Erin B. Corcoran, *Obama's Failed Attempt to Close Gitmo: Why Executive Orders Can't Bring About Systemic Change*, 9 U.N.H.L. Rev. 207, 208 (2011) (addressing the Obama Administration's failure to execute plans to close Guantanamo Bay and analyzing lessons to be learned from this alleged misstep by the executive).

28. Khalid Sheik Mohammad and four others have been arraigned in a military commission at Guantanamo Bay on charges of orchestrating the Sept. 11, 2001, attacks. *United States v. Khalid Sheikh Mohammed, et al.* (S 14) 93 Cr. 180 (KTD). For the Military Commissions case docket, *see*, http://www.mc.mil/CASES/MilitaryCommissions.aspx (June 28, 2012).

29. Raj Kannappan, *Eric Holder Defends the Assassination of U.S. Citizens*, WASHINGTON TIMES (March 12, 2012), http://communities.washingtontimes.com/neighborhood/

mugged-reality/2012/mar/12/eric-holder-defends-assassination-us-citizens/. John O. Brennan, President Obama's top counterterrorism adviser, said American citizens who join Al Qaeda may also be targeted [by drone strikes], yet failed to mention the killings of at least three Americans in drone strikes in Yemen last year. Charlie Savage, *Top U.S. Security Officials Says 'Rigorous Standards' Are Used for Drove Strikes*, N.Y. TIMES, Apr. 30, 2012, available at: http://www.nytimes.com/2012/05/01/world/obamas-counterterrorism-aide-defends-drone-strikes.html.

Anwar al-Awlaki, a radical American-born Muslim cleric was killed by a drone attack in September, 2011, along with his son Abdulrahman al-Awlaki, a 16-year-old born in Denver. Another American citizen, Samir Khan, who was from New York, was killed in October of 2011. Mark Mazzetti el al., *Two-Year Manhunt Led to Killing of Awlaki in Yemen*, N.Y. TIMES, Sept. 30, 2011, available at: http://www.nytimes.com/2011/10/01/world/middleeast/anwar-al-awlaki-is-killed-in-yemen.html?_r=1&pagewanted=all. *See also*, Peter Finn, *Secret U.S. Memo Sanctioned Killing of Aulaqi*, WASH. POST, Sept 30, 2011 (describing a "secret memo" written to justify consigning Awlaki to death) available at: http://www.washingtonpost.com/world/national-security/aulaqi-killing-reignites-debate-on-limits-of-executive-power/2011/09/30/gIQAx1bUAL_story.html.

30. And it allows the president to use the military to indefinitely detain anyone, including American citizens that may be suspected of committing or aiding in the commission of a future terrorist act without charges pending the disposition of the war. 157 CONG. REC. S 8088 (1st Sess. 2011) § 1021-1022. While the language of the provision appears not to extend to U.S. citizens, according to Armed Services Committee Chairman Senator Carl Levin, President Obama requested the removal of language that would have expressly exempted American citizens and legal resident aliens from section 1021. (Statement of Sen. Carl Levin), http://www.youtube.com/watch?v=4DNDHbT44cY. (last visited July 16, 2012).

31. Laura K. Donohue, *The Shadow of State Secrets*, 159 U. PA. L. REV. 77 (2010). *See also* Margaret Ziegler, *Note, Pay No Attention to the Man Behind the Curtain: The Government's Increased Use of the State Secrets Privilege to Conceal Wrongdoing*, 23 BERKELEY TECH. L.J. 691, 715 (2008) ("In recent years, the use of the state secrets privilege has been expanding, both in frequency of use and in the types of protection it provides").

32. *See, e.g.* Brandice Canes-Wrone, et al. *Toward a Broader Understanding of Presidential Power: A Reevaluation of the two Presidencies Thesis*. 70 *The Journal of Politics*, 1–16 (2008) (explaining that U.S. presidents exercise fundamentally greater influence over foreign than domestic affairs and that Congress has incentives to delegate foreign powers to the president. This paper discusses three major incentives: (1) the importance of the president to have the power to move without congressional endorsement in order to respond quickly to issues including foreign conflagrations, negotiate peace between nations, monitor development of nuclear programs and retaliate against terrorist attacks; (2) because the executive branch collects most information regarding foreign affairs and congress is more concerned with domestic affairs, presidents have more knowledge of foreign policy; and, (3) because the president is most visibly responsible for national welfare, foreign policy is persistently a major issue in presidential elections, whereas congressional elections are based more on domestic issues.) (available at: http://home.uchicago.edu/~/whowell/papers/TowardABroader.pdf).

33. How else do we account for the lack of public outcry to the extra-judicial killings of U.S. citizens by our government, and the prior dismissal of the case brought by his fa-

ther seeking justification for having his son on the kill list? *Al-Aulaqi v. Obama*, 727 F. Supp. 2d 1 (D.D.C. 2010).

34. The cost of the War on Terror extends well beyond the money borrowed for fighting the war which has led to bigger deficits and higher oil prices. *See* Linda J. Bilmes and Joseph E. Stiglitz, *America's Costly War Machine*, L.A. TIMES, September 18, 2011, available at http://articles.latimes.com/2011/sep/18/opinion/la-oe--bilmes-war-cost-20110918.

35. David Zeiler, *Election 2012: President Obama at the Mercy of U.S. Economy*, MONEY MORNING (June 27, 2012), http://moneymorning.com/2012/06/27/election-2012-president-obama-at-the-mercy-of-u-s-economy/, (last visited July 4, 2012) ("One thing that's clear from the polls is that voters consider economic issues by far the most important in the Election 2012 race."). Associated Press, *AP-GfK Poll: Half think outcome of presidential race won't mean much change for economy*, THE WASHINGTON POST, (June 5, 2012), http://www.washingtonpost.com/business/economy/poll-economy-is-election-issue-no-1-yet-half-dont-think-whoever-wins-will-do-much-about-it/2012/06/25/gJQAvfr60V_story.html (last visited July 4, 2012). ("... the candidates, the polls and the pundits agree—the economy is the issue of 2012.").

36. Jeffrey M. Jones, *Economy is Paramount Issue to U.S. Voters*, Gallup.com (Feb. 29, 2012), http://www.gallup.com/poll/153029/economy-paramount-issue-voters.aspx (last visited July 4, 2012) (The economy ranked highest (92% finding the economy as an extremely/very important issue in the 2012 election) of nine issues tested in a Feb. 16–19 USA Today/Gallup poll. Whereas terrorism was fifth on the list of issues below the economy, unemployment, the federal budget deficit, and the healthcare law.).

37. In reality, the harm caused by Nazis and Communists dwarf that caused by the modern terrorist. About 2,929 terrorism-related deaths have occurred since 2004, with 1,709 having occurred within 2004. It was estimated at the time of the report that these numbers would rise dramatically. Robert Rivas & Robert Windrem, *Worldwide terrorism-related deaths of the Rise*, MSNBC, September 2, 2004. http://www.msnbc.msn.com/id/5889435/ns/us_news-security/t/worldwide-terrorism-related-deaths-rise/. (last visited July 16, 2012). As pointed out by Fareed Zakaria, "If you set aside the war in Iraq, terrorism has in fact gone way down over the past five years." *The Only Thing We Have to Fear ...* NEWSWEEK (May 24, 2008). Available at http://www.thedailybeast.com/newsweek/2008/05/24/the-only-thing-we-have-to-fear.html (last visited July 16, 2012). Even if one counts the wars in Iraq and Afghanistan as including terrorist related deaths, the numbers nowhere approximate the fatalities caused by Nazi's and Communists. About 5,709,329 Jewish people were murdered in total during the Holocaust. In Germany alone between approximately 160,000 and 180,000 German Jews were killed. United States Holocaust Memorial Museum, Holocaust Expedia, *German Jews During The Holocaust, 1939–1945.* http://www.ushmm.org/wlc/en/article.php?ModuleId=10005469 (last visited July 16, 2012). In World War II, the United States had about 405,400 missing or killed. Germany had about 3.5 million missing or killed. Japan had about 1.7 million missing or killed. Russia had about 7.5 million missing or killed). Meredith R. Sarkees, *Correlates of War Inter-State War Data*, 1816–1997 (v4.0), http://www.correlatesofwar.org/COW2%20Data/WarData_NEW/InterStateWarData_v4.0.csv (last visited July 16, 2012); *see generally* Meredith R. Sarkees & Phil Schafer, *The Correlates of War Data on War: An Update to 1997*, 18 CONFLICT MGMT. & PEACE SCI. 123 (2000). In the Korean War, China had an estimated 422,612 battle-related casualties. North Korea suffered about 316,579 deaths. South Korea had about 113,248 deaths. Meanwhile, the United States had about 54,487 battle deaths. *Id.*

38. Choe Sang-Hun, *South Korean Law Casts Wide Net, Snaring Satirists in a Hunt for Spies*, N. Y. TIMES, January 7, 2012, *available at* http://www.nytimes.com/2012/01/08/world/asia/south-korean-law-casts-wide-net-snaring-satirists-in-a-hunt-for-spies.html?pagewanted=all. Of course, Nazis and Communists are no jokes to Europeans and South Koreans. See below section....

39. As late as 1985, Sting was writing that "he hopes the Russians love their children too" because this is the one thing that might help us avoid mutual destruction through nuclear war. Sting, "Russians" (1985). This was a plea for everyone to see our common biology and common humanity.

40. *See, e.g.* MAHMOOD MAMDANI, GOOD MUSLIM, BAD MUSLIM: AMERICA, THE COLD WAR, AND THE ROOTS OF TERROR (2004) (positing that terrorism is a product of the Cold War, because during the Cold War, U.S. foreign policy divided the Muslim world into those who were "with us" (good Muslims) and those who were "against us" (bad Muslims). Those who were "good," were not labeled such because they further our ideals of freedom, justice and democracy, but simply because they could be used in allies against the Soviets). Parvez Ahmed, notes that contrary to the official version of history, which reflected that we went into Afghanistan after the Soviets, Zbigniew Brzezinski, President Carter's National Security Advisor, said in a 1998 interview, that "the reality, secretly guarded until now, is completely otherwise. Indeed, it was July 3, 1979 that President Carter signed the first directive for secret aid to the opponents of the pro-Soviet regime in Kabul. And that very day, I wrote a note to the President, in which I explained to him that, in my opinion, this aid was going to induce Soviet military intervention." Parvez Ahmed, *supra* note 24 at 780.

41. The Foreign Intelligence Surveillance Act (FISA) allows federal officials to obtain a court order authorizing surveillance or a search to acquire "foreign intelligence information," of a "foreign power" or an "agent of a foreign power" 50 U.S.C. section 1801(e)(1), 1805(a)(3)(A) (2000). FISA defines "foreign power" to include "a group engaged in international terrorism or activities in preparation therefor," 1801(a)(4). To be an agent, one would have to be affiliated with such a group. The lone wolf amendment was incorporated in 2004 to broaden the definition of an "agent of foreign power" to include any non-US person who "engages in international terrorism or activities in preparation therefor" section 1801(b)(1)(C), meaning they do not need to be affiliated with any "foreign power." S. Rep. No. 108-40, at 2, 11 (2003). In May 2011, President Obama approved a four-year extension of the government's Patriot Act. Tom Cohen, *Obama approves extension of expiring Patriot Act provisions*, CNNPolitics (May 27, 2011), http://articles.cnn.com/2011-05-27/politics/congress.patriot.act_1_lone-wolf-provision-patriot-act-provisions-fisa-court?_s=PM:POLITICS (last visited July 4, 2012). *See also*, FoxNews.com, *Obama Signs Last-Minute Patriot Act Extension*, (May 27, 2011), http://www.foxnews.com/politics/2011/05/27/senate-clearing-way-extend-patriot-act/, (last visited July 16, 2012). For an argument as to how the Patriot Act has undermined U.S. democracy by replacing an open and free information society with one of surveillance, policing and repression *see* DOUGLAS KELNER, FROM 9/11 TO TERROR WAR: DANGERS OF THE BUSH LEGACY (2003).

42. Timothy Recuber, *The Terorist as Folk Devil and Mass Commodity: Moral Panics, Risk, and Consumer Culture.* 2009 J. INST. JUST. INT'L STUD. 158, 158, 160 (2009) (quoting S. COHEN, FOLK DEVILS AND MORAL PANICS, 10 (1980)). As he further explains, "In Cohen's model of moral panics, the mass media sensitize us to problematic social types and allow experts and authorities the opportunity to suggest various solutions." *Id.*

43. *Id.* 158. Other examples of moral panics with accompanying folk devils include: Communists, homosexuals, young black men, drug users, and of course, Satanists. *Id* at 159, citing to: E. Goode, & N. Ben-Yehuda, Moral panics: The social construction of deviance (1994); S. Ungar, *Moral panics, the military-industrial complex, and the arms race.* 31 The Sociological Quarterly 165–185 (1990); H.S. Heatley, *Commies and queers: Narratives that supported the lavender scare.* Master's thesis. Arlington, TX: University of Texas at Arlington (2007); Glassner, B. The culture of fear (1999); C. Reinarman, *The social construction of drug scares,* in P.A. Adler & P. Adler (Eds.), Constructions of deviance: Social power, context, and interaction (1994).

44. In January of 2011, Janet Napolitano announced plans to scrap the current terror alert system with its color codes and replace them with alerts that "will provide a concise summary of the potential threat, information about actions being taken to ensure public safety, and recommended steps that individuals and communities, businesses and governments can take." The idea was to post these alerts on Facebook and Twitter. *Secretary Napolitano Announces New National Terrorism Advisory System to More Effectively Communicate Information about Terrorist Threats to the American Public* (Release Date: January 27, 2011) available at: http://www.dhs.gov/ynews/releases/pr_1296158119383.shtm (last visited July 16, 2012).

45. As Jerry Brito and Tate Watkins warn us, "Security risks to private and government networks from criminals and malicious state actors are no doubt real and pressing. However, the rhetoric of 'cyber doom' employed by proponents of increased federal intervention in cybersecurity implies an almost existential threat that requires instant and immense action. Yet these proponents lack clear evidence of such doomsday threats that can be verified by the public. As a result, the United States may be witnessing a bout of threat inflation similar to that seen in the run-up to the Iraq." Jerry Brito & Tate Watkins, *Loving the Cyber Bomb: The Dangers of Threat Inflation in Cybersucurity Policy,* 3 Harv. Nat'l Sec. J. 39, 40 (2011).

46. Frederich Nietzsche, The Gay Science: With a Prelude in German Rhymes and an Appendix of Songs, § 130 (1882, Walter Kaufmann trans., 1974).

47. Again, as Nietzsche explains, "That which is done out of love always takes place beyond good and evil." Frederich Nietzsche, *supra* note 20 at 153.

48. There were little or no public pleas to forgive, to turn the other cheek, or to love they neighbors after 9/11.

49. J.L. Mackie, Ethics 130–31 (1990).

50. *See, e.g.* Richard A. Posner, Economic Analysis of Law 3 (3d ed. 1986). There is a spectrum of ends in the rational choice and economic literature that ranges from casting our preferences in terms of simply maximizing whatever ends one may have, or as maximizing expected utility, or as maximizing our own self-interest or individual welfare, and in the law and economic literature there is sometimes a tendency to boil it all down to a preference for maximizing wealth. *See, e.g.* Russell B. Korobkin & Thomas S. Ulen, *Law and Behavioral Science: Removing the Rationality Assumption from Law & Economics,* 88 Cal. L. Rev. 1051, 1060–67 (2000). For a critique of the idea that we are merely self-interested wealth maximizers, *see* Maurice E. Stucke, *Money, Is That What I Want?: Competition Policy and the Role of Behavioral Economics,* 50 Santa Clara L. Rev. 893 (2010).

51. Below, I will provide a critique of this prayer, but let it suffice at this point to note that we are all too happy to accept some things as too hard to change and to move towards those things that are easy to change.

52. This is one version of what is commonly referred to as the prisoner's dilemma. *See,* Steven Kuhn, *Prisoner's Dilemma,* in EDWARD N. ZALTA (ED.) THE STANFORD ENCYCLOPE-DIA OF PHILOSOPHY (Spring 2009 Edition), at http://plato.stanford.edu/archives/spr2009/entries/prisoner-dilemma/. The scenarios are sometimes cast in terms of two prisoners who are in separate rooms being interrogated. If they cooperate with each other and keep quite they have a good chance of being set free. However, if one of them defects and provides evidence against the other, then freedom for that one is assured through an immunity agreement, and conviction is assured for the other because of the evidence. When they both give evidence against each other, they are both more likely to be in trouble. The dilemma is that in trying to guard against the other defecting if one cooperates, both end up in a worse situation than if they cooperated. In the one off prisoner dilemma situations, both players will defect because they want to avoid the worst-case scenario. Sometimes the problem is put in terms of being armed or disarming (do you want to put down your gun first?) or cooperating versus defecting. Although they could have been in the second best situation, they end up in second worst situation.

53. Paul G. Mahoney & Chris William Sanchirico, *Norms, Repeated Games, and the Role of Law,* 91 CALIF. L. REV. 1281, 1291 (2003). As they go on to note, "this comports well with actual beliefs and behaviors." Id. The argument that tit-for-tat is a winning strategy for repeat players comes from the landmark work of ROBERT AXELROD, THE EVOLUTION OF COOPERATION (1984). As Mahoney & Sanchirico note further, "tit-for-tat gained the highest cumulative score in Axelrod's famous tournament, and Axelrod dedicates a fair portion of his book to explaining the attractive properties that account for tit-for-tat's victory." Id. Axelrod's tournament, however, was a tournament of one on one repeat players and did not account for multiple repeat player interacting with each other at the same time.

54. *Id.* at 1296. What they propose is a strategy that punishes both defection and deviations from expected behavior, and by this, they mean punishing those who cooperate with those who defect instead of punishing them. They call this "defect-for-deviate," or "def-for-dev" which they describe as: "1) Start in round one by cooperating with all opponents; 2) Defect against a player if and only if she deviated from the def-for-dev strategy in the immediately preceding round." *Id.* They provide an example to show how this works as a strategy for norm enforcement which is as follows: suppose that we have ten players, and all ten cooperate as to all others in round one. Because all have acted consistently with the strategy to date, the strategy instructs each player to cooperate with everyone in round two. If all ten do cooperate with all others in round two, then all have again acted in conformity with the strategy in round two, and the strategy then instructs each player to cooperate with everyone in round three. Assume, however, that Player 1 defects in round three against Player 8, but no other player defects. Then Player 1 has not followed def-for-dev in the third round: she has violated def-for-dev's instruction to defect against another player only if that player deviated from def-for-dev in the immediately prior round. Thus, in round four, def-for-dev tells Players 2 through 10 to defect against Player 1 and cooperate with all other opponents. Further, it tells Player 1 to cooperate with all opponents. Thus, Player 1 is to "play the sucker" against all opponents in round four as punishment for her deviation in round three. Now suppose that all players except Player 2 follow the strategy in the fourth round and defect against Player 1 (Player 1 also follows the strategy and cooperates with everyone). Player 2 cooperates with Player 1 in the fourth round. Then Player 2 and only Player 2 has deviated from def-for-dev in the fourth round. Thus, in the fifth round def-for-dev

tells Player 1 and Players 3 through 10 to defect against Player 2 and cooperate with all others. Further, it tells Player 2 to cooperate with all opponents. Thus, Player 2 plays the sucker in round five as punishment for failing to punish Player 1 in round four. And so on. *Id* at 1296–97.

55. http://news.bbc.co.uk/2/hi/1288230.stm "First, though, moderate Hutus who weren't anti-Tutsi should be killed. So should Tutsi wives or husbands." http://www.ppu.org.uk/genocide/g_rwanda.html. *See also* http://www.unitedhumanrights.org/genocide/genocide_in_rwanda.htm.

56. This attitude is known as Manichaeism, or viewing the world dualistically in terms of good and evil, light and dark. George W. Bush on September 20, 2001, stated that "either you are with us, or you are with the terrorists." *See,* President George W. Bush, Address to a Joint Session of Congress and the American People (Sept. 20, 2001), (transcript available at http://georgewbush-whitehouse.archives.gov/news/releases/2001/09/20010920-8.html). Soon after George W. Bush's speech, Tunisia and other Middle East and North African states declared and offered their support for the "war on terror." Based on this support and cooperation, the U.S. turned a blind eye to the numerous, documented human rights violations made by the Ben Ali régime. *See,* Corina Mullin, Azadeh Shahshahani, *Western Complicity in the Crimes of the BenAli Regime,* 68 NAT'L LAW. GUILD REV. 122, 123 (2011).

57. Hillary Rodham Clinton said on September 13, 2001: "Every nation has to either be with us, or against us. Those who harbor terrorists, or who finance them, are going to pay a price." Senator Hillary Clinton (Democrat, New York). During an interview on CBS Evening News with Dan Rather. Available at: http://freedomagenda.com/iraq/wmd_quotes.html#Sw8leOyTFo. (last visited July 16, 2012).

58. 18 U.S.C. § 2339B(a)(1) (2000), which reads:

(1) Unlawful conduct. — Whoever knowingly provides material support or resources to a foreign terrorist organization, or attempts or conspires to do so, shall be fined under this title or imprisoned not more than 15 years, or both, and, if the death of any person results, shall be imprisoned for any term of years or for life. To violate this paragraph, a person must have knowledge that the organization is a designated terrorist organization (as defined in subsection (g)(6)), that the organization has engaged or engages in terrorist activity (as defined in section 212(a)(3)(B) of the Immigration and Nationality Act), or that the organization has engaged or engages in terrorism (as defined in section 140(d) (2) of the Foreign Relations Authorization Act, Fiscal Years 1988 and 1989). *Id.*

59. It argues that restrictions on financial contributions are regulations of conduct and not direct regulations of association. *See, e.g.* David Cole, *Hanging with the Wrong Crowd: Of Gangs, Terrorists, and the Right of Association,* 1999 SUP. CT. REV. 203, 205.

60. *Holder v. Humanitarian Law Project* 130 S. Ct. 2705 (2010).

61. Many studies show that this in-group and out-group view of the world is shared by those who have strong religious affiliations. A recent meta-analytic review of 55 studies with over 22,000 participants between 1964 and 2008 found that the greater religious identification, the greater extrinsic religiosity (religiosity that is motivated by external factors such as social status, security and acceptance by others), and that greater religious fundamentalism, were all positively correlated with racism. Hall, D. L., Matz, D. C. & Wood, W. *Why don't we practice what we preach? A meta-analytic review of religious racism.* 14 PERSONALITY AND SOCIAL PSYCHOLOGY REVIEW, 126, 130 (2010). The participants in the studies were primarily White Christians from the United States. *Id* at 126, 135. Although intrinsic reli-

giosity "was linked with decreased self-reported hostility and vengeance to others," it was not linked to an "actual decrease in hostile, vengeful behavior." *Id.* at 128. As the authors note, "intrinsically religious people may report racial tolerance largely because of a desire to appear nonracist but nevertheless may show racial prejudice when it is indirectly measured." *Id.*

62. The one disposition that "consistently related to racial tolerance," was agnosticism, "as reflected in an open minded questioning of religious doctrine." *Id.* at 134.

63. *Id.* at 128.

64. As of 1998 only 12% of congregations had a modest amount of racial diversity and nearly half had no racial diversity at all. *Id.* at 126.

65. According to Scheitle, and Dougherty, nine out of ten congregations in the U.S. are segregated by race: CHRISTOPHER P. SCHEITLE AND KEVIN D. DOUGHERTY, *Race, Diversity, and Membership Duration in Religious Congregations.* 80 SOCIOLOGICAL INQUIRY, 405 (2010).

66. Hall, D. L., Matz, D. C. & Wood, W, *supra* note 63 at 134.

67. *Id.*

68. *Id.* Sadly, but unsurprisingly, psychological research shows that those with low self-esteem tend to have wrathful images of god, while those with high self-esteem tend to have loving images of god. Id at 134. This also explains why the majority often views hate crimes legislation as giving people "special rights" rather than as a mechanism to protect vulnerable groups. Traditional Values Coalition, "Special Report," *Hate Crimes Legislation: Unequal Treatment Under the Law* 4 (Oct. 2005). *See also Romer v. Evans* where Colorado defended Amendment 2 as simply denying "homosexuals special rights." *Romer v. Evans,* 517 U.S. 620, 632 (1996). "In an effort to stem the tide of municipal laws protecting sexual minorities from employment and housing discrimination, the people of Colorado passed Amendment 2 to the state constitution, outlawing all such laws. Framed as a 'no special rights' initiative, Amendment 2's proponents waged an aggressive campaign, warning against the evils of homosexuality and arguing that sexual minorities should not be entitled to special rights simply because of their practices." Victor Romero, *Immigrant Education and the Promise of Integrative Egalitarianism,* 2011 MICH. ST. L. REV. 275, 297. As the Supreme Court noted, Amendment 2 actually imposed a special disability on sexual minorities by forbidding them safeguards that others enjoy or take for granted. *Romer,* 517 U.S. at 632.

69. According to a 2011 report issued by the PEW Charitable Trust, Pew Forum on Religion and Public Life, *The Global Muslim Population: Projections for 2010–2030: Region: Americas,* "If current trends continue, the Muslim population in the United States is projected to more than double in the next 20 years, from 2.6 million in 2010 to 6.2 million in 2030." *See* http://www.pewforum.org/future-of-the-global-muslim-population-regional-americas.aspx#4. As of 2010 Muslims represented approximately .8% of the U.S. population. Id. Even if this number doubles in twenty years, they will still only represent 1.6% of the population.

70. Oddly enough, most people of Middle-Eastern descent are simply categorized as white under the U.S. Census. According to the U.S. Census Bureau "White" is defined as "A person having origins in any of the original peoples of Europe, the Middle East, or North Africa." U.S. http://www.census.gov/population/race/about/ (last visited July 16, 2012). Even though the Middle East is general considered to encompass Afghanis, Arabs, (including the Arabic speaking populations of North Africa), Armenians, Iranians, Israelis, Kurds, Palestinians, Turks, and other populations from the Middle East region. While these groups

from the Middle East are labeled white, those from the Far East, are labeled "Asian" and include those with "origins in any of the original peoples of the Far East, Southeast Asia, or the Indian subcontinent including, for example, Cambodia, China, India, Japan, Korea, Malaysia, Pakistan, the Philippine Islands, Thailand, and Vietnam."

71. There are groups that are attempting to combat these mischaracterizations. For instance, "My Fellow American" is an online film and social media project that calls on supports to spread the message the Muslims are not "the other." It's a project of Unity Productions Foundation which is a non-profit organization. See, http://www.facebook.com/MyFellowAmericanProject#!/MyFellowAmericanProject/info. They also have a twitter page http://www.twitter.com/usmuslimstories. The Council on American-Islamic Relations, a Muslim civil and human rights organization, also works to combat these perceptions of Muslim Americans. See www.cair.com.

72. See United States v. McVeigh, 153 F.3d 1166 (10th Cir. 1998); see generally Lou Michel & Dan Herbeck, American Terrorist: Timothy McVeigh & The Oklahoma City Bombing (2001) (describing in detail the life of Timothy McVeigh, his terrorist plot, and the indictments arising from the Oklahoma City bombing). See also, Alessandra Stanley, A Terrorist, Plain-Spoken and Cold, N.Y. Times, April 18, 2010, http://www.nytimes.com/2010/04/19/arts/television/19mcveigh.html?ref=timothyjamesmcveigh.

73. See Zackary E. McCabe, Northern Ireland: The Paramilitaries, Terrorism, and September 11th, 30 Denv. J. Int'l L. & Pol'y 547, 561–64 (2002) (describing the long history of violence and human rights violations committed by the IRA against the UK and the United States' difficulty in defining these Irish Catholics as terrorists). This paper uses the example of Quinn v. Robinson concerning an extradition request from Great Britain for a member of the IRA who conspired to cause explosions in London and murdered a police constable. The decision supported the position that these atrocities simply qualified as political acts and the United States would be obligated to give safe harbor to one who participates in such acts. Id. at 561 (citing Quinn v. Robinson, 783 F.2 776,806 (9th Cir.)). See also, Ronald A. Christaldi, The Shamrock and the Crown: A Historical Analysis of the Framework Document and Prospects for Peace in Northern Ireland, 5 J. Transnat'l L. & Pol'y 123 (1995) (presenting a historical perspective on the problems in Northern Ireland, many which deal with human rights issues).

74. Antiterrorism and Effective Death Penalty Act, 18 U.S.C. §2339B(a)(1) (2000) upheld by Holder, supra note 62 at 2719, 23.

75. See, e.g. Marie Brenner, Taking on Guant·namo, Vanity Fair (March, 2007). Available at: http://www.vanityfair.com/politics/features/2007/03/guantanamo200703 (last visited July 16, 2012).

76. Ziauddin Sardar & Merryl Wyn Davies, Why Do People Hate America? 5 (2003). Ahmed Rashid, And Hate Begat Hate, N.Y. Times (September 10, 2011) Available at: http://www.nytimes.com/2011/09/11/opinion/sunday/and-hate-begat-hate.html?pagewanted=all (last visited July 16, 2012).

77. See section I. above.

78. The Text of the joint resolution can be found at: http://www.gpo.gov/fdsys/pkg/PLAW-107publ40/pdf/PLAW-107publ40.pd (last visited July 16, 2012).

79. PBS Online Remembering September 11, (14 September 2001); at: www.pbs.org/newshour/bb/terrorism/july-dec01/remember_9-14.html (last visited July 16 2012).

80. Not only did we pursue "regime change" in Latin America during the cold war, (See,

e.g. MICHAEL GROW, U.S. PRESIDENTS AND LATIN AMERICAN INTERVENTIONS: PURSUING REGIME CHANGE IN THE COLD WAR (2007)) (e.g. Guatemala in 1954, Cuba, 1959, Dominican Republic, 1961, British Guiana, 1963, Brazil, 1964, Chile 1973, Argentina 1976, Grenada 1983, Panama, 1989, and Nicaragua throughout the 1980s) but we trained people to use torture techniques in Latin America in the School of the Americas. John T. Parry, *Torture Nation, Torture Law*, 97 GEORGETOWN L. J. 1001, 1014–1016 (2009).

81. We had no problem toppling governments in the Middle East when it suited us, including toppling the government in Iran, imposing the Shah, and then giving him asylum when he was overthrown. *See, e.g.* BBC, *Iran Profile: Timeline*, available at: http://www.bbc.co.uk/news/world-middle-east-14542438 (last visited July 16, 2012).

82. Sikander Ahmed Shah, *War on Terrorism: Self Defense, Operation Enduring Freedom, and the Legality of U.S. Drone Attacks in Pakistan*, 9 WASH. U. GLOBAL STUD. L. REV. 77 (2010); Parvez Ahmed, *supra* note 24 at 781.

83. H.Res 864 (Nov. 3, 2009). The *Goldstone Report* is available at: http://www2.ohchr.org/english/bodies/hrcouncil/specialsession/9/factfindingmission.htm (last visited July 16, 2012). Note that Goldstone reportedly did recant some of his report, stating that more recent evidence shows that Israeli's did not target civilians as a matter of policy. *See, e.g. Judge Goldstone expresses regrets about his report into Gaza war* The Guardian (April 3, 2011) available at: http://www.guardian.co.uk/world/2011/apr/03/goldstone-regrets-report-into-gaza-war (last visited July 16, 2012).

84. Rep. Dennis Kucinich (D-Ohio), *Standing against the 'wrong is right' Goldstone Resolution* THE HILL's CONGRESS BLOG (Nov.3, 2009). Available at: http://thehill.com/blogs/congress-blog/foreign-policy/66141-standing-against-the-wrong-is-right-goldstone-resolution-rep-dennis-kucinich (last visited July 16, 2012).

85. The poster for the conference hangs on the wall behind my desk at the Center for Applied Legal Studies at the University of the Witwatersrand School of Law.

86. Tom Lantos, *The Durban Debacle: An Insider's View of the UN World Conference Against Racism* 26 FLETCHER FORUM ON WORLD AFFAIRS 31 (2002) (Tom Lantos, U.S. Congressman from California, served as U.S. Delegate at the World Conference on Racism in Durban, South Africa). Lantos, put much of the blame on UN High Commissioner for Human Rights Mary Robinson, for "fail[ing] to provide the leadership needed to keep the conference on track" and he put some of the blame on the Bush administration for "Six months of unilateralist foreign policies" that "had created such a climate of hostility and mistrust toward the United States that marshaling support among our allies to prevent the conference from being taken over and abused became an almost impossible mission." *Id.* at 32. However, he put the "majority of blame for the failure of Durban, ... at the feet of several members of Organization of the Islamic Conference (OIC). These regimes, some U.S. allies, proved unwilling to yield in their campaign to scuttle the noble agenda of the conference and to turn it into a forum to shun, isolate and de-legitimize Israel, America's key democratic ally in the Middle East." *Id.*

87. *Id.* at 40.

88. Id. As Lantos explains:

> The EU ambassadors dutifully said they would do all they could to help—but alluded to the anti-U.S. climate at the UN resulting from American positions on climate change, the ABM treaty, small arms and a host of other issues. They expressed a collective sense that the Bush administration should not expect help on issues it

cared about after neglecting so many global problems of concern to Europeans. For some, the Bush administration's foreign policies provided a convenient excuse for acting on their anti-Israeli proclivities. For others, the complaints were genuine. *Id.*

89. *Id* at 41. The measure passed, 408 to 3, with 3 abstentions. *Id.*

90. Id. Lantos reports being "troubled by her response." Id. He reports that he "explained to her that the U.S. position was non-negotiable, that no individual country or political conflict should be singled out in the context of a World Conference on Racism." *Id.*

91. *Id.* at 44.

92. Id. For a critique of Lantos's position on the conference, *see* A. Posner et al. *A Response to Tom Lantos' "The Durban Debacle"* 27 FLETCHER F. WORLD AFF. 5 (2003).

93. *See, e.g.* Nina Philadeloff-Puren, *Genre's Judgment: Discrediting Torture Testimony in the War on Terror* 19 L. & LIT 229 (2007).

94. Natham C. Funk and Abdul Aziz Said, *supra* note 23 at 1. "On both sides of the troubled relationship between Americans and the Muslim Middle East, there is deep estrangement and a growing belief in the futility of communication."

95. Mitt Romney on Tuesday, July 5th, 2011 in a town hall in Wolfeboro, N.H. Politifact rated Romney's statements as mostly false. http://www.politifact.com/truth-o-meter/statements/2011/jul/20/mitt-romney/mitt-romney-says-president-obama-was-planning-visi/. Then Candidate Obama did say that he would meet with foreign powers—friend or foe—without preconditions. *See* Kate Phillips, Obama and the Preconditions Meme, N.Y. TIMES, May 23, 2008, http://thecaucus.blogs.nytimes.com/2008/05/23/obama-and-the-preconditions-meme/. The statement came in response to a question from the moderator in a YouTube debate:

> Moderator: Would you be willing to meet separately, without precondition, during the first year of your administration, in Washington or anywhere else, with the leaders of Iran, Syria, Venezuela, Cuba and North Korea, in order to bridge the gap that divides our countries?
>
> ....
>
> Mr. Obama: I would. And the reason is this, that the notion that somehow not talking to countries is punishment to them—which has been the guiding diplomatic principle of this administration—is ridiculous.

Id. Alan Cowell, U.S. Is 'Not Your Enemy,' Obama Tells Islamic World, N.Y. TIMES, Jan. 28, 2009, at A8. President "Obama said that it was his job 'to communicate to the Muslim world that the Americans are not your enemy.'" *Id.*

96. *See, e.g.* Julian Border, *UN racism conference boycotted by more countries*, THE GUARDIAN (April 20, 2009) available at: http://www.guardian.co.uk/world/2009/apr/20/un-race-conference. The Conference was boycotted because the draft document adopted a reference to the 2001 conference document which singled out Israel and arguable posed a threat to freedom of expression. Thus, our response was simple not to engage at all with the conference.

97. *Id.* Rep. Barbara Lee, D-Calif., the chair of the black caucus, said the group was "deeply dismayed ... This decision is inconsistent with the administration's policy of engaging with those we agree with and those we disagree with," she said. "By boycotting Durban, the U.S. is making it more difficult for it to play a leadership role on U.N. Human Rights Council as it states it plans to do. This is a missed opportunity, plain and simple."

98. We waited some time before entering WWI and WWII. Although our merchant marines had been attacked on numerous occasions by the Germans we waited several years before committing to WWII. Approximately 25 US ships were detained, sunk, or damaged by German naval vessels between 1939 and 1941, before the US actually entered WWII. Approximately 20 of those ships were either freighter ships or passenger ships. ROBERT CRESSMAN, THE OFFICIAL CHRONOLOGY OF THE U.S. NAVY IN WORLD WAR II 1–51 (Naval Inst. Press 2000); *see also* http://www.usmm.org/sunk39-41.html#anchor325668 (last visited July 16, 2012).

99. *Facebook users 'are insecure, narcissistic and have low self-esteem'* By Mail Foreign Service, updated: 04:43 EST, 9 September 2010 http://www.dailymail.co.uk/sciencetech/ article-1310230/Facebook-users-narcissistic-insecure-low-self-esteem.html. (last visited July 16, 2012). *See, also* Soraya Mehdizadeh, *Self-Presentation 2.0: Narcissism and Self-Esteem on Facebook* 13 CYBERSYCHOLOGY, BEHAVIOUR, & SOCIAL NETWORKING (2010). *Millennials Will Benefit And Suffer Due to Hyperconnected Lives* February 29, 2012 "While experts see many young people becoming nimble analysts and decision-makers because of their embrace of the networked world, they also warn that some constantly-connected teens and young adults will lack deep engagement with people and knowledge by being hyperconnected." "Hyperconnected young people do not retain information; they spend most of their energy sharing short social messages, being entertained, and being too distracted to engage deeply with people and knowledge." http://pewresearch.org/pubs/2203/hyperconnectivity-teens-young-adults-internet.

The full report is available at: http://www.pewinternet.org/~/media//Files/Reports/2012/ PIP_Future_of_Internet_2012_Young_brains_PDF.pdf. "Analysts generally believe many young people growing up in today's networked world and counting on the internet as their external brain will be nimble analysts and decision-makers who will do well. But these experts also expect that constantly connected teens and young adults will thirst for instant gratification and often make quick, shallow choices."

100. The cover story of the July 16, 2012 NEWSWEEK is *iCrazy: Panic, Depression, Psychosis: How Connection Addition is Rewiring our Brains.* The inside story is Tony Dokoupil, *Tweets, Texts, Email, Posts: Is the Onslaught Making us Crazy* NEWSWEEK 24–30 (July 16, 2012).

101. Timothy Zick, *The First Amendment in Transborder Perspective: Toward a More Cosmopolitan Orientation*, 52 B.C. L. REV. 941, 942–47 (2011) detailing the many limits on our freedom of expression in the transnational context. As he states:

> Under Supreme Court and lower court precedents, most dating from the post-war and Cold War periods, U.S. citizens: (1) have only a limited First Amendment right to receive and distribute foreign materials inside the United States, (2) may be denied personal access to foreign speakers for any "facially legitimate and bona fide" reason, (3) have merely a First Amendment "freedom" under the Due Process Clause to travel abroad for the purpose of gathering information about foreign cultures, (4) are understood by some courts not to have any First Amendment right to send communications to audiences abroad consisting solely of aliens, (5) have only a limited right to associate with aliens located abroad, and (6) have no First Amendment right to access and distribute inside the United States propaganda materials disseminated by their government abroad. Moreover, no court has ever invalidated the Logan Act, a criminal statute dating from 1799 that bans citizens' unauthorized communications with foreign regimes and their principals, the ban

on alien contributions in U.S. elections, or the federal requirement that certain U.S. institutions obtain a license prior to sharing certain scientific and technical information with aliens working in the United States Under current First Amendment jurisprudence, there is no clear and unambiguous precedent holding that communications or associations that cross borders are protected in any meaningful way.

Id. at 942–43.

102. Note the previous editor and one of the main contributors, who were US citizens were killed by predator drones.

103. *See, e.g.* DAVID HELD, DEMOCRACY AND THE GLOBAL ORDER (1995); CARL BOGGS, THE END OF POLITICS (2000); c.f. THOMAS FRIEDMAN, THE LEXUS AND THE OLIVE TREE (1999) (arguing that globalization is good for democracy).

104. *See, e.g.* Anu Bradford & Eric A. Posner, *Universal Exceptionalism in International Law*, 52 HARV. INT'L L.J. 1, 5 (2011) ("international law is best understood as an overlapping consensus of the otherwise 'exceptional' views of the great powers"). The authors go on to state that "the United States has undermined or seriously weakened the international order it has helped to create and has earned the resentment of countries not powerful enough to treat international law as an à la carte menu." *Id.*

105. *See infra* note 20.

106. *See, e.g.* in relation to the Military Commission's Act, Roger S. Clark, *The Military Commissions Act of 2006: An Abject Abdication by Congress*, 6 RUTGERS J.L. & PUB. POL'Y. 78 (2008) ("arguing that the Military Commissions Act represents a total failure of Congress to pay attention to some basic propositions of international treaty and customary law and a failure to exercise its powers under the Constitution."). *See, e.g.* in relation to the Authorization for the Use of Military Force Resolution, Nancy Snow & Philip M. Taylor, *The Revival of the Propaganda State: US Propaganda at Home and Abroad Since 9/11*, 68 INT'L COMMUNICATION GAZETTE 389, 390 (2010); in relation to the Patriot Act, *See, e.g.* KELNER, *supra* note

107. "How acceptable sound bad music and bad motives when we march against an enemy!" FRIEDRICH NIETZSCHE, THE DAWN OF DAY 379 (Johanna Volz trans., 1903).

108. *See, e.g. infra* note 27, 43–44.

109. As Justice Brandeis once wrote, "Those who won our independence believed … that the greatest menace to freedom is an inert people; that public discussion is a political duty; and that this should be a fundamental principle of the American government." *Whitney v. California*, 274 U.S. 357, 375 (1927) (Brandeis, J., concurring).

11. Obscenity, Community and the Internet

1. 354 U.S. 476 (1957).
2. *Id.* at 483.
3. *See id.* at 487.
4. [1868] 3 Q.B. 360.
5. 354 U.S. at 489.
6. 413 U.S. 15 (1973).

7. *Id.* at 24 (citations omitted).

8. *See* Pope v. Illinois, 481 U.S. 497 (1987).

9. *Miller,* 413 U.S. at 30.

10. *Id.* at 32–23 (footnote omitted).

11. 418 U.S. 87 (1974).

12. *Id.* at 106. This was not actually the first case addressing federal statutes regarding obscene materials. In United States v. 12 200–ft. Reels of Film, 413 U.S. 123 (1973), the Court said that the "contemporary community standards" requirement applies to federal legislation, as well as to local statutes and ordinances. But, as the Court said in a later case, it was *Hamling* that made it clear that "the fact that 'distributors of allegedly obscene materials may be subjected to varying community standards in the various federal judicial districts into which they transmit the materials does not render a federal statute unconstitutional because of the failure of application of uniform national standards of obscenity.'" Sable Communications v. Federal Communications Comm'n, 492 U.S. 115, 125 (1989) (quoting *Hamling,* 418 U.S. at 106).

13. 492 U.S. 115 (1989).

14. *Id.* at 124.

15. *Id.* at 125.

16. *Id.* at 125–26.

17. App. no.5493/72, Ser A24 (1976).

18. *See* Ginsburg v. New York, 390 U.S. 629 (1968).

19. Under United States law, works cannot be obscene because of the ideas presented but only if there is an appeal to the prurient interest. *See* Kingsley International Pictures Corp. v. Regents, 360 U.S. 684 (1959).

20. App. no.5493/72, Ser A24 (1976) para.32.

21. *Id.*

22. *Id.*

23. s.1. The test is subject to a public good defence in s.4.

24. European Convention on Human Rights, art. 10(1), (Nov. 4, 1950, 213 U.N.T.S. 221).

25. *Id.* at art. 10(2).

26. App. no.5493/72, Ser A24 (1976) para.48.

27. *Id.* at para.47.

28. The European Court of Human Rights also rejected a challenge to a conviction for importing indecent material into the United Kingdom. *See* O'Carroll v. United Kingdom, App. no. 35557/03, 41 E.H.R.R. SE1 (2005). The appellant's claim in that case was that a lack of specific definition for indecency made his conviction a violation of Article 7 of the European Convention on Human Rights, which has been held to include a requirement that offenses be clearly described by law, *see id.* at paras. 4–5. The court, in language similar to that in *Handyside,* said that "it is not possible to attain absolute rigidity in the framing of laws, particularly in fields in which the situation changes according to the prevailing views of society." *Id.* at para.5. Even with discretion left to the jury, the court concluded that there was no violation of Article 7.

29. App. no. 10737/84, Ser A 133 (1988).

30. *Id.* at para.14.

31. In a later case, Scherer v. Switzerland, App. no. 17116/90, Ser A 287 (1994), it be-

came clear that, at least for some material, under Swiss law, the issue of exposure to the general public was not central. The material at issue there was available only in the back room of a sex shop and only to those with a membership card. The Swiss court said that the fact that no unwilling adults would be confronted by the material was irrelevant and that punishment was justified. The European Court did not reach the issue of a violation of Article 10 but, instead, found the case effectively moot, because of the death of the defendant.

32. App. no. 10737/84, Ser A 133 (1988) at para.32 (footnotes omitted).

33. *Id.*

34. *Id.* at para.36 (footnote omitted).

35. 535 U.S. 564 (2002).

36. The statute was held to be unconstitutional on other grounds, when it returned to the Supreme Court after reconsideration by the lower courts. *See* Ashcroft v. American Civil Liberties Union, 542 U.S. 656 (2004).

37. 535 U.S.at 580.

38. *See id.* at 581–82.

39. *See id.* at 582–83.

40. *Id.* at 583 (citations omitted).

41. *Id.* at 586 (O'Connor, J., concurring in part and concurring in the judgment).

42. *Id.* at 589 (Breyer, J., concurring in part and concurring in judgment).

43. *Id.* at 597 (Kennedy, J., concurring in the judgment).

44. There was an earlier case involving the Internet and citing *Ashcroft*, but it was not an obscenity case. Instead, the defendant in United States v. Dhingra, 371 F.3d 557 (9th Cir. 2004), had been charged with using the Internet to solicit sexual activity from a minor. He argued that *Ashcroft* prohibited a community based approach as to what activities were illegal when minors are involved. The court rejected that contention.

45. No. 3:04-CR-181-M, 2005 WL 624381 (N.D. Tex. Mar. 16, 2005).

46. No. 1:06-cr-430-WSD, 2007 WL 1087337 (N.D. Ga. Apr. 5, 2007).

47. 548 F. Supp. 2d 332 (N. D. Tex. 2008).

48. Criminal No. 03-0203, 2009 WL 113767 (W.D. Pa. Jan. 15, 2009).

49. 584 F.3d 1240 (9th Cir. 2009).

50. *Id.* at 1254.

51. 365 Fed. App'x. 159 (11th Cir. 2010).

52. There were also counts based on DVDs shipped to an address in Florida, but those counts do not raise the same concern and are easily subsumed under *Hamling*.

53. 365 Fed. App'x. at 164.

54. App. no. 5446/03, 2005-XI.

55. *Id.* at 6.

56. *Id.* at 7.

57. *Id.* at 7–8.

58. App. no. 17419/90, 1996-V.

59. *Id.* at para.42.

60. *Id.* at para.58. *See also Otto-Preminger Institute v. Austria*, App. no. 13470/87, Ser A 295-A (1994).

61. See High Level Conference on the Future of the European Court of Human Rights, *Brighton Declaration* (http://hub.coe.int/20120419-brighton-declaration, 2012).

Index

A

ABC news, 43
    accessibility of information, 102–3
    identification and, 103
media rights and, 31
accessibility of/to Internet, 102–3
    egalitarianism and, 97
    geography and, 157–58
    government control over, 74–75
    net neutrality and, 97
accident scenes, 43
accountability
    anonymous blogging and, 45–46
    for content, 98
    media, 29
    terrorists/terrorism and, 143
accuracy
    24-hour news cycle and, 26
    professional journalism and, 55
advertising
    comparative returns on, 9
    decline in, 5–6
    as financing online publications, 23–24
    and groups/cohorts, 104
    newspapers, 5–6, 8–9, 10, 11
    and obscenity, 156
    on Web, 8–9

al-Awlaki, Anwar, 211*n*29
Alberts v. California, 146
Alvarez, United States v., 62, 63
Amalgamated Food Employees Union v. Logan Valley Plaza, Inc., 201*n*61
America Online (AOL)
    and libel, 116
    Politics Daily, 19
America Online, Zeran v, 116
American Society of Newspaper Editors, 8
Anderson, David, 50, 52, 58, 60
anonymity
    in blogs, 112
    and defamation, 101, 110, 115, 117–19
    First Amendment and, 111
    and freedom of speech, 100
    identified authors vs., 117–19
    and individuality, 100
    and ineffectiveness of legal remedies, 101–2
    of Internet, 99–102
    ISPs and, 110–12
    ISPs and disclosure of identity, 114
    and libel, 119–20
    and opinion, 100